A GOOD FIGHT

A Good Fight

SARAH BRADY

WITH MERRILL McLOUGHLIN

PublicAffairs

New York

Book design by Mark McGarry, Texas Type & Book Works, Inc.
Set in Perpetua

Library of Congress Cataloging-in-Publication Data
Brady, Sarah, 1942–
A good fight / Sarah Brady with Merrill McLoughlin.
p. cm.   Includes Index.
ISBN 1-58648-105-3
1. Brady, Sarah, 1942– 2. Brady, James S.
3. Wives—United States—Biography. 4. Presidential press secretaries—
United States—Biography. 5. Victims of crimes—United States—Biography.
6. Gun Control—United States—History—20th century.
7. Firearms—Law and legislation—United States—History—20th century.
I. McLoughlin, Merrill. II. Title.
E840.8.B715 G66   2002   973.927′092′2—dc21
2002017790 [B]

FIRST EDITION
2 4 6 8 10 9 7 5 3 1

To my family, the joy of my life—
Jim, Scott, Missy and Bill
and Emmy

"Hope" is the thing with feathers—
That perches in the soul—
And sings the tune without the words—
And never stops—at all—

EMILY DICKINSON

Contents

CONTENTS

Acknowledgments

First, my thanks to my family and to the many friends who have been with me through all the ups and downs of life. I am especially grateful to Emmy Bania, to Jan and Otto Wolff, to Debbie and Jerry File, and to the members of the Eating Club. Their support for me and my family have meant more than I can say.

Throughout Jim's many medical problems, there were dozens of doctors, nurses, and other medical personnel whose professionalism and expertise astonished me and buoyed our spirits. It is impossible to mention them all. But it would be unthinkable not to name the one who, first and foremost, saved my husband's life: Dr. Arthur Kobrine.

I, too, have been blessed with the best possible care during my battle with lung cancer. My thanks to all who have attended me, professionally and personally, at Beebe Medical Center's Tunnell Cancer Center and Johns Hopkins' Weinberg Cancer Center—most notably,

Drs. Srihari Peri, Andrejs Strauss, and David Ettinger and Isabel Benson and Paula Grouleff.

The Brady law never would have been passed without the dedication and generosity of many hundreds of people—the staff and board of the Brady Campaign and other supporters who gave countless hours of hard work to the fight. But there are four whose vision and leadership helped show the rest of us the way: Charlie Orasin, Gail Hoffman, Barbara Lautman, and Susan Whitmore.

Finally, my thanks to those who made this book a reality. Mark Rosenberg of the Centers for Disease Control and Prevention, a board member of The Brady Campaign, urged me to tell my story. Mike Barnes and Phyllis Segal provided critical help and encouragement. And because of Phyllis, I was fortunate enough to become part of the publishing family at PublicAffairs, including Peter Osnos and my editor, Lisa Kaufman, whose belief in this project and unrelenting support have been above and beyond the call of duty. And Merrill McLoughlin kept me focused, amused, and amazed at her uncanny ability to make sense of my rambling recollections of a life that has had its fair share of good fights.

SARAH BRADY
December 2001

A GOOD FIGHT

CHAPTER ONE

The Day That Changed Everything

As I begin this story, I am fighting for my life.

I have lung cancer. Three kinds of chemotherapy and one round of radiation have not knocked it out, and I am now on an experimental drug. I have very high hopes for it. And even if this one fails, I've been told there are others in the research pipeline that I'll be able to try. Certainly, I have no intention of giving up. By nature, I guess, I am a fighter, as my friends in the National Rifle Association will attest. All my life that has been true: Point me at a problem, tell me what needs to be done, and I'll give it everything. I love a good fight.

Meanwhile, I am taking life one day at a time. I feel wonderful right now—the best I've felt in quite a while. Probably I don't have as much energy as I had before this came up, but pretty close to it. I'm trying to pay closer attention to everything around me, to enjoy, fully, the people and things I love most, to appreciate every moment as much as I possibly can. I have always adored the shore and the sun, for instance, but now every walk on the gorgeous beach near our house in Delaware—the ocean is just a hundred yards away—seems extra peaceful and relaxing; I love to get out and watch that surf and smell that air, and I feel renewed every time I am down by the water. And I have always loved to eat—one reason my husband nicknamed me "the Raccoon," "'Coon," for short, soon after we met is that I have tiny hands that can get food to my mouth very quickly—but now my appetite seems sharper, if not larger, and favorite foods are pure joy.

My husband's irrepressible sense of humor is dearer to me than ever, and I enjoy the lazy pace of our life here in "slower lower Delaware," as people call it. My brother and I have grown the closest we've been in our lives. I want to live to see our son achieve his goals and get married and have children. I love life, and I do not want to leave any of this behind. But I am not some kind of Pollyanna nut. I am trying to keep a healthy balance between being realistic, on the one hand, and living without self-pity and constant worry, on the other.

Of course, this is not the first time I've been made acutely aware of how important it is to live in the moment. And it most certainly is not the first time I have realized how utterly impossible it is to know how things will turn out in your life. Both of those lessons were driven home to me, about as forcefully as you can imagine, on March 30, 1981. I know it's a cliché to describe that day as "fateful," but that's just exactly what it was. It was the day that changed everything.

Jim and I were pretty exhausted when we woke up that Monday morning. Jim had been Ronald Reagan's White House press secretary for only about ten weeks, but during that time, both of us had been busier than we'd ever been in our lives. The weekends typically brought little relief from the constant demands of Jim's position, and not much chance for either one of us to rest.

That particular Saturday had been the night of the Gridiron Dinner, the annual event in which practically everyone who's anyone in Washington, D.C., turns out in white tie and tails to watch the press roast the politicians. It's all in good fun, officially off the record, and the President and First Lady usually attend, along with a good part of the Cabinet and the White House senior staff. Ronald and Nancy Reagan went that year, his first in office, and Jim went, too, and had a ball. I wasn't invited. But on Sunday, one of the press people hosted a brunch that we both attended, and then, in late afternoon, the Gridiron Club staged a special encore for spouses and others who'd missed the dinner performance. Jim and I both went to that, too.

The Gridiron replay was over at 6:30 or so, and we decided to splurge and eat at Portofino's, a little Italian restaurant near our house where we'd had the rehearsal dinner before our wedding. It was a wonderfully fun and romantic evening that ended in a hilarious mess: It turned out neither one of us had brought any cash or credit cards, and even though Portofino's said we could come back later and pay, I left Jim there as a hostage, having an after-dinner drink, while I drove home and grabbed a credit card. We paid the bill and laughed about it all, then went home and let the baby-sitter go. There was no way to know that there was anything truly remarkable about that night—that we would never have another like it.

As always, Jim got up at the crack of dawn. Since we'd been out later than usual, I was thinking we'd let Scott, who was two, sleep in for a while. It would give me a little extra rest as well. But Jim felt he saw too little of our son now that he was so busy at the White House. Typically, he left for work by 6 or 6:30 every morning and didn't get home until 7:30 or 8 at the earliest. The weekend before the Gridiron, we had managed time for a great family outing, first to the National Zoo, then to a restaurant on Connecticut Avenue, where Jim and I drank margaritas and ate Mexican food out on a patio, with Scott sitting beside us in his stroller. But those times were few and far between, and that Monday, Jim was just determined to get Scott out of bed and play with him before he left for work. So after he showered, despite my protests, that's exactly what he did. Looking back, I'm so very glad.

Then Jim drove off in his yellow Jeep, his pride and joy. It took about ten minutes to get from our house in Arlington, Virginia, across the Potomac River to the White House. Once he arrived, he always collected all the morning papers and attended an early briefing, then went to breakfast at the White House mess. Many mornings, and I think that one was no exception, he'd hear a little tap on his office window and it would be Helen Thomas, the White House reporter for United Press International. He'd always invite her in for a cup of tea, and they would chat. He thought the world of Helen.

So it was a pretty normal morning for Jim—and for me, too. I took Scott down the hill to a little church playschool he attended two days a week. I finished my grocery shopping and put a chicken in the Crock-Pot for dinner. It was a family custom. Every weekend, Jim bought a chicken in a little open-air market in Georgetown. Every Monday evening, the Bradys ate Crock-Pot chicken.

As it happened, my mother was in Arizona for a nephew's wedding. She had a wonderful woman named Frances McKnight who helped her clean house a half day every two weeks, and since Mother was going to be out of town, she'd suggested that Frances work for me that Monday. I picked her up, then collected Scott from playschool. After lunch, Scott and I settled down in the recreation room in our basement, and I turned the television to my favorite soap opera, *As the World Turns*.

Suddenly, there was a bulletin from CBS news, a *Special Report*: Shots had been fired at President Reagan outside the Washington Hilton Hotel, where he had just addressed a meeting of the AFL-CIO. Apparently, CBS reported, the President had not been injured. So I wasn't at all panicky.

When the phone rang, almost immediately, I thought it was Mom, who watched the same program, and I picked up the receiver and said, "Did you hear that?" But it was not my mother. It was my good friend Jan Wolff, who said, in a very shaky voice, "Sarah, do you want me to come get Scott?" What for, I asked—why would she need to come get Scott? Then she told me: ABC News was reporting that Jim had been shot. I said, "Oh, Jan, hang up and I'll call the White House." Because of Jim's position, we had a special White House signal phone—a direct line to the switchboard at 1600 Pennsylvania Avenue—and I grabbed it. I explained to the operator that I'd just heard my husband had been shot. "Is that correct?" I asked—not believing it for a minute—and the operator told me to hang up, they'd call back. Within thirty seconds someone did. Yes, he had been shot, but he was alive. I asked whether he was stable, and the answer was yes. I asked where the ambulance was taking him, and the operator said to the George Washington University Hospital.

By now, I was really anxious, and I was just going to get in my car and take off. Then the phone rang again, and it was Jim's assistant, Sally McElroy, in the White House press office. Stay right there, she said. We're on our way. They were sending a White House "carpet" driver—a military driver—to get me. I asked Frances to take care of poor little Scott, who of course had no idea what was going on, and I raced around frantically, looking for my pocketbook, then ran outside to wait for the car.

It was a dreary day—dark, drizzling, nasty. I was wearing my usual staying-at-home uniform of jeans and penny loafers, a blouse and crewneck sweater. I don't think I'd even bothered to pick up a jacket. While I was waiting out there, people who had seen the news began to come by. One woman said she'd just heard about my husband and, identifying herself as "Jonathan's mother," wished me good luck. I had no idea at the time who on earth she was. Later, I realized that

Jonathan was our paper boy, and his mother, Didi, eventually became a friend.

Otto Wolff, Jan's husband, arrived just about the time the White House car pulled up, and I asked him to come with me. Sally McElroy and Mark Weinberg, another of Jim's aides, were already in the car, and as soon as Otto and I got in, we took off for the relatively short drive across the river to the GW Hospital. The driver, Sergeant Sam Sampsell, was in constant communication with the White House garage, keeping up with developments.

Sally filled me in. I asked where Jim had been hit, and whether she and Mark were sure he was still alive. People say that I was told Jim had been wounded in the head, but I truly don't remember hearing that until we got to the hospital. In fact, I remember thinking *he's just been winged*, just like in the old cowboy movies.

When we came to the circle on the Virginia side of the Lincoln Memorial Bridge, Sergeant Sampsell, still monitoring the radio, must have heard something that alarmed him. All of a sudden, he slapped a light onto the top of the car and sped up, taking the corner on two wheels. I was usually pretty terrified of fast drivers, but that day, it didn't bother me one bit.

On the other side of the river, we passed the Lincoln Memorial and headed up Twenty-third Street toward GW. We were about two blocks from the hospital when the traffic came to an abrupt standstill, absolutely bumper to bumper. I was getting word, via the radio, that I should go to the main entrance and someone would meet me, and I didn't want to wait. I jumped out, along with Sally, Mark, and Otto, and we ran the last two blocks.

At the main entrance was a woman by the name of Sandra Butcher, the head social worker at GW. The minute she spotted me, she introduced herself, then said she wanted to take me to the neurosurgeon in charge of Jim's case. We raced through the hospital to an area not far from the operating suite, and there I met Arthur Kobrine.

I'll never forget seeing him that first time. He looked so young—I was only thirty-nine, but he was even younger—a large, good-looking man. He was so tall that for several days, when I was still getting everyone at the hospital mixed up, I would call him "the big doctor," meaning it both ways—both that he was tall and that he was the one in charge. As long as I live, I will never forget his words. He said, "Your husband has been hit above the left eye. The bullet entered above his left eye, and has transversed to the right side. If the operation is successful, he may well walk out of here. However, we do know that he will lose total use of his left arm and partial use of his left leg." He told me the operation would take about five hours, but he wanted me to know that Jim could easily succumb to the surgery. He asked if I had any questions. He had covered so much, so succinctly, that I had none. I just asked him please to save Jim's life—our little son needed him.

Sandra Butcher took Otto Wolff and me to the emergency room, to a cubicle where ER personnel could get away from time to time for short breaks. A few of them were in there, and I remember apologizing for intruding—I felt so bad that we were interrupting their breaks, since they work so hard. The magnitude of what was happening hadn't really hit me yet, partly because everything had gone so fast. I had reached the hospital within a half hour of the time Jim got there, and Jim had arrived within six minutes of the shooting. Not even one hour had gone by since John Hinckley fired those lethal .22-caliber Devastator bullets at the President of the United States and took down my husband as well.

We hadn't been there very long when Michael Deaver, the President's deputy chief of staff, brought Mrs. Reagan to the little room off the ER. She rushed in and I, jerk that I was, thought she had come to see me because of Jim. I had heard in the CBS report that the President had not been hit. But as we hugged each other, I realized she was shaking like a leaf. Then I said, "Oh, I am so scared," and she replied, "I am, too." And I knew instantaneously that the President, too, had been shot. "They're going to be fine," I told her. "They are both strong men."

We talked for a few minutes, and then she left. About an hour later, I wandered over to the hospital chapel, just for a quiet moment, and again encountered the First Lady. After I came back to the room, Sandra Butcher, bless her heart, took it upon herself to keep me informed of what was going on with Jim. She'd go to the operating room, send a nurse inside to find out what was happening, then come back with a report: "Everything's going fine. He's gone into the operation." Eventually, around 5 P.M., they moved us from that ER lounge up to a more comfortable room that had been especially set up for us, and where we had a telephone.

Not long after that, Sandra Butcher said she was going to check to see if there was any further news. When she returned, she said, "They're still operating." I remember thinking how weird that was. Why wouldn't they be? He'd only been in surgery for a relatively short time, nothing near the five hours Dr. Kobrine had said it would take.

Little did I know that Sandra Butcher—and much of the rest of the world—had heard on television that Jim had died, a mistake that was not corrected for about fifteen minutes. At 5:10 P.M., CBS reporter Jed Duvall broke into Dan Rather's special report on the assassination attempt with that report. NBC and ABC followed. Only CNN's Bernard Shaw refused to announce Jim's death without official confirmation, either from the doctor in charge or from the White House. Miraculously, I never did hear those reports—I was totally unaware of what had happened.

But Otto Wolff had heard. He had called our house, where Jan and several other close friends—David Cole, Scott's godfather; his wife, Brandy, and Dennis Thomas—had gathered to keep watch and to take care of Scott. Jan, who was crying, told Otto they'd just announced on television that Jim had died. "Rubbish," said Otto, and hung up. He didn't say a word to me about the conversation.

Later, though, Jan told me the whole story. They had all congregated downstairs in our rec room, where Scott was playing around. Of course, they had the news on. And suddenly the network flashed a picture of Jim on the screen and someone began to read an obituary. Scott saw the picture, and rushed to the TV, yelling, happily, "There's Daddy! There's Daddy!" and for a moment, all of the grownups sat there helplessly, completely distraught, their eyes filled with tears. Then wonderful Dennis Thomas scooped up little Scott and took him upstairs. First, he just carried him around for a while, to keep him away from the TV. Then he put Scott in his high chair, and Jan came up and fed him dinner. Every time I think about that scene, even all these years later, it breaks my heart.

Meanwhile, back at the hospital, I was trying to get hold of all the people who needed to come to Washington. Most had already heard about the shooting. My mother had made arrangements to return from Arizona, along with her sister, my Aunt Helen. Governor Jim Thompson of Illinois had volunteered to send his plane down to Centralia, Illinois, to ferry Dorothy Brady, Jim's mother, to her son's side. I couldn't reach Missy, Jim's daughter from his previous marriage, who was a student at Colorado State University, so I called her mother, Sue Beh—Jim's ex-wife—and learned that Missy was on her way to Denver. Sue had gotten her reservations from Denver to Chicago, where Sue planned to meet her and accompany her to Washington. I also called my brother, Bill, who lived in Portland, Oregon. He, too, knew what had happened and was making arrangements to come.

During all this, I was in constant touch with our house. Jan and the Coles and Dennis Thomas had been joined by many other friends and neighbors, who dropped by to see whether they could help. I kept checking in, asking about Scott, reminding Jan that someone needed to take Frances home, letting them all know that there was a chicken in the Crock-Pot. And I kept them up to date on who would be coming in from distant places, who would need places to stay. The White House was making arrangements for drivers to meet all the planes.

Yet with all those phone calls, no one ever said "Oh, I'm so sorry Jim died," even though many of them had heard that news. Missy had, for instance—before she left Fort Collins for Denver. It wasn't until she got to the Denver airport that Sue was able to let her know her father was still alive. Bill had seen the report, too, but then heard the correction almost immediately. Jim's mother and father never did hear it, thank goodness.

My uncle's next-door neighbor and best friend was the airport manager in Tucson, Arizona, and he helped get my mother and Aunt Helen first-class seats back to Washington through Chicago. When they landed at O'Hare Airport, Missy and Sue boarded the same plane, and so did Bill Greener, who had been Jim's boss several years earlier at the Department of Housing and Urban Development and also at the Office of Management and Budget. He was kind of Jim's mentor, and he had heard the news that Jim had died and did not learn until he got to Washington that it was not true. When they landed, they were met by the White House cars. Mother and Helen went to Mother's house, and Missy, Sue, and Bill Greener went to ours.

Dorothy Brady had arrived on Governor Thompson's plane, accompanied by Marietta Broughton, a writer for the Centralia *Sentinel*. She was brought directly to the hospital, and up to the room where Otto and I were waiting. Jim was still in surgery. That Dorothy had heard this news, packed a bag, and flown to Washington, all during that five-hour period, seems incredible to me even now.

So now, at the hospital, it was Dorothy, Otto, and me—plus a priest who had been dispatched by Jim's Aunt Helen and Aunt Margaret, devout Roman Catholics who lived in Jacksonville, Illinois. The minute they heard the news of the shooting, they called the Washington Archdiocese and had a priest sent over. Later, when we were able to see some humor in all this chaos and terror, that priest played a role. His arrival had been spotted by the press and had added credibility to the "news" that Jim was dead. By the next day, reporters, badly burned by miscalling Jim's death, were trying to make absolutely certain that they got everything perfectly right, or at least hedged their bets—to the point of absurdity. They printed a photo of Jim's and my ministers, who'd come over from Christ Episcopal Church in Alexandria to pray with us, and captioned it "the Bradys' alleged ministers." Ever since, Jim and I have teased them about being only alleged ministers, not the real thing.

Of course, Sandra Butcher was in and out of the room constantly. I didn't realize it at the time, but one of the things she was doing was making sure we didn't have access to a television. After the death reports, she wanted to be certain that all the news we got was coming from good sources.

The time dragged on, and I grew more and more nervous. At some point, someone brought in food, sandwiches. I was sure I wouldn't want any, but to my surprise, we devoured that food quite quickly. Toward the end of the five hours, it became more and more nerve-racking. I paced a lot—could hardly sit still.

All of a sudden, the door opened, and there was Art Kobrine. I hardly recognized him. The first time I'd seen him, he was so solemn, so very serious. But as he walked through the door into that room, he was beaming. I knew, before he said a word, that things had gone well. He explained that Jim had done beautifully—so well that he was not even going to have to spend much time in the recovery room. They were going to get him ready to go to intensive care, and we'd be able to see him in about half an hour.

The hospital had arranged a room for Dorothy and me, so that we could spend the night practically next door to Jim. Jan was putting together some things to bring over to the hospital—a change of clothes, a toothbrush, and my bottle of Mount Gay rum and some tonic. I knew I'd need a drink when this was all over! So after talking to Art, Dorothy and I went over to that room and waited anxiously for them to bring Jim up. They did so quite quickly, but it was probably twenty minutes before we could see him, because they had to hook him up to monitors that would keep tabs on virtually every part of his body.

He was awake. I guess that was one of the things that had pleased Art Kobrine so much. Usually, anyone with a head injury as horrible as Jim's was—even someone who is going to recover—doesn't wake up for a long time. But Jim woke up right away. When the doctors finished the surgery, this man was awake and alert.

After what seemed like ages, at about 9:30 or 10 P.M., they said we could see him. I went in first, and was not at all prepared for what I saw. All told, of course, he looked pretty damned good to me. His head had been shaved, and it was almost entirely bandaged because of the craniotomy.* The entrance wound itself was tiny. I had thought I'd see more stitches on his face, but there were none. His face was just fine, except it was so black and blue, so swollen.

He was moving, and he recognized me immediately. "'Coon, 'Coon," he said. He was on a respirator, and it's almost impossible to talk on a respirator, but you could tell he was trying to get that out. I

*Unlike the bullets that struck President Reagan, District of Columbia policeman Thomas K. Delahanty, and Secret Service agent Timothy J. McCarthy, the one that hit Jim exploded, as Devastator bullets are designed to do. Art Kobrine later said that brain tissue about the volume of a walnut had oozed from the wound even before the operation. To get at the fragments of bullet and bone buried deep in Jim's brain, and to remove brain tissue—about the size of a second walnut—that had already died, the surgical team sawed open his skull across the forehead. They also drained the area around his left eye to prevent pressure from an enormous blood clot from blinding him, just in case he survived.

didn't realize how miraculous this was, but the doctors and nurses were completely overwhelmed. They could not believe that this man, who had been so gravely shot, whose brain had been damaged, could be so alert, could recognize people, was actually trying to speak.

He had tubes and monitors everywhere. And he was very, very restless. Sedating a head-injury patient is an extremely risky business, so they couldn't do much, pharmacologically, to make him less fidgety. But he did not seem to be in any pain. I was just so delighted to see him, so thankful that there he was.

Then, all of a sudden, I was afraid. For the first time, I realized how many monitors there were. They kept beeping, alarms sounding, and every time one went off, I'd ask what was wrong. It would be nothing, of course, but it just sounded so loud in there.

Jim was assigned a nurse named Alison Griswold. What a wonder she was. She was on the second part of what they call a "double double"—two double shifts in a row—and she volunteered to stay when the shift changed again, to stay the night with Jim. She was the one who had accepted him up there, and she just wasn't going to let anybody else take over.

Pretty soon, Jim settled down somewhat, and the noises in the room became more regular. Dorothy came in. She was almost seventy-five at the time, and quite frail, and the sight of Jim just crushed her—broke her heart. She stayed for only a minute or two, then went back to our room and refused to return. After that night, though, she visited every day, always bringing cookies and other treats for the nurses.

By this time the President, after some time in recovery after his own surgery, had been brought to a room at the far end of the Intensive Care Unit. In the room next to Jim was Tim McCarthy, the Secret Service agent who also had been shot. I met his wife, Carol, who, like me, was spending the night. And of course the whole place was teeming with White House personnel and security people. This ICU had been transformed almost instantly into a White House outpost. In fact, by the next day a special office had been set up about halfway between Jim's room and mine. It contained typewriters and telephones and televisions. It had snacks and sodas always available, along with just about anything else the President's people might need or want. It was a regular working White House, because the White House is wherever the President is. The whole hospital was under the tightest security you could imagine. There were SWAT teams everywhere, and hardly anyone was allowed in or out.

Even so, we had some visitors. The national security adviser, Richard Allen, and his wife, Pat, who were neighbors and friends, came by, and so did Bob Dahlgren, a very dear friend of Jim's, and his wife, Suzi. He worked at the White House, so I'm sure he got in using those credentials. Senator William Roth of Delaware also stopped by; Jim had once worked for him, and they were close friends. Senator Strom Thurmond and Nancy Thurmond came, too. And Sue Block, the wife of Jack Block, who was then the secretary of agriculture. She was just wonderful to us. The next morning, in fact, she took doughnuts over to Mother and Scott, and that afternoon she took them homemade chicken soup. A lovely lady.

At 10:30 or so, the lights dimmed and everything grew quiet. Not long afterward, someone from the hospital looked in and said now that everything's in order, we need you to come down and fill out the admittance papers. They had them all ready, and after showing our insurance cards, I started to fill out the forms. Suddenly, it struck me how absurd this was. The form asked the "Reason for Admittance." "Shot in the head," I wrote. The form wanted to know whether this was work-related. "Yes." Every question seemed to evoke a bizarre answer because it *was* bizarre, what we were going through. It was as if we were in some strange movie, or a dream. How had the injury occurred? "In an assassination attempt on the President of the United States." What a surreal experience that was.

After I got back to Jim, I stayed up all night, watching. I knew from what Art Kobrine had said that the next three days would be crucial. That's when brain swelling, infections, and seizures might occur, and they could be devastating. It was going to be seventy-two hours before the doctors would feel Jim was out of the woods. I had no intention of leaving his side.

CHAPTER TWO

"Miss Kemp, Don't You Worry"

A COUPLE OF YEARS after Jim was shot, I saw John Hinckley in person for the first and only time. I sat in a corner of a courtroom and watched him led in. When I saw him, I felt no vindictiveness; neither Jim nor I ever has. I just thought that there went the sick, sad son of another family. I was terribly glad he was off the streets, of course—that he would never have another chance to wreak havoc with his fantasies. God only knows what demons drove him to do what he did.

But who knows why any of us turn out the way we are? I can't explain my own case very well. All my life, for instance, I've been a hopeful person—although truth to tell, as a child, there weren't that many things about me that you'd think would inspire great pride or optimism. I was never beautiful, and I was terrible at sports—slow and awkward and usually the last one picked for dodgeball or kickball. Although my parents had considerable musical talent, I could never even carry a tune. But in spite of my shortcomings, I apparently had a healthy ego that kept breaking through. Somehow, I always thought that eventually, things would get better. Often, they did.

I was born Sarah Jane Kemp in Kirksville, Missouri, on February 6, 1942. At the time, my father, L. Stanley Kemp—always called "Stan"—was teaching at Kirksville High School and my mother, Frances Stufflebean Kemp, who had also been a teacher before they were married, was a homemaker. I was their first child.

About a month after I was born, Dad was accepted as an FBI agent and went off to Quantico, Virginia, for training. When he finished, we moved east—first to New Jersey, then to Virginia, and then, when I was two, to Buffalo, New York.

My earliest memories are of Buffalo. We lived in a fourth-story walkup downtown on Arlington Place, a little circle populated with single-family homes and our small apartment building. Each floor had four apartments, two in front and two in back. Ours had one bedroom. That was mine, although after my brother was born, we shared it. My parents slept on a Murphy bed in the living room. We hadn't been in that apartment for long when another FBI agent and his family—Kit and Barbara Carson and their kids, Sally and Scotty—moved into one of the back apartments on our floor. They became extremely close friends of my family and remained so for many years.

I was a devilish child. For instance, before my brother was born, in April 1945, Mother had to rest every afternoon, and she would put me to bed for a nap at the same time. As soon as she went to sleep, I'd escape. I would tiptoe from area rug to area rug so as not to wake her, then leave the apartment and visit other tenants in the building. I particularly loved Ike and Art Gatland, a retired couple who lived just across the hall. Ike was a wonderful baker, and every day, she made yeast rolls that smelled divine and tasted just as good. I also loved to water the flowers. Not real flowers, mind you—flowers in the carpets on the hallway floors. All the tenants rinsed out their milk bottles before putting them outside their doors for pickup by the milkman. There was always a bit of water left in the bottles, and that's what I used to keep those carpets blooming.

When we first moved to Buffalo, of course, World War II was still going on. Because the local factories were supplying the war effort, there was a constant fear of espionage, so our blackout shades went down every night. As an FBI agent, Dad was very active in counterespionage, and he was very conscientious about security.

Even with the war, Buffalo was a fun place to be during those years. Although all the manufacturing in the country was geared toward the war effort and commodities like toys were in fairly short supply, it didn't really seem to matter. My father built me a sled with his own hands, and I vividly remember how I loved our outings in the famous Buffalo snows. He also built us a phonograph. It was inside a chest, and you'd open the drawer to get at the turntable. And Dad's job helped spare us many of the war's worst discomforts. It took him to Canada fairly frequently, and he was able to get things there—bacon and butter, for example—that were strictly rationed in the United States.

We had one of those big old-fashioned radios with a felt front. I loved listening to shows like *Fibber McGee and Molly* and Charlie McCarthy. In some ways, I think that radio helped make me into an avid reader. While I listened, my imagination carried me away, and I could see in my own mind what I was hearing about. Later, when I was devouring series like *The Bobbsey Twins*, *Nancy Drew*, and the *Hardy Boys*, the same thing happened. Those books transported me to a different reality for a while, allowing me to imagine a romantic sort of life I suppose I wanted for myself. The heroes and heroines always seemed to be traveling to wonderful places, encountering fascinating people, experiencing adventures that never seemed to come my way.

That radio also brought us news of the war. The dispatches were always preceded by a sort of siren, and when it wailed, everyone was immediately quiet, eager to hear the latest developments. Even though I didn't understand the war news, I knew that I had to be absolutely still while the grownups listened.

I remember the end of the war quite clearly. We heard about it on the radio, and suddenly, everybody who lived anywhere near our neighborhood park just came running, and there was a huge, spontaneous celebration. I didn't really comprehend what had brought them all together, but the adult joy was catching, and I couldn't help feeling happy right along with everyone else.

After the war was over, life settled into a pleasant routine. There were lots of kids to play with. Our building was just a block or two from a street where there were vegetable and meat markets. So very early on, Mother would give me some money and let me go down to pick up a loaf of bread or some milk. I felt very grown-up. Looking back, I realize what a very different world we lived in, where a mother could feel confident about sending a little girl off by herself in a neighborhood she knew to be perfectly safe and secure.

My parents were very social. They loved music, dancing, and parties, and they frequently played bridge and poker. Almost all their friends were FBI families, and many of those early friendships lasted all their lives.

My father got two weeks of vacation every year, and we always went back to Brookfield, Missouri, where Mother had grown up and Dad had moved when he was a child. Those trips were a dream for my brother, Bill, and me. We visited both sets of grandparents, but spent most of the time with Othermommie and Poppy, my mother's parents. We went almost every day to the country club, to swim in the lake. Daddy golfed almost non-stop, and Mother visited all her old friends. There was an old-fashioned bandstand in a park several blocks from my grandmother's house. It was a real-life version of an all-American town and lifestyle that today exist mostly in the realm of nostalgia.

In 1948, my father was reassigned to Washington, D.C. We did not have enough money to buy a house immediately and moved into an apartment development called Parkfairfax in Alexandria, Virginia. We had friends there waiting for us: the Carsons had moved to the same complex about five months before.

It was an idyllic place for a child. The apartments were garden-style, and the entire development was about two miles long and two miles wide. The buildings were well spaced, with beautiful landscaping and plenty of hills and gullies. Everything was wide open. You didn't even have to cross the street to find plenty of room to play. But if you did, you found yourself in a stand of woods about a quarter-mile deep, and that was very exciting. Summers were particularly great. We played in the woods, collected sassafras roots, and made tea. We waited all day for Lucky, the ice-cream man, to come with his truck. We played canasta and put on plays. And come autumn, school was an easy walk away.

Because I had started school earlier in Buffalo than Virginia law allowed, I was almost a full year younger than everyone else in my second grade class. In retrospect, that was a huge mistake. Academically, I did very well. New York did such a good job teaching reading, for instance, that I was very proficient, while the kids in Virginia were still learning phonics. But I was much more immature than everybody else. So I was never very popular, and I got a bit chubby. Even so, I enjoyed school a lot. And back home in the neighborhood, I had good friends who were closer to my age. Two of them, Myrl and Betsi Burkett, are still close.

During those years, my mother stayed at home, always there for us. Our family ate dinner together every night. What time we ate depended on when Dad got back from work. He would go directly upstairs without a word to anyone. He'd change clothes, take off his gun, and lock it away in a briefcase. Then, and only then, he would come downstairs and say "Hi, Francie," to my mom, and they'd have a highball, as they put it, before dinner. He just wanted that gun to be no part of our family life.

The early '50s were the last years of the big polio epidemics—just before Jonas Salk invented the vaccine that finally stopped the virus. Every summer, thousands of children came down with the disease, which could cripple them, destroy their ability to breathe without mechanical help, or even kill, and terrified parents across the country tried to keep their kids safe by refusing to let them visit public swimming pools and movie theaters.

In 1950, the night before I was to start fourth grade, I came down with polio. Although I had a very mild case, I wasn't allowed to walk for a couple of months and was confined to bed. I spent my time reading and listening to daytime soaps on the radio—*The Second Dr. Malone*, *Our Gal Sunday*, *Guiding Light*, and *Search for Tomorrow*. It wasn't until Thanksgiving that I was allowed to go downstairs. That's where the television was, so I was happy as could be. I was too young to realize how dangerous polio could have been.

By the time I got to high school, I had grown up quite a bit and was having more fun in school. I went to Francis Hammond High in Alexandria, and it was there, during a slumber party, that I started smoking. I had no good reason. It was simply that everyone else was doing it, and it looked so sophisticated, so cool—made you look older. After I got over the initial dizziness, I went right on smoking, although my father called cigarettes "cancer sticks" and I was well aware, later, of the surgeon general's health warnings. It was the usual story. I was young, and thought I had plenty of time, that I'd smoke for a few years, then quit when I got older.

I graduated in the class of 1959. I had applied to two colleges, both of them in Virginia. Mary Washington, a women's college, accepted me right away; William and Mary, a coed school, first put me on the waiting list, then sent word that I'd been accepted. So in the fall of 1959, I went off to Williamsburg. Jim, to this day, refers to my alma mater as "Bill and Mary" and pretends to have grave doubts about its accreditation.

But it was a wonderful school, and I loved it—especially the social life. Of course, college was far different then. As freshmen, we were not allowed to talk to boys after 6 P.M., Sunday through Thursday—a rule designed to encourage studying. We lived in dormitories and had to be in by 10 P.M. on weekdays and 11 P.M. on weekends. William and Mary had the country's oldest honor code, and we took it very seriously.

I lived in a freshman dorm, in a three-room suite with four suitemates. We played bridge early and often. Then there was dating. In high school, we had socialized mainly in groups, but college was another matter entirely, and I really enjoyed dating. Usually, we'd go to the fraternity houses on Friday and Saturday nights, where we drank beer or Purple Jesus (grape juice and grain alcohol) and did lots of dancing.

There was a downside to all the fun. I did not, to say the least, develop very good work habits. Academically, I did terribly. In fact, I did not make grades and—to the great disappointment of my family—I had to stay out of college for a year.

By this time, my father had left the FBI and was working on Capitol Hill as an administrative assistant to Republican Congressman Walter Norblad of Oregon. Dad helped get me a job in his office for my year out of college, a very junior clerical position. I think I did that job well, and I know I learned a lot. It was the year of the Nixon-Kennedy election, and I got to sit in the Senate gallery as Richard Nixon, then vice president of the United States, counted the electoral votes that made John F. Kennedy's victory official. I remember thinking what a sad moment that must have been for him. Practically all the people I knew, from my grandparents to my parents' friends, were very strong Republicans, mostly because they thought of the Democrats as the party of big government and excessive spending. I was following right along in the family philosophy.

At the end of that year, I couldn't wait to get back to college. From that point on, I did just fine academically. I also continued to have a wonderful time—although I had one close call.

Sophomore year, a group of us decided to make the spring-vacation pilgrimage to Fort Lauderdale, Florida. We piled into two cars one Friday afternoon and headed south. Just after midnight, in rural South Carolina, the car I was in was hit head-on by a vehicle whose driver—on his way *back* from spring vacation—had fallen asleep at the wheel.

All five in my car were injured. Everybody but me had a broken pelvis. I had broken my right arm and all my ribs and had a concussion and serious cuts on my face. To this day, I have a radio dial embedded in one knee. One girl in the other car ended up losing both legs below the knees. I spent two weeks in the hospital in Manning, South Carolina, then was able to go back and finish school. I came out of that accident feeling extremely lucky. But it made me realize that even when you're doing nothing wrong, something terrible can happen.

I graduated from college in 1964, one year late. Then, with a group of friends, I moved to Virginia Beach, where I got a job teaching fourth grade.

I loved teaching. And I had a wonderful social life. Virginia Beach, which is adjacent to Norfolk, was filled with young naval officers. There were lots of parties, many fun evenings at the Norfolk officers' clubs. But by the end of the two years I spent there, both the world and I had changed quite a lot. The fellows we were dating were beginning to go off to Vietnam. One guy I went out with was killed in a fire aboard his aircraft carrier. That wasn't all. America's racial problems were beginning to come to the surface in a big way.

I had awakened to race when I first arrived in southern Virginia for college. The train stations there still had waiting rooms for "White" and "Colored," and at gas stations, there were separate bathrooms and separate water fountains for the races. I was shocked. I had never seen any of that in northern Virginia.

But at William and Mary, no one was very politically involved. It was a conservative southern school, and students were much more interested in the weekend parties than they were in civil rights. Of course there were no black students at the college. Freshman year someone did bring around a petition, stating that the signers believed people should be admitted regardless of race, color, or creed. I signed, even though my FBI agent father had always said, "Sarah Jane, don't you ever sign a petition, because it could come back to haunt you." That was as close as I got to political activism during college.

In Virginia Beach, my attitude began to change. I began to feel that maybe it was time to get more serious about life. So at the end of two years, I decided not to remain there. I needed something more substantial. I applied for—and got—a teaching job back home in Alexandria.

That was the year Alexandria began a massive school-desegregation effort. In my sixth-grade classroom, at Charles Ficklin Elementary School in the inner city, I had twenty-eight kids. Four were white and twenty-four were black. The African-American children had never been to a school with white kids and had never had a white teacher. Most lived in a federal housing project in downtown Alexandria.

Those kids were just phenomenal. They were a little reserved at first, but as the year went on, their defenses broke down and they began to see me as a friend. I remember one long discussion when they talked about going to Woolworth's in downtown Alexandria, just as I had done as a child, and how they were always shooed out by the shopkeepers because they were black. It hurt them, they found it profoundly unfair, and they did not understand. We worked a long, hard time on that, discussing in considerable depth matters like their individual rights, peaceful ways to get the law to stand up for you, and the hope that new generations and new attitudes would change things for the better.

It was a great year, and when it was over, I was very sad to see that class move on. I remember writing in their records how much potential they had. A lot of the girls wanted to be schoolteachers after that year. And several kids, inspired by the school newspaper we had put out, wanted to go into writing. They were beginning to develop a real sense that they could make it, and it was hard to send them off to middle school.

Most of my fellow teachers were black, and another white teacher my own age, Jane Vodoklys, and I got to be close friends with them. I drifted away from the friends I had known in Virginia Beach and from college days. Our interests were diverging, and I don't think they understood my increasing interest in civil rights. In fact, I became so entrenched in this community that I began to think white people looked anemic and weak. My parents were compassionate folks, but they were a little slower to get caught up in the spirit of social change. The first time I invited my school friends over to our home for a party, Mother expressed some concern about "what the neighbors would think." But as a former first-grade teacher herself, she had much in common with them, and as she got to know my friends, she thoroughly enjoyed our get-togethers. She loved to hear about our adventures at school.

I had an odd health emergency that first year at Ficklin. One morning I woke up seeing double. The next day, it was even worse—the world looked like a complete mishmash, as if everything was superimposed on everything else. My left eye had strayed as far to the left as it could possibly go and was paralyzed there. Doctors at the Georgetown University Hospital said it could be a stroke or an aneurysm or even multiple sclerosis. But it turned out to be a virus that had affected three cranial nerves, and after two weeks, they sent me home—unable to say whether it would ever get better. For the rest of the school year, I had to wear first a patch over the eye, then glasses with one blocked lens.

That ordeal caused me one night of bleak despair. Alone that evening, I watched the movie *From Here to Eternity* on television. I remember seeing that great love scene on the beach, and suddenly being sure that I was now so grotesque that no one would ever love me, no one would want to marry me, I would never have children, never have the kind of life I had always hoped for. I was disconsolate, and cried myself to sleep. But it was all over the next morning. I woke up and thought *it's going to get better—I know it's going to get better.* That summer, it did.

My second year at Ficklin, I got a class that had given its fifth-grade teacher a hard time. There were a lot of boys in that class, and they tested her. Ultimately, she found it too tough. After several months, she left, and a series of substitute teachers took over for the rest of the year. Not surprisingly, without the foundation of stability and trust they might have established with a single teacher, the students were a bit out of control when I got them, and my second year—although it was fun—was a lot more difficult.

Most of the kids at Ficklin came from intact, two-parent families. Fathers mostly worked, and mothers mainly stayed home. There was no fear of weapons or guns in schools in those days. And I never heard the kids talk about hearing shots in their neighborhood. Violence and drugs were just not part of the culture, not yet.

But you did pick up some feeling of unrest from the kids, as they told stories about older teenagers who were beginning to feel real resentment toward the white mainstream. My boys the second year were decidedly feisty—one moment they were babies who wanted love and attention, and the next, they were wannabe teenagers, trying, sometimes belligerently, to imitate the behavior of the older kids.

During lunch one day, three or four of them swiped several cases of sodas from the truck that delivered to the teachers' lounge and hid them in my car. After school, they showed me what they had done, obviously wanting to see my reaction. I said I wanted them to tell their parents and that I expected a note from each family the next morning. I also told them I had to think overnight about what disciplinary action to take.

That evening, I spoke with a local police officer, who agreed to come the next day after school to talk to the boys. I still remember the panic in their eyes as the officer came in; they were sure they were going to be arrested. It was a great lesson for all of us.

Just before spring vacation that year—on April 4, 1968—Dr. Martin Luther King Jr. was shot and killed. The next day, a Friday, we found the students just devastated by the news. In Washington, riots had broken out, and some of our kids were convinced that there would soon be rioting in Alexandria, too.

Ficklin was right in the middle of the projects, which were made up of brick townhouse units over about five blocks. I visited the kids' homes fairly often and had never felt that the neighborhood was dangerous. I wasn't worried about rioting there, and it never entered my mind that it could spread to my neighborhood, several miles away. But the kids were concerned for me. One boy named Harold—called "H. Rap" by most of his friends, in honor of the black militant H. Rap Brown—came up and said solemnly, "Miss Kemp, don't you worry. If they start rioting today while we're in school, we'll ride on the front of your VW and make sure you get out of here."

One of my first acts of civil disobedience came the following Monday, the day of Dr. King's funeral. Most schools in the Washington area had closed in honor of the funeral, but Alexandria decided to stay open. My fellow teachers were very unhappy about that decision and planned to protest by calling in sick that day. They asked whether I'd join them, and I did.

Of course, civil rights was hardly the only issue of those years. I also was having an increasingly hard time dealing with the war in Vietnam. I was totally against it—didn't believe that the United States should be involved. But my brother had been drafted, after getting sick and losing fulltime student status in his freshman year at the University of Virginia. By the time Bill came back from Vietnam, safe and sound, thank God, I was thoroughly disillusioned, and eager to do something that might make a difference on all the issues that concerned me.

Getting involved in politics seemed like the logical course. I decided not to renew my teaching contract for the next year, and to look for a job on Capitol Hill. During the summer, I volunteered for work at the Republican Congressional Campaign Committee, which worked to re-elect incumbent Republican congressmen and to help Republican challengers beat Democrats. It was 1968, a presidential election year, and I was assigned to count the money that was flowing in from contributors. Within a month, there was an opening for a paid job as a bookkeeper, and it was offered to me.

I was in charge of "special accounts"—which after Watergate, of course, became illegal. At that time, they were perfectly legitimate. I kept a book totally separate from the rest of the accounting system. A boss would hand me fifty to a hundred checks in an envelope, all in relatively small amounts, no more than two hundred dollars. Under the law, the checks had to be made out by individuals; corporate contributions were not allowed. The checks would be earmarked for a particular member of Congress. Sometimes, you could tell immediately, by the codes and geographical origin, what company the contributors worked for. Employees of General Motors, for instance, earmarked a lot of money for Gerald Ford, then a U.S. Representative from Michigan.

After the election was over, I was offered a job as an assistant to Ed Terrill, the director of the campaign division. Our main focus was preparing for the 1970 congressional elections. We had six field men, each responsible for a certain section of the country, who would help the local party recruit good candidates. Then Ed and I would rate the candidates' chances of actually winning and target campaign resources accordingly. Over those two years, I got to know every candidate in the country, as we brought them in for campaign school to improve their chances.

And that is how I met Jim Brady.

CHAPTER THREE

A Bear Named Brady

I HAD HEARD about Jim Brady. He was working in an advertising agency in Chicago that ran a lot of Republican campaigns, and he had a reputation for being very, very savvy. In 1970, he was running a congressional campaign for Phyllis Schlafly and came to Washington to see what sort of resources he could get for her. The Republican National Committee had a cocktail party for candidates and campaign managers, and Ed Terrill talked me into going to it. It was there that I met Jim. We hit it off immediately, and that evening ended up having dinner together.

We had so much in common, starting with our Republican politics. On top of that, he was the brightest, funniest man I had ever met. He wasn't hung up on college days and drinking, like so many others I had dated. His range of interests and knowledge was so much broader than most of the people I knew. There wasn't a single awkward moment that entire evening. He was in town for that whole week, and I kept seeing him. After he got back to Chicago, he called and asked me out there for the next weekend.

It was St. Patrick's Day. And that Saturday was the single most fun day I had ever had. Jim Brady loved to eat, loved to party, loved people—and everybody, in turn, loved Jim. He always had a smile on his face, was the life of any party he went to. He was just absolutely great fun.

Saturday morning, before the St. Patrick's Day parade, we went to a pub called Hobson's and had oyster stew and Irish beer. Then we went down to State Street to watch the parade. It was cold and windy, and there were snow flurries, so every now and then we would go inside—always into some restaurant—before venturing back out to the parade. Over the course of the day, we ate at a Jewish deli, a German restaurant, a hangout famous for hotdogs, a Mexican restaurant, and finally, Benihana, for a Japanese dinner. For me, coming from Washington, which at that time had hardly any ethnic restaurants, this was an unbelievable experience.

For the next year and a half, Jim and I dated long-distance. He was in Washington quite often on business—Phyllis Schlafly eventually fired his firm, but he quickly picked up other campaigns—and when he wasn't, I was in Chicago. I got to know all his friends. Once, he suggested a spur-of-the-moment trip to Florida. It was the first time I'd ever been there, since that horrible accident had cut short my trip in college. And that first year, in late May, he invited me to meet him in St. Louis. From there, we drove over to Illinois, and I met his parents, Dorothy and "Big Jim" Brady, and his daughter, Missy—Melissa Jane was her proper name—who was just a little girl.

That was my introduction to Centralia, Jim's hometown. He had loads of friends who still lived there, and there was always something going on. We went to all of Jim's favorite local haunts—the Elks' Club and Jerry's Bigger Jigger and Gheridinni's for roast beef sandwiches—and there were parties all the time.

We visited again that Labor Day weekend, which was also the occasion of Jim's birthday, August 29, and of the Hambletonian, a horse race in DuQuoin, south of Centralia. For years afterward, that Labor Day visit was an annual tradition.

Just before Christmas that first year, when I was visiting in Chicago, Jim suddenly suggested that we go to Aspen, Colorado, for the holiday. I had never missed Christmas at home, but I called Mom and Dad, and they didn't seem to be all that upset at the idea. So I borrowed ski outfits from Jim's secretary, and that was the first of many Christmas skiing trips to Aspen.

Meanwhile, I had changed jobs. After the election in the fall of 1970, I got lots of offers from the victorious candidates we had funded, all of whom needed people to work for them on the Hill. I accepted one from James D. "Mike" McKevitt of Denver, a popular district attorney who had managed to win in a traditionally Democratic district. He only lasted for one term; two years later, he was beaten by Pat Schroeder. But he was a good member of Congress, and I liked him tremendously.

The 1968 Gun Control Act had just become law. It banned the importation of Saturday night specials, but it did not ban importation of their parts. So after the law went into effect, some American companies and foreign companies with plants on U.S. soil began importing the parts, then putting them together here. Mike, the ex-D.A., having known firsthand the devastation guns were causing in the inner city, wanted to close that loophole. He thought these small guns, used almost exclusively for crime, should be done away with entirely. As a member of the House Judiciary Committee, he made that our number one project. It was my first real brush with the issues of gun control.

We had a very close-knit staff. All of us were young, and we often socialized outside the office. One of the staffers was a caseworker named Janet Dent, who was dating a fellow named George, and when Jim was in town, the four of us often went out together.

Evidently, George had given Janet a gun for self-protection. One Sunday, the two of them got into an argument. According to police records, Janet said, "George, if you feel that way, why don't you just shoot me?"—and he did. Picked up the gun and killed her. The second it was done, he fell apart and called 911—he didn't run—but it was one of those domestic disputes that can so easily end in tragedy when a gun is readily available. That incident moved Mike and the rest of us to work even harder to improve the gun laws.

By the summer of 1972, Jim and I had been dating for two years. But all of a sudden, it seemed we weren't seeing each other so often. Then I found out from mutual friends in Illinois that Jim had been seeing another woman.

He had always been something of a ladies' man, and I had known about it from the start: Ed Terrill had warned me the minute he realized I was seeing a lot of Jim. I knew he'd been married briefly in college. After his divorce, he'd become a fairly famous man about town. *Chicago Today* magazine had named him "Bachelor Cook of the Year," and when I attended parties with him in Chicago, I met many women he had dated before me. On my first visit to Centralia, I learned from his friends and family that I was hardly the first female he had invited out for a visit.

So when I heard he was seeing someone else I wasn't entirely shocked. But we had gotten pretty serious by then, and I was deeply hurt. I decided I'd wasted two years, and the whole affair was over. When he called the next day, I told him I knew about the other woman. I didn't want to see or hear from him again, I said, and I certainly would not be coming to the annual Labor Day celebrations in Centralia. He was stunned. He said I had to come—his mom was expecting me. I said absolutely not—it's done with—and we hung up. I wasn't going to waste any more time with him. I was convinced that this was the end. But I was just devastated. And that weekend was absolute hell. I didn't think I would ever make it out of my apartment again, I was so depressed.

Then, Sunday night or Monday, Jim called. If you come to Centralia, he said, we're going to get engaged. He promised never to see the other woman again. I knew he had been deeply afraid to get married again, since the breakup of his first marriage had been so painful. So that proposal—overcoming how gun-shy he felt—meant a great deal to me. I believed him when he said the fling had meant nothing to him. And I agreed to go.

He ordered a ring, and we decided to keep our engagement quiet until it actually arrived. That fall, when he got the ring, he was running a campaign out in Missouri. He couldn't leave the campaign, so I met him in Kansas City and we stayed at a Holiday Inn. There was a malamute convention there—maybe a hundred dogs and their owners staying at the motel—which made it a particularly interesting weekend. All night long, if one dog barked, they all barked. But we didn't mind. We had dinner at an Italian restaurant, and during the meal, after jokingly presenting me with a cigar band in a fancy box, he gave me my ring, and it was official. Within a few weeks, we went back to Centralia, where friends and family members threw a big party for us. And Jim started planning to move to Washington.

After Mike McKevitt was defeated in 1972, his whole staff moved over to work for another incoming member of Congress, Joe Maraziti of New Jersey. He was a grandfatherly Italian in his early sixties. He had a darling Irish wife, Eileen, as sweet and motherly as you can imagine, and they had seven children and seven grandchildren. Joe had been majority whip in the New Jersey State Senate, very instrumental in redistricting in 1970, and he had carved out a nice little Republican dis-

trict that essentially matched his old Senate district and elected him to
Congress.

Joe was very good to the staff, so we were quite happy for a while.
Then we started noticing unusual things. He lived at the Capitol Hill
Hotel, and his wife and family were up in New Jersey. One Thursday
afternoon, he left to go up to his hometown for the weekend. The next
day, his wife called, asking for him. He hadn't shown up in New Jersey.
All of a sudden, we started getting worried.

It didn't take long to figure out what was up. Over Cherry Blossom
Weekend, the congressman had introduced us to a very attractive
young woman named Linda Collinson. We started getting a lot of
phone calls from her. Throughout that spring, he seemed to be seeing
her, and then he decided to buy a townhouse up on the Hill. It was in
his name only, and he wanted it kept quiet from his wife. Linda moved
in with him.

Another thing: Joe Maraziti had the strangest way of handling the
payroll. I had taken care of payroll matters for Mike McKevitt and did it
for Maraziti as well. In those days, each member was allotted a certain
amount of money per year to pay employees. There was a stipulated top
salary, and no one person could be paid more than that. But apart from
that, a member of Congress could distribute the money any way he or
she wanted. You could have five employees and pay them all very well,
or you could have a much bigger staff and pay them much less.

Our Washington staff was stable; we all had our salaries and they remained the same except when we got raises. But every month you had
to fill out payroll changes, if there were any. And with Joe Maraziti,
there always were—all of them up in his New Jersey office. The first
month he was in office, he put a man who had worked for him during
the campaign on the payroll for a very high salary. I remember that the
fellow signed up for the retirement plan, which suggests that he
thought he'd be on the payroll for some time. But it was just one

month before Joe took him off and substituted someone else. This continued. Joe would pay each one of these people a lot for one month, then that would be it. It was very strange.

Eventually, Joe's affair caught up with him. He had put Linda Collinson on our payroll under a fake name. He did have her do a little work, and she wasn't earning much money. But during the Watergate summer of 1974, when Joe Maraziti was one of the last members of the House Judiciary Committee standing by Richard Nixon, we began to get press calls asking about her. Joe would make us close the office door, turn off the lights, and stop answering the phones so that the press couldn't get to us, and he himself essentially hid out in the Republican cloakroom. Finally, it all hit the headlines: "Beautiful No-Show Adorns Maraziti's Staff." Joe's constituents voted him out of office after his first term.

After a relatively short job hunt, Jim got a political appointment at the Department of Housing and Urban Development, and he moved to Washington in the winter of 1973. That spring, we went house-hunting, and we found a house on Mother's Day. I gave up my apartment and moved in with Mother and Daddy, and Jim lived in our house until we were married.

The wedding was on July 21, and it was everything I wanted it to be. It was in Old Town Alexandria, at Christ Church, where George Washington had attended services. We were married at noon, and the reception was across the street at an old ship captain's home. We spent our honeymoon night at the Watergate, in a lovely suite. The next morning, Jim—true to his incredibly social nature—suggested that we invite some of the family over for brunch. So his parents and mine, my aunt and uncle and cousin, his aunt and uncle, and my brother all came over. On top of that, we spent the week after our wedding at our own house—

along with Dorothy and Big Jim Brady and Missy. Jim went back to work immediately. I took one day off. It was actually a perfect beginning for the kind of marriage we were going to have. We never took time off for the kinds of vacation most people seem to want. We'd take long weekends to go skiing or visit Centralia, but that was about it.

After Joe Maraziti lost his election, I was back in the job market. I was just getting ready to accept a job with the columnists Robert Novak and Roland Evans, when I had a call from Eddie Mahe, an old friend I'd worked with at the Republican Congressional Campaign Committee. Eddie asked what I was doing. I explained about Evans and Novak, and he said, "Get your tail over here." He was the new executive director at the Republican National Committee, and he was putting together a staff. He offered me a job in the campaign division, and I accepted immediately. Working with Eddie again was certain to be fun, and I'd also be working with the new RNC chairman, Mary Louise Smith, a moderate Republican I was quite sure I'd enjoy.

I was definitely still a Republican, although the Watergate scandals had disillusioned me somewhat. My feelings about President Nixon himself remain somewhat complicated to this day. When I was growing up, the Nixons had lived just a couple of blocks away from my family back in Alexandria, so in some sense, I thought of them as neighbors. When he was first elected, I thought he would get us out of Vietnam quickly, and I supported him. But he didn't move fast enough for me on the war front. As time went on, I began to hear stories about the arrogance of the people around him. But I continued to think that Nixon himself was a good man, and the only time I met him—at an event where Republican candidates could have their pictures taken with the President—he was very fatherly and kind to me. When Watergate broke, I just couldn't believe at first that that nice family man would be involved.

Years later, the day after Jim was shot, President Nixon wrote me a lovely letter. "As the eyes of the nation are understandably riveted on the condition of the President," he wrote, "I want you to know that millions are deeply concerned about Jim and are praying for his recovery." I was very touched by that note. It was straight from his heart.

The house Jim and I had bought was in Arlington, Virginia, on South Hayes Street, about a mile from where my parents lived. We loved it because it was so easy for both of us to get to work. Without even getting onto a highway, we could hop onto the Fourteenth Street Bridge over the Potomac to Washington. It had cost a bit more than we'd intended to spend, but Jim had insisted, and I'm glad. It was a lovely three-story brick home on a hill. Our bedroom was on the first floor, along with a living room, dining room, kitchen, and sunroom—plus a great screened porch, which later was glassed in. Jim was always known as "the Bear." He gave everyone animal nicknames, and that one was his, probably because he was so bear-like in stature. I called him "Pooh Bear," or "Pooh." He would lie in the corner of this wonderful porch to watch television, and he called it Pooh Corner.

For our first few years together, Jim was at HUD, and many of his colleagues became our close friends. Among them were his boss, Bill Greener, and his wife, Charlene, and Liz and Hugh O'Neill, Dick and Bobbie McGraw, Ron and Stephanie Weber, and Bob and Suzi Dahlgren. The guys all had a great sense of humor and were very outgoing. They were all workaholics, but they really wanted to relax at night.

We did an awful lot of entertaining during those years. Jim thought it was as easy to have twelve or fifteen people to dinner as it was to have two. So he was constantly inviting people to our house. And he was a huge spender. He didn't spend money on himself, although he certainly was well-dressed. But he was very generous. He thought nothing of buying rounds of drinks, of buying me gifts, of buying things for the house—anything that popped into his mind. I paid the bills, and it was kind of nerve-racking for me. Jim seldom recorded the checks he wrote, so I was never quite certain how many of them were out there. And there were a lot of things we had to do without because so much of our money went to entertainment.

From HUD, Jim moved to the White House Office of Management and Budget. From there, he went to the Defense Department, as a special assistant to President Gerald Ford's Secretary of Defense, Donald Rumsfeld, who would take the same job a quarter century later under another Republican president.

In that job, he had to do a lot of traveling. One of those trips was to Hawaii. While he was there, I got a call from the woman who had opened our bank account when we got married. She told me our mortgage check had just come in, and there wasn't enough in the account to cover it. I said that couldn't possibly be true—I'd kept pretty good tabs—and I asked her to read off the other checks that had come in. The first couple of items were pretty ordinary: the gas and electric companies. Then, all of a sudden, I heard "the Don Ho Singers," and I said, "Wait a minute—how much was that for?" And my Lord, it was for $7,000. No mystery about the identity of the culprit: He was over there in Hawaii, even as we spoke, on business with the U.S. secretary of defense.

I was panic-stricken. I was much too embarrassed to ask my parents for money, so I left the office at lunch hour and went back to the house. I gathered all my silver, the television, stereos and everything else of value—except my wedding ring. There was a pawn shop not far away, and I went to the back door because I was so embarrassed. I hocked all that stuff and got enough cash to cover the mortgage check.

Needless to say, I was humiliated—and furious at Jim Brady. That evening, I cooked dinner and sat there all alone. There was no television to watch, no radio to listen to. When Jim called, I let him know in no uncertain terms what had happened and how I felt about it. It turned out that he had written a check for a party Secretary Rumsfeld was giving for the president of Korea. He had thought a personal check would be easier than trying to arrange a government check. After we hung up, Jim called his military assistant in the Pentagon, and by the next day I had a reimbursement check and was able to retrieve all my treasures from the pawn shop.

When Jim got home, I went to pick him up at Andrews Air Force Base, and what a sheepish look he had on his face! Typically, he had brought me a gift—muu-muus. Not one, which would have been plenty. Being Jim, he brought five.

You could never stay mad at Jim Brady for very long. But I dreaded every trip after that. When he went to Africa, I begged him not to spend a lot of money. When he got back, the secretary of defense got off the plane first, and then I saw Jim's rosy cheeks, and in his hand was a big shield and a spear. In the hold with his luggage, he had the biggest black pot I've ever seen in my life.

In 1976, of course, President Ford lost the election, and Jim knew that he would be without a job. He took his money out of the government retirement fund, a nice-sized check, and invested it in some stocks. So at least we had some money put away, and I was working. But it wasn't quite the same as having Jim bring home a paycheck.

Still, it seemed the less money Jim had, the more he would spend. He'd have lunch with his buddies, who also were out of work, and after they'd had a couple of drinks, he'd go shopping and bring home nice things we didn't need. He also took up the hobby of smoking cigars and pipes, and seemed to put a lot of money into that.

One day I called home to see how he was doing, and he said, "Oh, I'm fine; Bob Dahlgren and I are here bricking the kitchen." Our kitchen was wallpapered, with some wood paneling, and I loved it. But Jim and Bob had decided that it would look good if one of the walls were brick. I was madder than a hornet, because I loved that wallpaper, and I knew Jim often started projects that he never finished. This time, knowing how upset I was, he did finish, and after a while I learned to like the brick wall.

Eventually, Jim signed on as press secretary for Senator Bill Roth of Delaware. He loved that job, and enjoyed the people. While he was there, they worked on a bill sponsored by Roth in the Senate and by Jack Kemp in the House. Jim always called it the Roth-Kemp bill, and the House folks always called it Kemp-Roth. It was the supply-side tax cut that ultimately became law under Ronald Reagan. Jim really made a name for himself in the press conferences they held to sell that bill to the public.

In 1978, I found out that I was pregnant. It was the greatest moment of my life. I had wanted more than anything to have children. And for my mother, it was nothing short of a godsend.

In January of 1975, my dad had retired at the age of sixty, with visions of playing lots of golf and traveling. But he didn't feel well all spring, and lost weight, and coughed a lot. By that summer, it was clear that he was very ill, and Mother finally persuaded him to see a doctor. A chest X-ray showed that he had lung cancer. He had smoked for years, and knew it was bad for him. He was always trying to get me to quit.

He was diagnosed on July 18 and died on November 20, and it was a miserable four months. He was such a vibrant, athletic, youthful man at the start, but totally changed in such a short time, through all that agony. It went so quickly—traveled to his brain and to his liver. Through almost the whole ordeal, I was sure they were going to come up with something that would reverse this. It was only right at the end that I completely realized he was not going to make it. For my mother, it was just devastating. They had been so close, and she'd depended so heavily on him.

After that, she had never been the same. She started seeming much older. The only thing that helped was my news in '78. She was going to be a grandmother, and she couldn't wait. It gave her reason, once again, to live.

Scott—James Scott Brady Jr.—was due on Christmas Day, and I worked right up to the end. He was born on December 29, by Caesarean, and he was gorgeous. It was what I had wanted more than anything. I wanted to live the way my parents had. And I didn't want to work anymore. I wanted to stay home with that wonderful, happy baby.

About this time Jim was getting restless. The presidential elections were coming up, and he wanted to go back into what he hoped would be a Republican administration. Then Eddie Mahe offered him a job as press secretary for Texas Governor John Connally's presidential campaign. Jim took it, and in no time, he was traveling almost constantly. He'd be home for weekends, but that was about it.

Jim always says John Connally raised and spent twelve million dollars to get one delegate. Everyone had expected Connally to give Ronald Reagan a run for his money, but he didn't. The campaign ended in March 1980, and Jim came home. Just a few days later, he had a call from Ed Meese, a Reagan adviser. Jim had been recommended by the Connally folks, he said, and he asked Jim out to California, where he was offered the job of media person for Ronald Reagan. Jim accepted. For the rest of that year, he was gone almost constantly.

After Reagan won the Republican nomination, his campaign moved its headquarters to Washington. Happily, that meant we saw a little bit more of Jim. And as time grew closer, it became apparent that Reagan might well win.

That fall, the candidate had been getting some heavy criticism from environmentalists for saying that trees put out more sulfur dioxide than cars. One day, the campaign plane was flying over a forest fire somewhere and Jim looked down and yelled, "Killer trees! Killer trees!" The press picked that up, and everybody thought it was hilarious except for William Casey, the campaign chairman, who pulled Jim off the campaign for a couple of days. But it quickly became apparent that if anything, Jim's joke had *helped* Ronald Reagan, and he was soon back on the plane.

A few days before the election, knowing Reagan was going to win, Jim called and said I had to come to California for election night. So I flew out and went to the hotel. There was going to be a campaign party at 6 or so, and I was looking forward to it, having spent so many election nights at parties over the years. Usually, you'd wait all evening, and if your candidate won, you cheered and it was so exciting. But that day, the news that Ronald Reagan had won came early, in late afternoon, because of the East-West time difference. So although we went to the party, it was a bit anticlimactic.

The next day, Jim rode back on the campaign plane and I flew back commercially. He was then named East Coast media coordinator, and the Reagan people started the arduous task of picking Cabinet members and staff. Jim worked day and night. And I think the Reagan team was credited with doing an outstanding job on the transition.

But one position that they didn't fill quickly was White House press secretary. There was lots of speculation, and Jim's name was being floated. He had been offered jobs as assistant secretary of defense for public affairs and assistant secretary of the treasury for public affairs, but he held those at bay because of the chance—he thought it was a long shot—that he might get White House press secretary.

One day, early in January, Jim came home and said he thought Reagan was going to name the press secretary the next day. We were having a drink when the phone rang. It was Reagan's designated chief of staff, James A. Baker III, who asked, "If Ronald Reagan called and asked you to serve, would you?" Jim, of course, said yes. Not five minutes later, Ronald Reagan called and offered him the job. And my Lord, you should have seen Jim Brady! At the University of Illinois, he had been a standby for "Chief Illiniwek," the Indian dancer who performs on the sidelines, and he did this great Native American dance, in which he ended up doing the splits in the air. On that campaign, he had gained a lot of weight—I think he was up to 250 pounds—but he was still agile, still able to dance like nobody's business, and Chief Illiniwek was alive and well in our living room that night.

Jim Baker had called back to say that the announcement wouldn't be made until the beginning of the following week. So the only people we told were Jim's mother and mine, and they of course were sworn to secrecy. But somehow, word began to get out that it was going to be Jim Brady. One of the TV networks sent a crew to talk to Dorothy Brady in Illinois, and they asked whether it was true that Jim has been named White House press secretary. Dorothy, thinking it must be official, gave them the nod.

That morning, I had a haircut appointment at Elizabeth Arden. I had on a dreadful old gray coat, which was covered with fuzz balls—my mother detested it—and I wasn't wearing any makeup. My hair was just about to be washed, when the White House called. They were going to announce Jim's appointment in thirty minutes, and they would send a car to get me. So I wrapped that horrible coat around me and rode over to Blair House, where the announcement was made. It was the first time I met Ronald Reagan, and I understood instantly why millions of American voters had found him irresistible. He was charming. He had a gentle look in his eyes and seemed genuinely interested in me, and he spoke of Jim with great sincerity. There was nothing phony about him.

Just before the Inaugural, Jim flew out to California so that he could accompany the Reagans to Washington. It was his first time on what would become Air Force One, and he typed a letter to Scott while he was in the air. It's a document we all cherish.

January 13, 1981
Tuesday

Dear Scott,

I am flying aboard Air Force One to the West Coast to pick up President Elect and Mrs. Reagan and bring everyone back to Washington for the Inauguration.

Only three of us are taking this big bird on the flight which takes us over St. Louis (probably Centralia and Gram's and Pop's house), Kansas City (where your mommy and I got engaged) and Gallup, New Mexico (where there are a lot of Indians) . . .

I have so many things on my mind. I have only a few days left to staff up the White House Press Office, decide when to have the first press conference, develop a press plan for the first 90 days, and have time to keep current on everything I must know to brief. (The briefings, I notice for the first time yesterday, are getting harder. I had an uneasy feeling when I didn't know all of the answers . . .)

I haven't really come to grips with it yet but I'm sure it will all work out. It always does. (Remember, The harder you work, the luckier you get.) . . .

I am going to call Mommy and you soon from the plane. I hope you are awake now and having waffleswaffleswaffles. The Creep-mouse is going to get your feetfeetfeet. . . .

I miss seeing you because you are asleep when I leave for the office and asleep when Daddy gets home. Last night I had the flu and didn't even get to ask what you did while I was at the office. . . .

Well, son. I have not written you the most interesting letter but I feel better getting my worries off my chest and thinking of you and mommy at home with the nice kitties. It was cold this morning when I left and dark too. There will be a lot more days like that.

I love you truly,
Daddy

CHAPTER FOUR

An Inaugural Whirl

I T IS ALMOST impossible to overstate how much our life changed after Jim was appointed White House press secretary. The announcement was made less than two weeks before the inauguration, and immediately, we began to be invited to things, left and right. I had almost no appropriate clothes. After all, I'd been a stay-at-home mom for the past two years. I had exactly one pair of heels—black. And I had that one, miserable gray coat. Jeans and loafers were my usual daytime clothes. So I had to get out and do some shopping almost immediately. I did, and was able to find several good, conservative cocktail dresses that served me well.

One of the first parties I remember was at Bob Novak's place. I knew Bob himself, because I'd almost gone to work for him and also because he and his wife owned a beach house next to one we rented in the summers, in Bethany Beach, Delaware. But apart from the Novaks,

I knew almost no one. Jim, of course, knew everybody, and he was the number one attraction, because the guests, apart from a few members of the Reagan team, were mostly from the press.

I was standing on the sidelines, feeling incredibly awkward, when a woman came up to me. She, too, looked a little uncomfortable. She asked whether I was Sarah Brady, Jim's wife, and introduced herself as Kay Graham. She said she was having a small dinner party later that week—it was Inaugural Week—and wondered if we would like to come. She said to check with Jim, and asked me to give her a call.

On the way home, I told Jim that a woman named Kay Graham wanted to know if we could come to dinner. Jim looked at me with utter astonishment, and said, "My God—why didn't you tell her yes right off?" Any press secretary, he added, would kill to go to Kay Graham's house. Then I realized what he meant: Kay Graham must be Katharine Graham, chairman of the *Washington Post* and probably the most powerful woman in the United States.

Kay Graham's party was an education for me. To begin with, there was valet parking, even though they parked the cars right there on the beautiful grounds of her Georgetown house. I had never been to a party with valet parking. Then there was the fact that Mrs. Graham had called it a small dinner party, which made me expect maybe twelve people, at most. But there were at least fifty there, maybe seventy-five. At the parties I was used to, if the crowd grew so large that the guests' coats couldn't fit in the front closet, they got piled on one of the beds. Mrs. Graham, in stark contrast, had her library set up as a cloakroom, complete with a coat check person. The house was lovely, all lit with candles, and the guest list was spectacular. There were members of the press, members of the Senate and the House, ambassadors, even movie stars. At the time it was all so new to me that just seeing these people boggled my mind.

But that was just the beginning of our incredible new life. Since Jim was a member of the senior White House staff, he was assigned a military aide and driver for the inaugural festivities. And since much of the time Jim himself had to be with Ronald Reagan, the aide and driver often took care of me.

Dorothy Brady and my mother's sister, Aunt Helen Dehner, had come to town for the festivities, and I had bought tickets for them, me, and my mother for the inaugural gala that Friday night. That was the first time we used the driver, and what a way to travel! The aide and driver made sure we got in and found our seats, which were terrific, without any obstacles, no waiting in lines. Everything was smooth and pleasant as could be. Jim, of course, couldn't sit with us, since he had to be with the Reagans. But he did make a point of stopping by our seats to say hello.

The next day, Inaugural Day, the driver and aide were again at our beck and call. Because of Jim's position, we got to sit right behind the President during the swearing-in on the steps of the Capitol. When that was over, we were invited to the luncheon inside, with the President and Vice President George Bush, other senior staff members, and some ambassadors—plus the leadership of the House and Senate.

At that historic luncheon, all the other women were wearing gorgeous suits and St. John's knits and mink coats. And there I was in a camel pleated skirt, looking like a college girl. But it didn't seem to bother anyone. All the people there, including Mrs. Reagan's glamorous Hollywood friends, were incredibly friendly and pleasant. Nobody seemed to notice I wasn't dressed anywhere nearly as well as anyone else. That is true, generally, about Washington: Clothes are not the thing. It's who you are, or the power you wield. Being Jim's wife, I was just automatically one of the crew, no matter how I looked, and they were lovely to me that day and from that time on.

After lunch at the Capitol, we went to watch the parade. Again, Jim had to be with the President at first, and I was kind of alone. But I was seated in the box right behind the Reagans, and once the President arrived at the reviewing stand, Jim came and sat with me.

When the parade was over, we went to the White House. Jim, like many of the other White House staffers, was eager to see his new office. It was lovely—beautifully decorated. It had a fireplace and it overlooked the grounds where so often you see television correspondents doing stand-up reports for the evening news. Jody Powell, Jim's predecessor under President Carter, had left a bottle of champagne, which we enjoyed later.

Then it was time to get ready for the ball. Jim, once again, had to go with the President and his family; they would attend every one of the inaugural balls. But Dorothy and I were going to the Illinois event, along with tons of Jim's friends who had come in from Centralia and were all staying at our house. Because of Jim's position, we could buy pretty much as many tickets as we wanted, and all those folks wanted to come.

The house, needless to say, was a disaster. All these people were staying in our downstairs recreation room, and Scott, who had just turned two, was racing around like mad. It was very hectic. I kept wondering what on earth that military aide and the driver must think of us. Probably, they had thought they were going to be taking care of someone more like Mrs. Reagan's friend Betsy Bloomingdale—very sedate and formal—and instead, here were we, in this suburban madhouse, with people and kids just everywhere. But if that's what they were thinking, they never showed it. They were marvelous to us. The driver watched Scott and chased him around the block, and the military aide—an officer—even pressed Jim's tuxedo pants.

That evening, the driver and aide first took Jim to the White House to be with the President. Then they came back and got Dorothy and me and a few others and drove us to the Illinois ball. Now as anyone who has ever been to an inaugural ball knows, it is not at all what you expect. It is not an elegant affair with beautiful music and gorgeously dressed people twirling around the room. It's more like a huge stand-up cocktail party, with hundreds of people bumping into each other and standing in lines to get a drink. But it was fun, nonetheless, and we enjoyed ourselves thoroughly.

I brought Dorothy home fairly early, and I never saw or heard most of our guests come in that night. But the next morning, I did notice that they had brought home a pretty impressive cache of souvenirs— not just napkins or little plastic cups commemorating the occasion, but also several acrylic tables decorated with the Presidential seal. I didn't really think they should have taken things like that. But I'm sure a lot of people did. I, personally, didn't even get a napkin.

The next night, Scott learned to get out of his crib by himself. Having all these people around was just heaven for him, such fun, and once he figured out how to get out, he came running downstairs to show us what he'd done. We all admired the feat, then I took him upstairs and put him back to bed. Thirty seconds later, he was back. This went on for forty-five minutes or more. Sometimes he almost beat me back downstairs.

Eventually, all our guests went to sleep and so did Jim, who had to get to work very early the next day. But I didn't dare go to bed. By now, Scott was on about his fifty-second trip downstairs, cute as a button in those pajamas with feet, and none of my reprimands had any effect whatsoever. All I could think about was the possibility that he'd escape altogether—leave the house and take off for parts unknown. Finally, I went down to the basement and got a drill and a hook and eye. I put Scott in his crib, then attached the hook and eye on the outside of his bedroom door and locked it. He cried for about ten minutes, and that was it.

The next morning, I called our pediatrician and told him the terrible thing I had done. I felt so guilty. But he said that's exactly what I should have done—that kids need limits and that Scott's well-being was the most important thing. That made me feel much better. Later on, Scott figured out how to open the hook and eye, and the problem started all over again. I had to get stronger and stronger locks to keep him in. He was just not ever going to be a sleeper. He had quit taking naps when he was just one year old, and then he never wanted to go to bed at night. And that's the way he has been ever since: always late to bed and late to rise.

That winter, Jim worked extremely hard. He loved every minute of it, of course—was having the time of his life. Almost every night, he was on television, and Scott loved to watch him. He was a little confused, though, about exactly what his father did for a living. He thought Jim was working for Ronald McDonald. He had a Ronald McDonald puppet, and in his mind, the two Ronalds were one and the same.

Many nights, there were dinners and other affairs that both Jim and I had to attend together. The parties—especially the embassy affairs—became more and more exotic. I couldn't help noticing how different I was in many small ways from the people we started associating with as soon as Jim became White House press secretary. The truth is that it was a lifestyle I wouldn't have chosen for myself. I like to eat earlier, I like to go to bed earlier. I like things much more casual. I'd much rather stay home. I love rock and roll, not classical music. I know this sounds terrible, but there it is. I don't like big formal cocktail parties. I like small, casual affairs with friends. I really don't feel comfortable in big groups of people I don't know.

But for those first few months, in the winter of 1981, it was all new, and wonderfully exciting. It was a true whirlwind, and that's the way I still see it in my mind's eye.

And it lasted fewer than seventy days.

Along with that bottle of champagne Jody Powell had left in Jim's office, he had also left a second gift, which had been passed down to him by Ron Nessen, President Ford's press secretary. It was a hideous bulletproof vest of blue brocade, clearly designed to be worn under a tuxedo. Pinned to it was a note: "Jim, it's not the guns that'll get you in this job; it's the gnats and the ants," meaning the endless tiny annoyances that came with the position.

On Inaugural Day, we laughed, as Jody had meant us to. But it was the bullets that got Jim Brady.

CHAPTER FIVE

God Bless the Greenfield Umbrella

THE NIGHT AFTER Jim was shot, I never slept at all. By morning, he still seemed to be doing very well, despite being on a respirator and hooked up to all those monitors, so I stepped across the hall to where the White House had set up its hospital command post. They had orange juice and coffee and doughnuts there, and also television sets, which gave me a chance to catch up with the early-morning news reports about the assassination attempt. Every time they mentioned Jim, they would talk about "the gravely injured Jim Brady," and stress that his survival was doubtful. And I kept thinking *Why do they say that? He's doing so beautifully.*

There were lots of visitors that morning, mostly White House people and Cabinet members on their way to see the President—who was doing so well that he actually signed a bill into law—but all of them stopped to say hello. There was one stranger who hovered around that morning and every day for the rest of the week, a man so somber that to me, he seemed almost ominous. I noticed that he was talking with various doctors, and he kept looking in at Jim, almost as if he were waiting for him to die. Finally, he disappeared, and I asked someone who he was. The answer just chilled me: He was a homicide detective.

Despite that horrible moment, my spirits were quite high. Jim seemed so alert. I went into his room at one point, and he said—quite clearly, even with the respirator, "feet, feet." I knew exactly what that meant. He wanted me to scratch them.

Finally, that afternoon, somebody said I simply had to get some rest. Around 3 P.M., I did lie down, and I fell asleep for a while. Suddenly, in the midst of a very odd dream, I heard an incredible burst of noise. I woke up instantly, and saw nurses and doctors rushing toward Jim's room. I realized that they had called a code on him, and for a few moments, I was utterly terrified.

I needn't have been. What had happened was that Jim had decided he didn't want to be on that respirator any more, and he had extubated himself—pulled the contraption out of his throat. By then, Alison Griswold was back on duty as his nurse, and she jumped over to stop him. She grabbed his arm, but Jim was so strong that he lifted her right up and she went flying across the bed—and of course, she called a code, bringing all the doctors and nurses running. They were about to reinsert the respirator when Bill Knauss, the physician in charge of the intensive care unit, suggested that they wait a few minutes to see how Jim did without it. And lo and behold, he did just fine.

By that night, I was beginning to feel more secure. I went to bed in the room they had given me and slept pretty well. The next day, Jim continued to get better. The hospital personnel made a ball out of adhesive tape, and he started bouncing it around the room and throwing it at people, so they knew that his cognitive abilities were in fairly good shape despite the damage to his brain. It was going to be the next day before he was truly out of danger, but all of us felt very good about his progress.

Then, all of a sudden, late Wednesday afternoon, Jim just collapsed and went to sleep. When he woke up, he wasn't the same. He was extremely quiet and kept wanting to sleep. Dr. Kobrine had told me that one of the signs of brain swelling is that the patient becomes slow and groggy, so when he came by on rounds, I mentioned the change, and he ordered a brain scan. Thank God, it was a false alarm. The scan was perfect—no brain swelling or infection. According to the doctors, Jim had simply worn himself out, and it wasn't long before he was alert once again.

The next day, Thursday, I finally felt I could leave the hospital for a while. By this time, Scott was at my mother's house, so a White House car took me directly over there. Of course, Scott had no idea what was going on. They'd told him his father had been hurt, but he didn't understand. I played with him and loved him as long as I could, then had the car take me over to our house so that I could pick up a change of clothes.

The house looked incredibly dark and lonely, not at all its usual self. We had chintz curtains, which usually were tied back, but apparently there had been so many members of the media hanging around outside that someone had pulled them all closed for privacy.

Our friends and family members had set up a schedule so that somebody would always be at the house to answer the phone and accept deliveries. And things were arriving practically by the truckload. There were flowers everywhere. I remember with particular fondness a tree sent by Barbara Walters. It lasted for years, and I always called it "Barbara."

By the end of that first week, Jim was moved out of intensive care and into a regular room on the fifth floor of the hospital. He was doing well, but cerebrospinal fluid had begun accumulating in his forehead, behind the flap of skin they had opened during his craniotomy, and it was causing a truly horrible swelling. The fluid would flow in whatever direction he leaned, and the swelling was bizarre looking. During that time, I didn't think he should have any visitors from the outside world, and the Secret Service watched carefully so that no one but doctors or nurses came into the room. But at least once, the agents slipped up. Our friends Dick Allen, who was the President's national security adviser—probably the reason he got past—and Gary Schuster, a reporter with the *Detroit News,* suddenly appeared in the room. Jim, with that dreadfully distended forehead, was sitting on the side of his bed, and I know the sight scared Dick and Gary nearly to death.

Eventually, Art Kobrine drained the fluid, but for a while, I was pretty careful about who got to see Jim—he was still very confused, very sick. People did come by to see me, though. Among them was Barbara Bush, wife of the vice president. I was reading in Jim's room when she arrived, and went out to greet her. She apologized for disturbing me, and when I said she hadn't at all—I'd just been reading— she replied, "Oh, I hope it's a good, dirty book!" Barbara was very good to us for years afterward, always making sure that I was included in any women's get-togethers and inviting Jim and me to several affairs at the vice president's house.

Another person who stopped by was Bryant Gumbel, who had just been named anchor of NBC's *Today* show. He and Jim were fellow fans of the Chicago Cubs, and he simply wanted to wish us the best. Not long after that, John and Nellie Connally came to visit. I did allow them to see Jim, since Jim had worked for Governor Connally. When he left, John Connally had tears in his eyes—in part, I am certain, because it brought back such painful memories of Dallas on November 22, 1963, when he was severely wounded and President John F. Kennedy was assassinated.

Meanwhile, support was pouring in from all over the world. Bears were the gift of choice because of Jim's nickname; all told, we received more than three hundred of them, including one six-footer from Canada. There were mailbags filled with letters and cards from schoolchildren. Restaurants all over town sent food, since everyone knew how much the Bear loved to eat. Our dear friends Dick and Germaine Swanson, who owned Germaine's Restaurant, sent meals frequently.

It was interesting to watch Jim during this period. You could see his mind trying to put everything together. He would switch back and forth, from periods of clear understanding to moments of utter confusion. I made it a point to try to keep him in touch with what had been going on in his life before he was hurt. I would talk about family or friends and read him articles about President Reagan or politics, and most of the time I kept his television tuned to news programs. They had started occupational and physical therapy, which would have to teach him how to do, with one hand, all the things he had done all his life with two. He had not yet begun speech therapy, which he desperately needed.

Because of the damage to Jim's left frontal lobe, which affects your emotions and your ability to mask them, strong feelings of any kind could bring on what we called a "wail"—a very unnerving noise somewhere between crying and laughing. As his brain healed, he was increasingly able to control it, and in later years, he would wail only during extremely emotional moments—sad or happy—such as the singing of the national anthem. But in those early days, it happened all the time: he would start to say something, and suddenly his voice would just wail off.

For anyone, that noise was disconcerting. For Scott, the first time he heard it was terrifying. I brought him in to see Jim the second Sunday after the assassination attempt. He was so excited to see his dad, and of course Jim was extremely glad to see him. As I put Scott up on the bed, Jim started wailing helplessly. He couldn't stop—it just went

on and on. Imagine how that little boy must have felt. He could remember, two weeks before, his great big father playing with him, jok-
ing with him, telling him stories, carting him around on his shoulders,
taking him for rides in the Jeep. Suddenly, here he was in bed, not
looking much like himself, and making this horrible noise. Jim couldn't
finish one whole sentence without breaking into the wail. Scott was
scared to death and burst into tears—something I had very rarely seen
in this happy-go-lucky child. But it was not long before he got used to
the new Jim, and from then on he went to the hospital a lot.

Things went very well until just before Easter, when suddenly Jim's
temperature shot up. It turned out to be a fever triggered by Dilantin,
an anti-seizure drug often prescribed for patients with head injuries.
They brought him a cooling blanket and put him on Tylenol, but nothing worked. That fever just kept going higher.

The nurse Jim was closest to was a darling young woman named
Susan Deyo, who had not yet passed her nursing exam. He called her
"Flash." When she left that evening, she came up and hugged me and
was in tears. By that time, Jim's temperature had reached 105. But she
hadn't been gone an hour when the fever broke, and once it did, Jim
was on the mend once again. We had Easter dinner there at the hospital.

It wasn't long before I decided it would be good for Jim to see
more friends. During the presidential campaign, he had gotten to
know Bill Plante of CBS very well, and Bill had been eager to visit. So
Sally McElroy, Jim's loyal White House assistant, arranged it. When Bill
arrived, Art Kobrine was in with Jim, so Bill and I waited outside. All
of a sudden, the door burst open and Art and the nurses ran Jim's bed
down the hall and into the elevator. "I'm taking Jim to surgery," Art
shouted. "He has air in his ventricles"—brain cavities that should have
been filled with cerebrospinal fluid. Art had tried to let the air out
with a syringe, but there was so much of it that he suspected a major
leak in the dura mater, the membrane that covers the brain. To fix it, he
had to do a second craniotomy. It took more than six hours.

Once again, Jim came through the ordeal beautifully and began to recuperate. But now it began to seem as if something life-threatening was destined to hit him every two or three weeks. He would be gaining strength and eating well, and some new enemy would strike him down. The next setback was pneumonia. And then, for quite a while, he was having trouble swallowing. He lost a lot of weight. He was down to skin and bones—a skinny little soul, which for my Bear is not normal. He ate lots of pudding, and gradually built himself back up.

By this time, I was spending most of every day at the hospital with him, but going home to sleep and spend at least a little time with Scott. One night, for some reason, I woke up in the wee hours and on an impulse, called the nurse to see how Jim was doing. She said it was so strange that I'd called; he had been wheezing a bit, and she had sent him down for a lung scan. I figured it was pneumonia again. But by the next morning, the scans showed blood clots in his lungs, perhaps the most serious complication so far.

Art Kobrine and the rest of the medical team decided that they couldn't use heparin, a very effective blood thinner, because it was so soon since Jim's head injury, and it could cause a hemorrhage in his brain. Instead, they proposed to insert a device called a Greenfield umbrella—essentially, a sieve that would strain out blood clots—into his vena cava, the large vein that returns blood to the heart from the body's lower half. There wasn't a Greenfield umbrella available at the GW Hospital, but doctors were able to locate one in Richmond, Virginia, and ordered it flown to Washington. That was a very scary day, waiting for that operation to take place, because at any moment Jim might throw a deadly clot—a big one that could block the pulmonary artery and kill him. But once it was inserted, Jim was safe once again, and we went back to our normal routine. That Greenfield umbrella remains inside Jim to this very day.

Fairly early on, in the midst of all these medical problems, we had a bomb scare. One evening, a squad of police officers suddenly rushed down the hall, bringing bomb-sniffing dogs, and they told me that they had to get into the room, that someone had called in and said there was a bomb there. The Secret Service stood outside the door while the dogs came in and sniffed, and of course there was nothing there. But just as they were leaving, one of Jim's White House assistants—an older woman named Kathy Ahern, who visited him every day—arrived to see him. She was Southern, and she adored Jim—thought of him as a son. She saw the bomb squad and the dogs and the Secret Service agents clearing out of Jim's room, and she thought Jim had died. It was very hard on her.

As long as there were no immediate emergencies, I felt pretty good about things. For one thing, I had a terrific support system in our wonderful friends and family. My brother, who was living in Oregon, came to Washington the day after the shooting and stayed for a month, on leave from his job. Later that spring, Bill decided to move back permanently because he knew I would need help in the months and years ahead.

There was just one night when I truly felt sorry for myself. It was maybe the second week after Jim was hurt, and a friend of mine, Bobbie McGraw, had come for a couple of days to help take care of Scott in the evenings so I could be with Jim. That one night I came home and just fell apart: *Oh, why me? Why did this have to happen to us?* By the next morning, the wave of self-pity had passed, and I remember feeling very ashamed. Once I got that out of my system, I never felt that way again.

Quite the contrary, in fact. I was afraid at times, of course, and acutely aware of how close to death Jim had been and how fragile he was. But always, in my heart, I felt he was going to get back. I tended not to think ahead very much, but to take each day as it came. In that hospital, and especially with Art Kobrine in charge of us, you almost felt as if you were in a womb, and it was easy to believe that Jim was going to be safe.

And something else: I felt lucky. Jim was on a neurosurgery floor, where everyone has a brain injury or spinal cord damage or cancer of the brain, or any number of other devastating disorders. Being there, you saw every day that you weren't the only one, that hundreds of others faced the same drastic changes in their lives. Many of them didn't have anything like the support system we had, and many were young people, in their late teens or early twenties. So I didn't feel worse off than anyone else. In fact, I felt much luckier.

Often, my spirits would get some unexpected boost. In April, Bill Greener asked me to join him for the annual White House Correspondents dinner. I wore a navy blue silk dress, not nearly as formal as it should have been, and drove to the hospital after feeding Scott. A White House car was going to pick Bill and me up there and take us to the dinner. Just before we left, I was saying goodbye to Jim. One of his problems in those early days was incontinence, and he urinated all over me. The whole front of my dress was soaked. But after patting it dry as best I could, I went on to the dinner.

Although the President usually attends that event, that year Ronald Reagan was still recuperating from his own wounds, and he was resting at Camp David. But he and Mrs. Reagan called in during the dinner and their words were broadcast to the crowd of nearly 2,000 over loudspeakers. Then—in front of everyone—Mrs. Reagan spoke to me, personally, saying how much we shared and sending her love. Tears started streaming down my face, and I had to stand up, and the crowd clapped and roared and toasted Jim. It was an extremely emotional tribute, unlike anything I had ever been through. There I was, in that soiled blue silk dress, but I know no one noticed, and I certainly didn't care. I was thrilled that they loved Jim so much.

As Jim improved, we began to have a regular happy hour every Friday night. Dominique's Restaurant would send over a couple of men in black tie with big silver trays laden with fantastic hors d'oeuvres—

shrimp, caviar, lobster, patés, even exotic delicacies, like ostrich. We had wine and beer in the room, and everybody came who could. It was a wild assembly of people—doctors and nurses and family and press friends and regular friends and people visiting other patients on the floor and some of the patients themselves. Jim always enjoyed it. Sometimes he wasn't as well as other times, so wasn't very talkative, but many Fridays he seemed almost his old self.

In early June, President Reagan came to the hospital for a visit. Jim was really excited, as was the hospital staff. We spruced up the room, which was filled with bears, plants, and cards, and I decided that Jim ought to wear a pair of nice pajamas for the visit rather than one of those horrible hospital gowns. Someone had sent him a pair of designer PJs, and they seemed just right for the occasion.

The President, accompanied by Michael Deaver and Jim Baker, brought Jim some jelly beans, and they had a nice chat. In the course of it, Jim asked the President to thank Mrs. Reagan for the pajamas. Somehow, in his still-muddled mind, he must have linked any fancy apparel with the First Lady, who was famous for her own designer clothes. After the visit, Deaver and Baker briefed the press and mentioned that Jim had thanked Nancy for the PJs. The *Washington Post* printed it. I have always wondered whether Mrs. Reagan read it—and if so, what on earth she thought.

By summer, Jim was doing so well—even beginning to walk with a cane—that we were able to take a Fourth of July outing. We were invited to the White House, where there was a big party on the South Lawn for staffers and their families, with hotdogs and balloons and entertainment and bands. Because of Jim's condition, we couldn't actually be out on the lawn, so we were invited to use the second floor at the residence, along with the people who came with us—my mother and brother, Art and Cindy Kobrine and their kids, Otto and Jan Wolff, Bob and Suzi Dahlgren and their children, and Dick and Jeri Church, old friends from out of town. Scott, typically, was racing around like mad, having a ball. I told him not to run, that this was the White House. But the ushers took Scott's side. This is the people's house, they said, this is his house—let him do what he wants.

We took Jim, in his wheelchair, out on the balcony that overlooks the South Lawn, because we wanted him to be able to hear the music and see all the activity. The crowd noticed, and suddenly, there was just thunderous applause. Later, our entire entourage went over to the Hay-Adams Hotel, where we had rented several rooms. From there, we could see the fireworks. It was Jim's first trip out of the hospital, and it was a wonderful experience for him—made him realize that he really was going to get home.

One day in July things were going so well that I thought I might be able to spend just a couple of hours relaxing in the sun, which I've always loved. It had been such a hard four months that I needed a little R&R. So I went out to the Army-Navy Country Club, which was quite near our house, and settled down by the pool and was enjoying the beautiful day and listening to the normal, happy sounds around me. In some lounge chairs next to me, there were several Navy wives a little older than I was, very nice-looking women. Suddenly, one of them said, "Oh, I have a good joke." One of the others asked what it was, and the first woman said, "What's Ronald Reagan's favorite vegetable?" No one knew, so the woman delivered the punch line: "Jim Brady."

It was as if somebody had stabbed me through the heart. I lay there for a minute, then picked up my bag and my cover-up and moved to the other side of the pool. Of course, it must have been a joke that was going around; I just hadn't been out in public much and had been surrounded by super-supportive people, so the shock was terrible and the pain was very deep. The longer I lay there, the more I hurt. And the more I hurt, the angrier I got. So when I was getting ready to leave, I marched over to them. I said, "Hi, my name is Sarah Brady, and I just wanted to say one thing: I heard the joke you told about my husband, and I want you to know that my husband is one of the brightest, most wonderful men in the world, and I would hope in the future you won't tell that joke again." Oh, the look in their eyes. They were just stricken.

It was a stupid thing for me to do, so immature. I know they didn't mean it. I know we've all done cruel things. But at the time, boy, did that one hurt.

CHAPTER SIX

"Free the Bear"

I N A u g u s t , Jim's father came to visit for the first time since the shooting four months before. Big Jim was not in very good shape. Several strokes and a heart attack had taken considerable toll on his health, and the horror of Jim's injury certainly hadn't helped. But in his heyday, my father-in-law had really been something. He was one hundred percent Irish, a railroad man—yardmaster for the "Q," as folks called the Chicago, Burlington, and Quincy Railroad. Coincidentally, my grandfather had been a conductor for the same line. Big Jim worked, drank, and gambled hard all his life, but he was a good man who truly loved Dorothy and my Jim, their only child. He was a wonderful dancer, even long after he had to walk with a cane. I remember many an evening at the Centralia Elks Club, one of his favorite hangouts, feeling as if I were dancing with Fred Astaire.

But when he came to visit that summer, Big Jim was old and frail, and he had also become a bit deaf. He arrived with his brother, Ed Brady, and their two living sisters, Margaret Burke and Helen Cain, the aunts who had sent the priest to Jim's bedside the day he was shot. Ed, the youngest of the four, drove them all to Washington from Centralia, and he took a whole week to do it. Every day, the four of them would get up, have breakfast, and drive for about four hours, then stop at a motel in time for Big Jim to have a nap and Helen and Margaret to watch the soap operas. They had told me they would not stay with us, but wanted two rooms at a motel close to our home. Helen and Margaret never wanted to impose.

It was great to see Jim and Big Jim together. Jim was doing well by that time, and I think his father was relieved to find him in such relatively good shape. In fact, in many ways they seemed to be in much the same condition—somewhat slowed down and considerably restricted in their movements. Like Big Jim, Helen and Margaret were also hard of hearing, and I'm not sure the three of them really understood what my Jim said while they were there, but they interpreted his wailing noise as laughter—and they all laughed along together for the entire visit. It was good for them all.

By the end of that month, I had grown pretty complacent. It was my custom to call the hospital from home first thing every morning to find out how Jim was doing, but one day I didn't get around to it until about 9. To my horror, I was informed that he had just had a grand mal seizure so severe that he had been taken to one of the operating rooms. He didn't have surgery, but he had to stay in the recovery room for two days. He was seizing so hard that he was put in a respirator and dosed heavily with Valium and narcotics.

All the seizing jogged loose something up in Jim's sinuses. His skull in that area had been shattered by the shooting, and although it had healed somewhat in the intervening months, the grand mal episode had cause new damage. Cerebrospinal fluid began leaking from his nose, indicating that there was an opening between the brain and the outer world—an extreme danger because of the possibility of infection.

To fix the problem, Art Kobrine undertook a series of operations, trying every technique he could think of to close the hole. One of them involved packing the cavity with fat from Jim's abdomen. Others included anesthetizing Jim with cocaine, which led an intern to present him with a bright red T-shirt that declared, "I toot coke." All of Art's procedures seemed to help for a while, but then the leaking would begin again. Art was very discouraged because he knew better than any of us just how great the danger was. Eventually, however, the leaking stopped once and for all. The gap between Jim's brain and the outside world seemed at last to heal on its own.

But Jim did start having a few "breakthrough seizures" every now and then, minor episodes in which one arm would start trembling and his head might shake. So the doctors upped his medication. That, in turn, made him a little sleepier, a bit less active. Those medications are very debilitating. Nonetheless, it was clear to all of us that Jim was now getting near the point where he might come home, and I realized that I had to get ready.

I started with our wonderful porch, home of "Pooh Corner," where I knew he'd want to spend most of his time. I glassed it in with good, airtight windows and had it heated, and I arranged to have an elevator installed that could carry Jim from the garage to the first and second floors. The third floor, from that time on, would be inaccessible to him. Also, I knew that because of his ongoing seizures I needed to be able to give him shots of phenobarbitol. The nurses taught me how to do it, giving me lessons on oranges. After Jim came home, we never went anywhere without a syringe and a supply of phenobarb, just in case. I carried them in a purple bag with a golden drawstring that had originally contained a bottle of Crown Royal whiskey.

In preparation for going home, Jim made several day visits to the house. We were able to keep those visits secret from the press, so that they would be free of outside interference, and we invited family and friends over for the time he was there. Jim just loved those trips, short as they were. He grew increasingly impatient—he just couldn't wait to get home for good.

At some point that fall, one of Jim's friends made a large petition headlined "Free The Bear," and everyone who entered Jim's hospital room was required to sign it. Of course, there was only one person whose signature could actually set the Bear free, and that name remained conspicuously absent from the growing list. But on November 23, just before Thanksgiving, Art Kobrine came into the room on what was clearly a special mission. "OK," he announced, "I'm signing it"—and he did. After eight months in the George Washington University Hospital, Jim could go home.

What a celebration we had! Jim was able to walk out of that hospital, with the aid of a crutch on his good right arm. Television crews filmed the whole thing, as we got him into a van provided by the White House and took off with a Secret Service escort. It was a real homecoming. A neighbor had made a huge sign—WELCOME HOME BEAR—that was hung across the front of our house. And there we were. I knew a new life was beginning, but I never dreamed how difficult it was going to be, and what an awesome responsibility I would find it to have Jim in my care, away from the warmth and security of the hospital.

The doctor had written orders that Jim was to have a registered nurse on duty during the daytime. At night, we could have a "sleeper," someone who would just spend the night and check on Jim periodically. From the start, that second person seemed kind of silly to me, since I would be in the bedroom sleeping with him and was perfectly capable of doing the checking.

But the reality was not just silly—it was dreadful. I don't remember the real name of that sleeper, since we quickly started calling her

"Hitler." She was a horror. All she did was sit in the living room and read a Bible, and once in a while she would come in to see if Jim needed to use "the whizzer," as he called the toilet. She disapproved of pretty much everything about us, and did not hesitate to make that clear.

On Thanksgiving, for instance, I had a huge dinner, with family and friends, and we were all having a wonderful time. Everyone was having a drink—and oh, the looks she gave us because of that. You would have thought we were the worst sinners on earth. She was also very critical of how I treated Scott. He should be quiet, she thought, and never make any noise, and I should be much more strict with him. After a week or so, I simply couldn't stand the constant barrage of criticism. I called the agency that had sent her and said I did not want her back, adding that from that time on, we would take care of ourselves at night.

The RNs were very good, but—understandably—very nursey. To me, it was very important that our house not become a hospital. I wanted it to be Jim's home, not a place where he had to do therapy, and I wanted it to be as normal as possible for Scott, too. Right from the beginning, I felt it was important that Jim go in to GW every day for physical, occupational, and speech therapy. So five days a week, the RNs would arrive early in the morning and get Jim bathed and dressed and off to the hospital. He was there from about 10 each morning until 3:30 in the afternoon.

Although they were lovely women, the nurses were in charge, and I found the adjustment very hard. A lot of little things got on my nerves. For instance, they were always putting Jim's medicines where they wanted them, not where I had chosen to keep them. And I wanted the family to have as much privacy as possible, which was difficult when relative strangers were constantly in our midst. It was very hard to make peace with the fact that I really did need the help. But I did need it. I couldn't possibly have taken care of both Jim and Scott by myself.

The second week Jim was home, I had a big blowup—not at the

nurses, but certainly as a result of the building pressure. We had an enormous amount of laundry all the time, what with Jim's linens and clothes and Scott's things, and one day my dryer quit working. I called Sears to see how quickly someone could repair it and was told it would be about a week. I had a fit. I got hold of the head of Sears and yelled at him, then finally, still seething, went out and bought a new dryer, which I could have delivered right away. It took me an hour or so to get over that fury, and then I was fine again. Slowly, I began to adjust.

One thing that seemed important was maintaining a lively social life. We returned to a fairly normal routine, going out to eat with friends quite often and, at Christmastime, even attending black tie parties at the White House. That period also saw the start of what came to be known as the Eating Club. Shortly before Jim was hurt, Marian Burros—now the great food columnist for the *New York Times*—had written an article for the *Washington Post* about Jim's love of food and cooking. After he got home, she decided to put together a group, mostly folks we'd gotten to know during the Reagan campaign, that would come to regular dinners at our house, each bringing part of the meal.*

I thought it was good for Jim to be around everybody, to keep in touch and not lose his sense of who he had been and was slowly becoming again. There were still some great deficiencies in his brain and would be for many months—even years—to come. Art Kobrine had told me that as it healed, Jim's brain would forge new neural channels to replace old, injured pathways, that in effect, it would figure out on its own new ways to handle thoughts and behavior. But when Jim first got home, that process was far from complete.

---

*The original group included Marian and Don Burros, Germaine and Dick Swanson, Mollie and Jim Dickenson, and Bill Plante and his wife, Robin Smith. It eventually expanded to include Ed and Barbara Fouhy, John and Sara Mashek, and Beverly and John Sullivan. In recent years, we lost Don Burros to a premature death from cancer and we added one other new member, Dr. Roy Coleman.

A perfect example came in early December of that year. At the age of eighty-four, Big Jim Brady died of a heart attack. Of course, I told Jim right away that his father had died, and he did cry for a few minutes.

Jim couldn't possibly have taken a long trip at that point, so I went to the funeral by myself and stayed in Centralia for several days with Dorothy. But when I came back to Washington and tried to talk to Jim about the funeral, he stubbornly insisted that his father was not dead. His brain, still in that uncertain stage of recovery, was unable to process the information. In fact, I am quite sure that he never truly believed Big Jim had died until 1994, when Dorothy died, and he saw his mother's and father's graves side by side.

At some point around Christmas, I decided that we no longer needed the registered nurses and could rely, instead, on nurses' aides. I arranged with Americare Health Services, our in-home care agency, to switch to two nursing assistants—one for early morning, to help Jim get ready and off to the hospital, and one in the early evening hours. The first to join us was Linda Day. We were thrilled with her; she was so nice to all three of us and seemed instinctively to understand our need for privacy. Shortly after that, Emmy Bania arrived. As it turned out, she was to be our own personal angel.

Emmy had just moved to the United States from the Philippines. She was working days at a local drugstore and weekends on the switchboard at a nearby apartment building, and she wanted evening work, as well, so that she could save enough money to bring her family to America. She was college-educated and had been a teacher in the Philippines, but her teaching credentials were not valid in the United States.

She began coming to us weekday evenings around Christmas. And she was a dynamo. For the next twenty years, she saved her money, went to computer school, got an excellent day job using her new skills, and brought her husband, three sons, sister, and parents to the United States. She learned to drive, bought a car, invested in real estate, and sent three sons to college. Through all this, she remained with us. She is, to this day, a beloved member of our family.

Linda and Emmy worked out perfectly during the week. But I also needed help on weekends, which was more difficult for the nursing agency, since many people don't want to work weekends. We had a succession of temporary fill-ins. Some were fine, but most were real doozies. Quite a few got pregnant and had to quit, and I began to wonder if there was something peculiar about our drinking water. One of these was young and quite capable. But for several months, although we realized she was pregnant, she denied it, insisting that she had a major constipation problem. Finally her mother caught on to her real condition, and we lost her.

One of our favorite weekend aides was Margaret, a terrific woman who worked constantly to support her son, who was then about twelve. Margaret didn't drive and was so good-hearted that she would accept nursing jobs that lasted only three hours, the minimum the agency would assign. So she might work three or four jobs a day, taking buses from one to the next, all over the Washington area. By weekends, when she came to us, she was exhausted. Whenever she sat down for a break, her poor eyes would just cross right in the middle of a conversation, and she was asleep. She played the numbers and taught us all about dream books, which try to explain the symbolism behind dreams and help people interpret their own.

It took years for us to come up with a perfect group of people who fit in, could relieve each other, and were completely reliable. Linda Day died during her second year with us, a very sad loss. But by 1985 we finally found Mary Dickerson and Dee Hardy, who, along with Emmy, became our permanent employees.

Given what I know about home nursing care, I have incredible empathy for anyone who needs it. For one thing, the cost is prohibitive. That alone can put good care out of reach for those who don't have good insurance, as we did, and my heart just aches for them. For another, finding *anyone* to take the job—let alone people who are responsible and who fit comfortably into your home life—is incredibly difficult. When we finally managed to get it right, it seemed like a miracle. Once again, I felt incredibly lucky.

We were also blessed in another important way. For the entire eight years Ronald Reagan was in office, Jim remained the official White House press secretary, and therefore was eligible to use White House cars. That first summer after the shooting, the White House garage leased a wheelchair-accessible van mostly for Jim, although other White House visitors, including Vice President Bush's mother, also used it. When Jim had to be transported somewhere—from home to the GW hospital, for instance, or to the White House, once he returned to work on a part-time basis—two drivers were dispatched. Over the years, we got to know the entire group pretty well, and they were all wonderful to our family.

In mid-January 1982, an Air Florida plane crashed into the Fourteenth Street Bridge, then plunged into the Potomac River during a terrible snowstorm. Jim was at physical therapy at the time, and I had Scott outside because I wanted to shovel out the driveway to make it easier to get Jim into the house when the van brought him home. While we were out there, we kept hearing sirens, but had no idea what on earth was going on.

As it began to get dark, Scott and I went inside. Jim, who usually got back at 3:30 or 4, still wasn't home. My mother called to tell us about the plane crash, and I turned on the television and saw the picture of the Fourteenth Street Bridge. I panicked. Usually, Jim's van used the Lincoln Memorial Bridge, but the drivers did change routes occasionally, and I was suddenly convinced that they had been on the

Fourteenth Street Bridge when the Air Florida plane plowed into it. I called the White House to ask whether they had heard from Jim's van. They hadn't. For a couple of hours, I was terrified. But at 8 that night, the van finally rolled in. It had simply been caught in the snarl of traffic caused by the crash.

Throughout the winter Jim continued to do well. One of his problems during that period was that he had trouble distinguishing between people who looked somewhat alike. I don't know how the brain categorizes such things, but I noticed that we would be out and Jim would call some blond, for instance, by the name of another blond, or he would confuse someone of a certain age who wore glasses with somebody similar. If you told him the right name, he was just fine—remembered everything there was to know about the person in question—but he often couldn't get it right at first.

One night, we went out to eat with Alan Woods, a good friend. The restaurant was Middle Eastern and served wonderful food. There was a hostess who was exceptionally pleasant to us. All during the meal, Jim called her "Helen." At the end of the evening, Alan asked me how on earth Jim had known the hostess's name.

I, of course, had realized from the start what was going on. Jim loved and respected many members of the press corps, but there was no one he loved and respected more than Helen Thomas of United Press International. They had a wonderful relationship, and from the very earliest days after the shooting, he had often mentioned her. That night, I had recognized that the restaurant's hostess looked quite a lot like Helen Thomas. Jim, who thought so highly of Helen, had made them one and the same in his mind. And bless her heart, the hostess never spilled the beans.

All told, Jim's first winter at home was fun and social. By March, I thought it was finally time to have Scott christened. We had postponed the ceremony after he was born, since Jim had been so busy with the

1980 presidential campaign, and it had been out of the question during Jim's hospitalization and his first few months back home. But now Scott was three years old, and I decided we should finally have it done.

The church we belonged to, Christ Church in Alexandria, where Jim and I had been married, is small, with lots of nooks and crannies and beautiful woodwork, including little doors that lead into the pews. It was a monumental task to get Jim into a pew that Sunday and, as always, a real effort to get Scott settled down. The minister came over to the pew before the service, and told Scott he had a present to give him when the christening was over. Then the service began.

The organ played a few chords of a familiar hymn—and Jim Brady began to wail. As always, he couldn't help it. He was aware that he was doing it, but helpless to stop. About the same time, Scott realized that he was closed in by the little doors to the pews, and noticed simultaneously that he could escape by climbing under the pews. He did, and proceeded to crawl on hands and knees all the way to the front of the church. Seeing the minister there, Scott tugged on his robe and asked where his present was. The minister, instantaneously, made an extremely wise decision: He would go ahead with the christening immediately, rather than wait until later in the service.

I was a wreck. My husband was wailing. My son had taken over the service. The entire congregation was totally rattled by the combination of events. Somehow, we managed to get through the christening itself, and I then made the second wise decision of the day: to hightail it out of there as quickly as possible. So out we went, Jim still wailing and Scott vociferously complaining that there were no pictures in the book the minister had given him as a present—a Bible.

No wonder folks have champagne after these occasions. I could have drunk an entire case.

CHAPTER SEVEN

"I Hate John Hinckley!"

NOT LONG AFTER the christening, I noticed that Jim seemed to be slowing down. One night, for example, some friends had a party for us. There wasn't a single person there whom we didn't know extremely well. In the van on the way home, Jim asked, "Who *were* all those people?" I was stunned—and a little alarmed.

The next day, I was painting furniture with the daughter of a friend out on the Pooh Corner porch. Jim was watching television in the living room right next to us, and at some point, I wandered in to check on him. All of a sudden, he started having a seizure—the first I had ever actually witnessed, since by the time I got to the hospital after his grand mal episode, he had already been snowed under by drugs. His right arm and leg began to shake crazily. I ran for my vial of phenobarbitol. I knew I had to inject it intramuscularly into a fatty area, and I had to do it as quickly as possible. So I aimed for his thigh, and gave him that shot right through his trousers. Then we called 9 1 1. By the time the ambulance came, he was doing much better, and although he went in to the hospital to get checked out, he didn't have to stay.

But the following Monday, Jim just wasn't himself. As we got him ready to go to GW for physical therapy, he seemed to be having trouble breathing. We called an ambulance, which took him to the hospital, and he was readmitted—a year to the day after the shooting. He was very frightened by being brought back. He told Art Kobrine that he hoped this didn't mean he was going to die.

It didn't. But poor Jim had to stay in the hospital for almost a month. His whole system seemed to have gone into fatigue, and of course the seizures indicated that something that wasn't immediately apparent was going on inside. Once again, he turned out to have tiny blood clots in his lungs; apparently, they had slipped through the Greenfield umbrella. As part of Jim's treatment, Art Kobrine ordered his legs elevated. That, in turn, helped cause an irritation of the esophagus that made it difficult for him to keep food down. He lost weight—sixty pounds in all—and grew more and more discouraged. So did I.

I had given up smoking when I was pregnant with Scott, and had never gone back to that horrible habit all through that first difficult year. But during this period I did. It was a new kind of stress that drove me to it; for the first time, I found myself thinking, *will this never, ever end?*

But something good also came out of that episode. During Jim's bout with esophagitis, Art Kobrine recommended Dr. George Economos, an internist who would oversee Jim's treatment, coordinate all his medications, and be in charge of his general health, both in the hospital and after he went home. Like Art and Cindy Kobrine, George and his wife, Lou, were to become great friends.

When Jim came home from the hospital, he was still recuperating from the esophagitis. So the head of our bed had to be raised with cin-derblocks and his feet were raised to avoid blood clots. He looked very funny in bed—like a jack-knifed tractor-trailer. I remember constantly waking up in the middle of the night and having to climb back up to my pillow, as the raised head caused me to slide toward the foot of the bed. Jim was on a very restricted diet for a while, too: no fat, nothing spicy, no acids, no milk, no sodas, and no juices except for apricot and prune, both of which he despised. I can't imagine what I fed him. And he had to take heparin every day for the blood clots. I gave him the shots in his stomach. They were tiny needles, but he hated them.

For me, the biggest problem during this period was the lack of in-dependence and spontaneity we were facing. We couldn't just decide at the last minute to do something—go out for pizza, for instance. If we wanted to go anywhere, we had to call for the White House van and driver. Everything had to be planned. And Scott and I couldn't go any-where if Jim was at home, unless we had arranged ahead of time to have someone stay with him. Even that made me extremely nervous, since most people couldn't give him shots, and I worried about the lit-tle seizures he continued to experience.

Art Kobrine wrestled for more than six months to stop those episodes. He wanted to reduce Jim's dosage of phenobarbitol, since anti-seizure drugs are extremely debilitating, but every time he did, Jim would have one of these "focal seizures," as distinguished from the grand mal variety. He had one in the hospital lobby, and one at Nathan's restaurant, and several at home. Sometimes, he would come out of it even before I gave him a shot. But there was always the possi-bility that he would go into a life-threatening seizure, so Art worried long and hard about a solution. Finally, he hit upon a combination of drugs that did the trick, and after the summer of 1982, Jim never had another seizure. To this day, we're very superstitious, afraid to change the regimen that has worked so well.

Thank God Scott didn't have to grow up with those seizures. We always tried to protect him from scenes and experiences—with ambulances and police, for instance—that can be very scary for little children. For the most part, I think we succeeded. Still, as he got older, Scott was increasingly aware of Jim's problems, and sometimes it was difficult for them to relate. For example, Jim would read to him from time to time, but he couldn't put any drama into his voice and he read quite slowly, and Scott would simply get bored.

In fact, about that time I began to realize that Scott was much more active than other kids his age. He was not good at listening, and not at all good at sitting still. He was a free spirit who did whatever popped into his mind. That summer, I decided to put a fence in our back yard so that he could be outside without me and I could keep an eye on him from the kitchen window. But he outsmarted me at every turn. That fence hadn't been up for more than five minutes when he discovered a small opening where it met a wall, and he was out that hole before I knew it. The next day, my brother came over to close the gap so Scott couldn't escape again. It was a very hot day, and Bill was working hard. Just as he finished, he heard Scott say, "Whatcha doing, Uncle Bill?"—and there he was, on the outside of the fence, looking in. My dreams of a safe haven for Scott were never to be.

I was overprotective, I know. And it wasn't just a reaction to Jim's being hurt, although I'm sure the shooting made me even more fearful about our safety. Right after Scott was born, I had tried going back to work for just a few hours a day as volunteer coordinator for Governor Connally's presidential campaign, but it lasted only a week or so. I couldn't bear to be away from Scott and worried every minute he wasn't with me. As he grew, I took all the safety precautions I could think of, including installing special locks that were supposed to prevent the windows in his room from opening. Scott, however, figured them out. One afternoon he came down and announced proudly that he had explored the entire roof, and it was really neat up there.

By this time, I knew there was genuine cause for concern about his safety; you could never be sure what his fearless little mind would de-termine to do. But I was also simply neurotic. I became very nervous about driving if Scott was in the car. I wouldn't go on any highways at all and began to fear the Fourteenth Street Bridge, where cars went so fast and changed lanes constantly. I loved fresh fruits and vegetables, and that summer went quite often to a farmers' market at Robert F. Kennedy Stadium across the Potomac. Using the Fourteenth Street Bridge, it was only fifteen minutes away. But I became so afraid of that route that I would go entirely out of my way, making it at least a forty-five-minute trip each way.

That fear of driving lasted for years. If I was near the airport, I was convinced a plane was landing on me. If I drove up a hill, I slowed down at the crest, half believing that the road would disappear entirely on the other side. I was even more afraid when someone else was behind the wheel. The White House drivers thought I was a real head case, since I was always after them to choose a route that wouldn't put us on the beltway—the big highway that loops around the District of Columbia.

Scott, of course, was the focus of much of this neurosis, and I know he suffered in other ways as well. It must have been heartbreaking not to be the center of attention the way most cute, curly-headed toddlers are bound to be. Here was this precious child—the brightest, most wonder-ful kid you ever saw—who was very rambunctious, doing normal little-boy things all the time. And everybody wanted him to be quiet, to be careful not to disrupt his dad. He must have felt that he was constantly being shushed. He must have desperately missed having a father pick him up and put him on his shoulders and play ball with him, although my brother and our friends tried very hard to fill the gap. Meanwhile, I was tired all the time. And when you're tired, you get fussy.

One night I was reading to Scott in his bedroom, and he wasn't pay-ing attention. I guess I jumped on him a bit, and said, "Quiet down now, it's bedtime," and he had a rare temper tantrum. He started crying, "I hate John Hinckley, I hate John Hinckley!" I was completely shocked, because that name had been spoken so little in our home. I said, "Honey, why? We don't hate anyone," and he said, "Well, if John Hinckley hadn't shot Daddy, then you wouldn't be so tired all the time." And I just lay there with Scott in the bed and we cried together. It was a real expiation, I guess, for both of us. He was so little and yet so understanding.

Probably the reason John Hinckley's name was on Scott's mind was that his trial took place that spring. Jim and I truly didn't pay any special attention to it. Strange as it may seem, the outcome just didn't seem important to us. What was important was our future and how we were going to live and make our life better. But Scott, clearly, had paid more attention than we realized. We always tried to be open with him and to talk about his feelings so that any fears or resentments wouldn't get pent up, and he was always expressive, able to get things off his chest. But that outburst came as a complete shock to me, revealing as it did how he had put it all together in his mind: This John Hinckley was to blame for Mommy being tired all the time and for his life being so drastically changed.

That spring was also hard on Jim's daughter, Missy. She had been a freshman at Colorado State when Jim was shot and had come to Washington right afterward and stayed for three or four days before going back to school. But later that year, not long after Jim first came home from the hospital, she had decided not to go back to college for the second semester of her sophomore year. Instead, she came to Washington to be with us. She arrived just after Christmas and stayed through the spring of 1982. I got her a job as a photographer's assistant at the Republican Congressional Campaign Committee, where I'd worked years before.

I had a good relationship with Missy. Jim and Sue Beh, Missy's mother, had married in college, but Sue had left him after only about two years. By the time I met Missy, she was about seven, and her mother had remarried. Jim often had Missy for weekends during the time we were dating. During the summers, Jim had her for longer periods, and they'd spend time with Dorothy and Big Jim in Centralia, which Missy just loved. When Jim and I got married, she was a junior bridesmaid in our wedding. Over the years, Missy visited every summer. She would spend Thanksgiving with us and Christmas with Sue one year, and vice versa the next, and she often came skiing with us in Aspen. Since the divorce had hurt Jim very much, I ended up being the one who communicated with Sue to make all the arrangements, which was a little odd. But it worked out fine. Jim was devoted to his daughter.

That spring, though, was really tough for her. Here was Scott—something of a handful, to put it mildly. And I was struggling just to keep the household running and exhausted half the time, hardly good company for a young woman. Worst of all, Missy was seeing Jim in such devastating shape, and she was there when he had that relapse and had to go back into the hospital, a terrifying event for all of us. My heart has always ached for her, because that time—one of the longest periods she ever spent with her father—was so difficult. She stayed with us just for that one semester, and then, come summer, she went back to Colorado.

Late in the spring, we went to the beach house in South Bethany that Jim and I had rented each spring for several years before he was hurt. It was a wonderful house right on the beach, and our dear friends Otto and Jan Wolff and Dave and Brandy Cole came with us. Jenny Wolff was three months younger than Scott, a good playmate for him. We looked forward so much to that weekend. In past years, it had been such a treat. Jim, of course, had always been at the center of things, up at the crack of dawn, cooking breakfast, flying kites, surf fishing, making chili, getting everyone organized, making everything happen.

This year, from the moment we got there, the difference was obvious, and for me, terribly painful. For one thing, of course, Jim had to enter the house in a wheelchair. In past years we had always had the master bedroom upstairs, but this time, since he couldn't get up there, we took one of the downstairs rooms. That was fine—just different.

But after the drive, Jim had to take a nap. He didn't seem to be showing much excitement about being there; mainly, he wanted to rest and eat and rest some more, and it got no better as the weekend progressed. It was such a stark change that it hit me very, very hard. In the past, Jim had been the one who would push me into doing things with people. Jim had been our leader, full of life and joy and energy, the most fun of anyone. Now he was just a sleeping participant. It was extremely sad, and as the weekend went on, it got worse and worse. That was one of the few times I've ever showed how bad I felt in public, even with close friends. But I think they all felt the same way.

That weekend taught me a lesson I needed to learn: After a disaster like Jim's you shouldn't try to go back and live exactly the way you did before. We had always loved the ocean and sea life, and we certainly didn't want to give them up entirely. In the future, I decided, it would be best to go somewhere else. So the next year we went with another group of friends to Dewey Beach, Delaware, where we had rented a condominium—and had a ball! It is important not to give up the things you love, but you have to do them in a different way. You want to make new memories, not allow yourself to be haunted by old ones.

Late in June, John Hinckley was found not guilty by reason of insanity. I have since read that Art Kobrine thought the verdict depressed Jim. It was certainly true that he was visibly slowing down at the time, but I don't think it was the trial that got to him—and I think subsequent events proved me right.

Several months before, Art had noticed on Jim's CT scans that the ventricles of his brain were larger than they should be, a sign that excess cerebrospinal fluid might be building up and putting pressure on his brain. Early in July, he decided to bring Jim in for some further surgery, this time under local anesthesia, to install a shunt that would siphon off excess fluid. It worked like a dream. Almost immediately, Jim was more alert and energetic, and he quickly resumed making progress in physical therapy.

In Jim's case, Art has pointed out, "Everything bad that could happen seemed to happen." This time was no exception. Less than two weeks after the shunt was installed, Jim suffered compression fractures in four vertebrae, an occasional side effect of heparin, which can leach calcium from the bones. For the next year, poor Jim had to wear a full-body brace, which he hated. He called it the Iron Maiden.

That was the bad news. The good news was that the compression fractures turned out to be the last of Jim's serious setbacks. From that time on, he was steadily on the mend.

CHAPTER EIGHT

The Turning Point

JIM HAS A FRIEND named Steve Neal, a newspaperman from Chicago whom he'd gotten to know well during the presidential campaign. Steve knew what a big Cubs fan Jim was, and in the fall of 1982, he arranged with the Cubs to have Jim throw out the first ball at one of their games.

Jim could not fly, because Dr. Kobrine thought fluctuations in the air pressure on a plane might shatter those delicate bones near his sinuses. So the Cubs folks set up a wonderful train trip. They arranged to have the Anheuser-Busch private car attached to the end of an Amtrak train, and that magnificent car was all for us—Jim and me, Scott, Emmy, and Bob Dahlgren, our old friend from Jim's days at the Department of Housing and Urban Development, who had helped arrange the trip and came with us.

It was absolutely beautiful. At the very end of the car was a little balcony you could go out on the way presidential candidates did in the old days to speak to the crowds. We kept it locked because of Scott. Inside, there was a gorgeous living room with wonderful chairs and sofas. Jim and I had a bedroom with a real bed and private bathroom, and there were a couple of other smaller bedrooms—although larger than regular train compartments—with upper and lower berths and their own bathrooms.

There was a marvelous cook on board who had his own quarters at the back of the car. He called it the "dog house." He served us cocktails and a wonderful dinner—we could order anything we wanted, since there was a fully stocked freezer—and Jim was in seventh heaven. For us, both from railroad families, trains were always a huge treat. We'd taken many in the past, including The City of New Orleans, the famous Illinois Central train from Chicago to New Orleans, and, just before it was retired, we had ridden the Southern Crescent from Washington to Atlanta and back. So we would have enjoyed this trip even if there hadn't been anything special at the other end.

But there was. Our old friends Dick and Jeri Church threw a party for us at their home in Glen Ellyn, a Chicago suburb, and invited lots of our old friends, kids included. It was gorgeous weather, so we were inside and out, and it was a great family affair. In college, Jim had been a member of Sigma Chi, and Dick Church was a fellow Sigma Chi. One of his sons was in a local boys' choir, and that night they sang the Sigma Chi sweetheart song to me. It was lovely, and Jim enjoyed hearing that. It was a wonderful evening.

The next day we went to the ball game. We both enjoy baseball, and to be able to go to a Cubs game—with Jim throwing out the first ball—was a thrill. He did a pretty darn good job, too. During one of the breaks, a little girl who played "Annie" in the musical sang "The Sun'll Come Out Tomorrow" to Jim. I sat there crying, of course. And that wasn't all: George Halas, the owner of the Bears, knew Jim was in town and invited us to the football game the next day. We sat in Mr. Halas's box, and he offered Jim a lifetime seat on the fifty-yard line. He refused it, since we weren't going to be living anywhere near Chicago. But it was a very special day.

While we were in Chicago, Amtrak went on strike, and all passenger rail service shut down. We were a bit panicky at first, because we didn't know how we'd get back to Washington. But it turned out that our private railroad car could be hooked to the end of a freight train, and that was fun, because it meant we took a different route back home. That trip meant a great deal to us. It wasn't just the wonderful new experiences we had had. More than that, it meant something to our future: Now we knew, for certain, that in spite of the shooting, the Brady family was going to be able to get out and travel together.

If anything, that trip reinforced my desire to have a more normal life. Although we were always encouraged to use the White House drivers, I felt guilty every time we had to call them. About that time, the car manufacturers introduced the first minivans, and I thought they might be the solution—a way to achieve more independence. So I traded in our old station wagon and got a minivan, then took it to a medical-supply firm that specialized in making places wheelchair-accessible.

I had an idea. Because Jim's left side and his left foot are stiff, it is very difficult to get him into the front seat of a vehicle. I thought that if you made the front seat so it would spin out, he could sit down on it from the curb, then sit back, and you could push the seat—Jim and all—back into place. I told Freddy from the medical supply place what I wanted, and he made it. It was so exciting. I thought we'd start living a normal life again, that we'd be able to go out whenever we wanted without calling for special vans and drivers. And it was true: We were able to do quite a bit more.

At first, though, my ambitions may have been too high. We soon had an experience that made me realize I had to not try to do too much. During this period, Jim's mother was visiting fairly regularly. The change in her since Jim had been hurt and Big Jim died was dramatic. She had always seemed so active and vibrant before; now she was quite frail. But she could see that Jim was getting better, and she was a real trooper, and we looked forward to her visits. She usually stayed for about a week.

During one of those trips, I suggested that we all go to George Washington's estate, Mount Vernon—just a typical American thing to do. So one weekday morning we got Jim into the minivan and packed his wheelchair into the back. And we took off—no help—just the four of us: me, Jim, Dorothy, who herself needed help, and Scott, an over-active four-year-old. I must have been crazy.

We drove to Mount Vernon, and I let them all out and got Jim settled in his wheelchair, then parked the car. We started into the grounds, and we had to go slowly, for both Dorothy's sake and mine, as I was pushing the wheelchair. It wasn't long before Scott got impatient and took off—and all of a sudden we realized he'd been gone quite a while. We had already been through the house itself, which was very difficult; we needed a lot of help getting Jim's wheelchair through. Then we realized Scott was gone, and I went to pieces. The Mount Vernon grounds are huge, and they slope down to the Potomac. All I could imagine was he'd gone down to the river and fallen in and drowned. The Mount Vernon guards put out an all-points-bulletin for a little boy, and pretty soon someone radioed that they had found him. When they brought him back to us, Scott looked at me and demanded, "Mom, why did you have me arrested?"

By now, it was time for lunch, so the four of us went to the dining room where visitors to Mount Vernon can eat. All by myself, I helped Jim walk up three or four steps, and then we got the wheelchair up. I thought this was fine, but Jim, who didn't have much stamina, was actually exhausted. After lunch, as we got ready to go back down those few steps, he reached the bottom one, then suddenly lost his balance. I could see that he was about to go over, and to make sure he didn't fall on his head on the cement, I pushed him as hard as I could into a big bush off to our right.

Scott immediately went to a telephone and called 911 and said, "Help, my Daddy's fallen," so an ambulance arrived and took Jim to Mount Vernon Hospital. I piled Dorothy and Scott into our minivan and we followed him out there. He seemed fine, but the hospital wanted X-rays to make sure. I knew I couldn't keep Scott in that hospital for two or three hours, so I drove him and Dorothy home, then came back to find that they were ready to release Jim. There really was nothing wrong, although the hospital personnel were worried about his left foot, and had bandaged it up. That's the foot he doesn't use, of course, and it was always sore; it had nothing to do with the fall.

That experience taught me another good lesson: I couldn't do everything on my own; I did have to have some help. In the future, I was much more careful, since Scott's and Jim's safety were far more important to me even than regaining our independence.

In 1984, after all those years working for the Republican Party, I finally got to go to my first presidential convention. It was Ronald Reagan's convention, and the Republican National Committee said they wanted us. I'm sure the White House was behind the invitation.

The convention was going to be in Dallas. Since Jim still couldn't fly, the RNC arranged to have a company called Coachman provide a brand new, thirty-two-foot motor home and a driver, Tim, who happened to be the son of one of Coachman's top executives. It was exquisite. It had a kitchen, a dining room table, a lounging area right behind the driver, and two or three bedrooms. The largest had a king-size bed and private bath, and Jim called it his "attitude-adjustment room"; he was still short on energy and loved to go back there and nap. Emmy came along on the trip, and we also brought Jocelyn File to babysit for

Scott. Jocelyn, the daughter of our friends Debbie and Jerry File, was sixteen at the time.

Ron Ziegler, who had been Richard Nixon's press secretary, was now head of the National Association of Truckstop Operators, and he alerted all the truck stops along our route that we might be coming through. All across the country, they were ready for us, with welcome signs and plenty of hospitality. It made the trip such fun for us.

Along the way, we did some sightseeing. In Nashville, we stayed at the Opryland Hotel and went to Opryland itself, where we heard some great music. Then we went on to Memphis, where we ate barbecue and stayed at the Peabody Hotel, which is famous for the ducks that parade through the lobby on a red carpet twice a day. We visited Graceland, too, and Scott and Jocelyn rode on Elvis Presley's bus. From Memphis, we drove all the way to Dallas in one day. We stayed at the Anatole Hotel, which was the headquarters for the White House. That put us right in the middle of the action.

My first night on the convention floor was incredibly exciting. It was the evening President Reagan accepted the nomination, and we were invited to sit in Mrs. Reagan's box. Next to me were Willard Scott and his wife, Mary. Willard, like me, was from Alexandria, and we had known him long before his fame on NBC's *Today Show*, back when he worked for one of the local radio stations. Having Willard there made the evening all the more enjoyable.

Before we went up to the box, we all met in a holding room. A lot of the Reagan folks popped in and out while we were there, and that was the first time we met Charlton Heston, who later would become my chief adversary as chief spokesman for the National Rifle Association.*
I think he was going to say the Pledge of Allegiance for the convention

---

*The only other time I met Charlton Heston was at a Reagan-sponsored tennis tournament in California in 1993. He seemed to avoid Jim and me, but at one point, we found ourselves face to face. He looked down at Jim and said, "Hello, Mr. Brady." He didn't say a word to me—or even make eye contact.

that night. He struck me—I remember it vividly—as a pompous ass. He was raised somewhere in the Middle West, and I know he didn't grow up speaking in that forced, theatrical way. He sounded very phony to me.

After the President made his acceptance speech, the Reagans threw a celebration party. It was in a tent, and only family, close friends, and White House staff were invited—about fifty people in all. President and Mrs. Reagan walked around, chatting with their guests, and it was the first time I had ever been with them on such a casual basis. Before then, I'd mostly seen them at White House functions or other formal occasions, although I did know Mrs. Reagan a bit better and was well aware of what good care she'd taken of Jim and me. But that night, I truly realized for the first time what a decent and wonderful person Ronald Reagan himself was. He loved to tell stories. You'd be standing in a group, and you could just see the sparkle in the President's eyes, and you could almost read his mind: "I probably shouldn't do this, but I've just got to tell this joke!" Such a personable man, always amusing.

That trip was one of the most interesting ever. I considered my first convention a great success. And on the way back, we even dropped in to Centralia for a visit.

We returned to Centralia in the summer of 1985. This time, I drove us out, and we all looked forward to our stay. Our visits there had always been fun. Almost everyone in town knew everyone else, and Jim had so many friends. It was a typical small midwestern town.

We had been there for a day or two when a dear friend, Dorothy Mann, came to get us for an outing. The Manns were transplanted Texans who owned a construction company that built railroad ties for the southern railroads—a very lucrative business. When I first met them, they lived next door to the Bradys in a huge, charming Victorian house. The matriarch, Marie, was in her seventies at the time, a widow. The rest of the clan included Marie's daughter Dorothy, Dorothy's husband, A.C., and their three living children, who were a bit younger than Jim and me. Dorothy and A.C.'s youngest child, Mike, had killed himself in the early 1970s, when he was a student in high school.

The Manns had been friends of Jim's for years. They threw an engagement party for us, and we always spent lots of time with them when we were out there. In the years since I first met them, they had sold the Victorian homestead and bought a new place on the edge of town. It had lots of land and a swimming pool, and it became the center of social life for many people in Centralia. It was one of those houses where, the minute you enter, you head straight for the kitchen. Marie, who'd had a stroke, was always there, always cooking. There was plenty of food and lots of liquor. They were hard-working, hard-playing people, and to be with them was always fun.

On that summer day in 1985, Dorothy and the manager of the construction company were out doing errands, and they stopped by in their pickup truck with the idea that maybe Scott and I would like to come out to the house and go swimming. We loved the idea, so we got our suits and went out to the truck. Scott got in first, and I climbed in behind him. He picked up off the seat what looked like a toy gun, and started waving it around, and I thought this was a perfect chance to talk to him about safety. So I took the little gun from him, intending to say he must never point even a toy gun at anyone. As soon as I got it into my hand, I realized it was no toy. It was a fully loaded little Saturday-night special, very much like the one that had shot Jim.

I cannot even begin to describe the rage that went through me. To think that my precious little boy, six years old, had actually held a loaded .22—that somebody, that manager, had *left* it there, out on the seat, pushed me right over the edge. The Manns had little children around all the time, kids who were always in and out of everything. It wasn't as if they lived in some kind of adult cocoon. And here was this gun—I couldn't believe it!

Dorothy hopped in next to me, and the manager got in. I handed the gun to Dorothy and asked her to put it away. I didn't want to see it again, I said—get rid of it. They both could tell that I was extremely angry. The manager made some lame excuse about how he had to have that for self-protection against union members in St. Louis. I didn't reply.

All the way out to the Manns' I could think of nothing else. When we got there, I could hardly speak to anyone. I was disappointed and shocked. My father had been an FBI agent, and I'd grown up with a gun in my home. But I had never, ever seen such stupidity—someone just allowing a gun to lie around. I loved Dorothy Mann with all my heart. But her own son had shot himself. How could she have allowed that fellow to have a gun where a child could get hold of it?

Suddenly, I just wanted to get out of Centralia. I know I over-reacted, but I was panic-stricken on Scott's behalf. I called my mother and told her what had happened. Bill and my father had owned an Enfield rifle, and I asked Mother where it was. I said please just make sure that rifle is not there at your house. It wasn't; it was at Bill's place. But by the time I got back to Washington, I was at a point where I didn't want Scott anywhere unless I could watch him every second. Anyone might have a gun lying around. And anyone could get hold of it.

A couple of days after we got back, we were spending a typical August evening at home. We'd finished dinner, and I was washing the dishes while listening to the news on television. I heard a report that the National Rifle Association was pushing a bill called McClure-Volkmer—after its sponsors, Republican Senator James A. McClure of Idaho and Democrat Harold L. Volkmer of Missouri. The bill, according to the report, would do away with the 1968 gun control act.

Instantly, all the fury that had hit me that day in the pickup truck came rushing back. I knew the 1968 law well, from my days working for Congressman Mike McKevitt. It had been passed after the deaths of two of my heroes, Dr. Martin Luther King Jr. and Robert F. Kennedy. It was a small, sensible measure that essentially set age limits for gun buyers—you had to be eighteen to purchase a long gun and twenty-one to get a hand gun—imposed some inspection and bookkeeping requirements on gun dealers, set up some guidelines for interstate sales, and banned the importation of Saturday night specials. It was not, by any means, a restrictive law. In fact, it had no teeth. Even though it required you to fill out a federal form when buying a gun from a dealer, a form that asked your name, address, and age and whether you were a fugitive or felon, there was no mechanism for checking out the truth of what you wrote, no background check. You were on your honor.

A sensible law, hardly an abrogation of anyone's rights. Yet here was the NRA, pushing this bill to rescind it.

I didn't even stop to think. I picked up the phone and called the National Rifle Association's Washington headquarters. I have no idea who answered; at that time in the evening, it may well have been a cleaning person. I didn't care. I just said, "My name is Sarah Brady, and you've never heard of me, but I am going to make it my life's ambition to try to put you all out of business."

The next day, I went to work.

CHAPTER NINE

The Birth of the Brady Bill

DURING THE 1984 campaign, there had been a gun-control referendum on the ballot in California, and Peter Hannaford—Michael Deaver's partner in the Republican public relations firm Hannaford and Deaver—asked me to help get it passed. He wanted me to endorse the proposition or perhaps even do an advertisement on its behalf.

I was very intrigued by the idea, but I happened to mention it to a reporter, a good friend of Jim's and mine, who gave me some excellent political advice. He reminded me that Jim worked for Ronald Reagan. Although the President had taken no position on the referendum and was not involved in any way, our friend argued, California was his home state, and if I took sides on the issue, I might be perceived as speaking for Jim. In the end, I did not get involved, and it's a decision I have never regretted. I would have looked a bit like a carpetbagger, suddenly intruding into California state politics. Besides, knowing what I now know about gun laws, it was not, in retrospect, a very good proposal. It was too complicated—not the kind of law I would want to endorse.

While I was considering the idea, however, I had become familiar with Handgun Control Incorporated, which had been founded in 1974 by Dr. Mark Borinsky, a victim of gun violence.* Peter Hannaford was a member of Handgun Control, and its Washington headquarters was doing what it could to help with the California proposition and had sent me lots of information about the issue. So my first thought, after I called the National Rifle Association that night, was that I'd see whether HCI could use my help.

I called Handgun Control the next day, told them who I was, and asked whether I could do anything to assist them on this McClure-Volkmer issue. HCI's president, a wonderful man named Charles Orasin, immediately said yes. What he'd like me to do, said Charlie, was draft a letter, to be sent out over my signature, to the members of the Senate, who would be considering the measure within the next week.

The following day, I went to Handgun Control's headquarters and we drafted the letter. We had no time for any serious lobbying effort, although I did make a few phone calls trying to persuade senators to vote against McClure-Volkmer. I watched the vote from the Senate gallery. The outcome was shocking. Only seventeen Senators voted against McClure-Volkmer. Eighty-three voted to do away with that piddling little 1968 gun law. Next, the bill would go to the House. There wasn't a doubt in my mind that I wanted to be involved in the fight there. My career as an advocate had begun.

Working against that bill was the first real lobbying effort I put in,

*At the time of its founding, the organization was called the National Council to Control Handguns.

and when it finally came to a vote, I felt gratified. McClure-Volkmer did pass, but in a version that was so watered down from the original that we considered it a victory. The new law allowed mail-order sales of ammunition, for example, but still banned sales of guns through the mail. And dealers could now sell certain guns to people from out of state, as long as the sale was legal in the buyer's home state. But we felt that the most important elements of the 1968 law had been preserved. What's more, in a voice vote the House passed a total ban on machine guns, a measure that hadn't even been debated. On balance, it was quite clear that with some hard lobbying work, we might be able to prevent the National Rifle Association from having its way over the next four years—something its leaders thought was possible with Ronald Reagan's administration in power.

In the old days, the NRA had been primarily a sportsman's group. Its magazines were geared toward hunting and outdoor life and the sort of guns sportsmen use. It wasn't until after passage of the 1968 law that it got into the business of fighting, tooth and nail, against restrictions on any kinds of firearms—no matter how mild a proposed measure might be or how much common sense it made.

In the wake of the 1968 law, extremists within the organization were panic-stricken by what they saw as possible erosion of rights to gun ownership. Little by little they mobilized, and eventually took over the NRA's board from the sportsmen who had dominated it. The group's legislative arm became very strong, and through NRA publications and direct-mail appeals, it began painting everything in terms of black and white—either pro-gun or anti-gun. In their eyes, there were no shades of gray, no middle grounds for compromise.

Over the years, the NRA had grown into a formidable force. The organization could draw on huge amounts of money, and it used that money to fund candidates it approved of and to fight candidates it did not. It had been incredibly successful with these tactics, and by the mid-1980s, members of Congress were famously afraid of standing up to the gun lobby, even though opinion polls consistently showed that the American public overwhelmingly supported sensible gun-control measures. What's more, for many years the NRA had worked hand in hand with police and other law enforcement groups, which had given it extra credibility in the halls of Congress.

Just about the time I started helping Handgun Control, however, that was beginning to change. The first three issues I worked on—all common sense measures, no-brainers with wide public support—produced a growing gap between the NRA and its old allies in law enforcement. The first, of course, was McClure-Volkmer. A number of law-enforcement groups had been disturbed by that attempt to roll back the 1968 law, which they had found useful, and they had been fairly outspoken about their disagreement with the NRA.

Handgun Control's next target was "cop-killer" bullets, the kind of ammunition that could pierce the armor police wore. On this issue, not surprisingly, law enforcement was very much on our side. The NRA was not, and its opposition to a ban on the bullets drove a further wedge between the gun lobby and its former police allies. Congress banned those bullets in 1986.

The third issue was plastic guns. Handgun Control, the airline industry, and nearly every law enforcement group in the country agreed that the law should require any gun manufactured in the United States to contain enough metal to set off the magnetometers at airports. Again, it was a matter of common sense—and again, the NRA opposed it, further alienating many law enforcement groups.

By the time I joined HCI, its chairman and heart and soul was Nelson "Pete" Shields, whose son had been murdered in San Francisco by one of the "Zebra" serial killers back in the early 1970s. After his son's death, Pete was appalled to discover that there were no big lobbying groups for gun control. So he quit his job in Delaware, where he had been an executive for DuPont, took an apartment in Washington with his wife, Jeanne, and, starting with their Christmas card list, began recruiting members and contributors for Handgun Control Incorporated. The murder of John Lennon in 1980 brought the organization an infusion of support. But that had petered out after a while, and reporters never tired of pointing out that HCI was definitely David in the face-off with the Goliath NRA.

If Pete was the heart and soul of HCI, Charlie Orasin was its brain. Like me, he was a moderate Republican. He had once worked for New York's Senator Jacob Javits, and he understood politics like nobody's business. He was a big-picture thinker with good gut instincts and a genius for direct-mail fundraising.

Charlie thought Handgun Control should continue doing what it had done all along: supporting sensible gun-control measures offered by others and working to defeat initiatives from the National Rifle Association. But he also argued that we needed something to capture the public's imagination. It was his notion that we should develop a landmark piece of legislation that would be all our own.

In Charlie's view, there was at least one obvious need. What had been sorely lacking in the 1968 law was any mechanism for making sure that someone who was buying a gun was truly eligible under the law. All you had to do was show proof that you lived in the state where you were buying the gun and swear that you were not a lunatic or a criminal and the firearm was yours. Jim always refers to the law in those days as "lie and buy." What was missing, in short, was any real background check, and closing that loophole, Charlie thought, would be a good basis for our bill.

I completely supported the idea. It is impossible, of course, to say for certain that a background check would have saved Jim Brady from the nightmare of March 30, 1981. But I do know this: John Hinckley bought the gun he used in Washington in a Dallas pawnshop for twenty-nine dollars, and he lied by giving an address that was no longer his and showing an old Texas driver's license as "proof" that he lived there. A background check would have caught that lie. And because lying on a federal form is a felony, John Hinckley would not have been able to buy a gun.

Charlie decided to make this new legislation the highest priority of Handgun Control. That was when we began working on what eventually became known as the Brady Bill. The original piece of legislation Charlie drafted called for a seven-day waiting period between a gun's purchase and the buyer's taking possession. It didn't actually require a background check, but the whole idea was to give local officials the time they would need to run one.

Now we had to figure out how to sell this idea. At the time, Handgun Control was a very small organization. There had been only about twelve employees when I first signed on as a volunteer, and although we had nearly doubled in size since then, our resources were still extremely limited.

Our first order of business was to look for congressional sponsors for our bill. Charlie thought that Representative Morris Udall of Arizona would be a great sponsor in the House, so he was one of the first people we approached. We learned, in the process, an extremely valuable lesson about how important it is to do your homework and make sure that you have all the facts absolutely straight.

We had won some early support for our idea from law enforcement groups, but it was still a very new bill, and many police organizations, public officials, and members of the public weren't even aware of it. Mo Udall listened carefully to what we had to say. This was a difficult issue for him. He was a liberal, but he was also a westerner, and gun control is a very touchy issue in the West. After hearing us out, he beat around the bush a little, then said he'd like to call Chief Peter Ronstadt out in Tucson. Chief Ronstadt, who happened to be the brother of

Linda Ronstadt, the singer, was a very highly respected lawman in Arizona. So right in front of us, Congressman Udall picked up the phone and explained the whole thing to Chief Ronstadt, who said that the bill didn't sound bad to him—he wouldn't oppose it—but that on the other hand, he didn't think it would do much good. Not surprisingly, as a result, Mo Udall turned us down on being a sponsor. That was just about the most humiliating thing I'd ever been through.

The truth was that we were novices at this lobbying game. The members of Congress didn't know me personally, and Handgun Control, the organization, was hardly a household name. The people whose support we were trying to win couldn't simply trust what we were saying. They needed to have a feel for what our bill would do, and to get it, they would have to be checking with the experts back home. From that time on, I vowed, I would never go in to lobby a member of Congress without getting totally briefed on his or her district, and without knowing just exactly where the local law enforcement people stood.

In the end, we found a wonderful House sponsor for the seven-day waiting period—Democrat Edward Feighan of Ohio. It worked out perfectly, because our head sponsor in the Senate was Howard Metzenbaum, of the same state. Our Ohio team worked well together. Ed was a sweet, easy-going person, an incredibly hard worker. He believed so much in our cause. And I could never say enough about Howard Metzenbaum. It's so strange, because his name was kind of a red flag to every Republican; we considered him one of the most liberal members of the Senate—almost the opposite of everything the Republicans admired. Among people I had known, he was widely feared and disliked. But as I got to know him, I realized he was one of the most cultured, educated, dedicated, no-nonsense people you could ever hope to encounter. He was, quite simply, a prince of a person.

Our next task was to figure out how to get our message to the public at large. The National Rifle Association had enough money to buy ads on TV, in newspapers, and in magazines. That was one of the tactics they used in congressional races: They would mount huge campaigns that just saturated the media with their message. We, by contrast, couldn't afford anything close to that kind of advertising blitz. For the most part, we had to depend on press conferences and news stories, which meant we had to think of ways to get the press's attention. That's not an easy thing to do. As Jim says, you don't just "commit news." You really have to work at it.

And dedication and imagination alone were not going to be enough to win our David-Goliath struggle. In order to really get this going, Charlie Orasin knew we had to raise some real money. He came up with an idea for an advertisement that would carry a photograph of me along with an open letter to the people, asking for their support. The headline was a quote: "A bullet from a Saturday-night special shattered my life."

Charlie went to a few of HCI's more generous contributors and was able to get enough money to run the ad in the *Washington Post* for a couple of days. At the bottom, there was a coupon that read, "Yes, I'll join and help the fight," inviting people to send in money and become members of Handgun Control. That ad did so well that it provided enough funds to pay for more advertisements—not just in the *Post*, but quite a few other places. By now, people were beginning to hear about our initiative.

Before I go further, it might be a good idea to make absolutely clear where I stand on the issue of gun ownership. There's an awful lot of nonsense floating around out there, most of it spread by our opponents in the gun lobby, who like to say that Sarah Brady is to guns what Carrie Nation was to alcohol—determined to enact some kind of sweeping Prohibition against them. But I am not a gun-banner.

This is a chance to put my beliefs on the record once and for all. So here is a kind of Brady credo that Jim, too, would endorse:

I believe in the Constitution of the United States, including the ten amendments that make up the Bill of Rights. That means, among other things, that I completely support the right of those who disagree with me to do so using every peaceful means at their disposal: debating, protesting, picketing, even heckling—although I confess, I don't much enjoy that last one.

It also means that I believe in the Second Amendment: "A well-regulated Militia, being necessary to the security of a free State, the right of the people to keep and bear Arms, shall not be infringed." But let me be clear about this: I believe—and historically, U.S. courts have consistently ruled—that the language of the Second Amendment does not mean individual citizens have an absolute right to own guns. The courts' interpretation has always been that the amendment refers to the right to bear arms for purposes related to serving in an organized militia. No court has ever struck down a gun law on the ground that it violated a general right to bear arms.

Opponents of gun control argue that this interpretation is wrong, even though the legal precedent is so strong. And in October 2001, for the first time, a federal appeals court agreed with them, ruling that the Constitution guarantees the right of an individual to bear arms for purposes unrelated to militia service.* If that case goes to the Supreme Court, I suppose it is conceivable—although unlikely— that the High Court will agree with that interpretation, so at odds with legal precedent. So for just a moment, let me engage the issue on my opponents' terms.

---

*The ruling, by the Fifth Circuit Court, came in the case of *Emerson v. United States*. It is worth noting that during the same year, the Courts of Appeals for the Fourth, Eighth, and Tenth Circuits ruled the opposite way in cases before them. All three reaffirmed the long-accepted principle that there is no individual right to be armed for personal purposes.

Suppose the Founding Fathers did mean to declare gun ownership to be a basic right of citizenship. Even if that were true, I would happily and energetically argue for sensible gun control laws.

Because I also believe part of the genius of the Founding Fathers was that they laid out some basic principles that Americans have been able to reinterpret in light of changing times and customs. In modern times, for instance, the courts have been perfectly comfortable with certain carefully defined limits on free speech—those pertaining to political campaign contributions, for instance, and to child pornography.

I am quite certain that if Thomas Jefferson, John Adams, Benjamin Franklin, and company could somehow be with us today, it would be obvious to them that gun ownership is not quite the same issue that it was in frontier America. Take just the simple word "arms." To them, it meant a fairly small array of weapons, and there was little distinction between the sorts of arms owned by civilians and those carried by national armies. Today, would they write the Second Amendment in quite the same way? Would they use language that some extremists read as a blanket endorsement of the right of people to bear *all* arms? How about surface-to-air missiles, or tactical nuclear weapons? I don't think so.

I also think that in their wisdom, the Founders would understand that a nation that has grown far more heterogeneous and urban than they ever could have imagined needs to think somewhat differently about public safety. Would they, today, endorse the right of *all* people to bear arms? Including terrorists, felons, and the mentally deranged? Again, I don't think so.

My stand is pretty simple. I believe that law-abiding citizens should be able to buy and keep firearms. And I believe there are sensible standards that we can and should insist upon when it comes to gun ownership.

First and foremost, we should try to keep guns out of the hands of those who should not have them, including criminals, lunatics, and children.

Second, there are certain classes of weapons that should be out of bounds for private ownership. They include Saturday-night specials, which are used almost exclusively for crime, and assault-style weapons, which serve no ordinary sporting purpose. There may be a few Americans who actually use such guns in hunting. In my view, those people have moral issues of their own they need to address, and they most certainly do not deserve to be called "sportsmen."

Third, I believe that those who do own guns ought to be held to the highest standards of safety. They should be well trained in the use of their weapons, as those of the Founders' generation almost automatically were. And they should be required to keep the weapons secure, so that neither innocent children nor not-so-innocent adults can get hold of them.

Finally, I believe that the Founding Fathers would come down solidly on my side.

CHAPTER TEN

Learning the Rules

W HEN I FIRST started working at Handgun Control in 1985, I was a volunteer. I remained a volunteer until nearly 1989, partly because I wanted to be able to spend as much time as possible with Scott, and partly because it didn't feel right to me to take money for this cause. This was something I believed in, and I was glad to be able to give it all the time and effort I could spare.

Charlie Orasin, however, kept worrying about my status, and eventually, he came up with an idea that turned out to be great both for me and for Handgun Control. He said a speakers' bureau might be able to get me some speeches around the country. I would be paid for the speeches, which would accomplish two goals: It would help out my family financially and also help HCI spread the word.

I was hardly an accomplished speaker. The first speech I ever gave was a year or so after Jim was hurt, to my mother's garden club. I think my mother was astonished that anyone wanted to hear me, and she sat through the entire talk—which was essentially about what had happened to us, and about how suddenly and unexpectedly life can change—with an incredibly pained expression on her face, looking as if she were about to die. I thought I must be terrible. But afterward, she said it was good. She was just suffering, as mothers always do, thinking how hard it must be for me. My good friend, Debbie File, also came to that speech and recorded it.

Not too long after that, Senator Bill Roth, Jim's old boss, called to say that Wilmington College in Delaware would like to give Jim an honorary doctorate and they hoped I would say a few words at the ceremony. Thinking I'd just be thanking the college on Jim's behalf, I agreed to do it, then asked who would be giving the commencement address. I would, he said. I spent weeks and weeks writing that speech, all in longhand. And this time, I decided I could use some help. Burt Bartlett, a friend of Jim's, was in the business of training people for public speaking, and I asked him to come over one afternoon and coach me a little. He gave me some very useful pointers on how to relate to an audience. He told me to be sure to look in each direction and to catch the eye, early on, of someone who looked friendly—someone smiling, perhaps. Then, whenever I needed reinforcement, I should look for that person again to help reassure me that I was doing fine.

My only other speaking experience before Handgun Control came about three years after Jim was shot, when the National Republican Women's Federation asked me to appear at their convention in Phoenix. It was my first little vacation from Jim and Scott, and I was exhausted. I thought it would be good to get away from the stress for a bit, so after the speech I flew to Albuquerque, where I had spent some time as a child. I stayed there a night or two, then drove to Santa Fe and Taos. I was miserable the whole time. I kept thinking how Jim and Scott would love to be there. That trip taught me that first and foremost, I wanted to be near my family.

So when I began my travels for Handgun Control, I tried not to be away from home too many nights. Whenever possible, I would do the entire trip, speech and all, in a single day, and get home that same evening. Most of my appearances were at universities, city clubs, or civic organizations. We always tried to plan them so that in addition to giving the speech itself, I could also meet with the editorial board of the local newspaper to explain our legislation and perhaps attend a fundraiser for some local gun-control group.

In the beginning, most of the groups that signed me up through the speakers' bureau wanted me to give inspirational talks about Jim's and my life, before and after the shooting. Then, as time went on, more and more of those who invited me to speak wanted to hear about gun control as well. Eventually, I combined the two themes into a speech I developed and perfected over the years.

Even at the beginning, I was never afraid to appear in front of groups. Speaking about something you know very well is quite easy. Telling people about something you're really committed to is also easy if you know your business and are sure of the facts. In my experience, even though there are usually a few dissenters present, the majority of audiences are friendly. They want to hear what you have to say.

Still, those trips could be frantic. One of the first speeches I gave for Handgun Control was at the Commonwealth Club in San Francisco. Barbara Lautman, communications director for HCI in those early days, went with me. We took the earliest possible flight to California and went immediately to a luncheon with supporters at the house of an HCI board member who lived right outside San Francisco. That afternoon, I did three or four radio and TV interviews. We weren't going to spend the night in San Francisco—we had to be in Los Angeles later that evening—but Barbara had arranged a hotel room downtown so that we could freshen up a bit before the speech. By the time we got there, after all those interviews, we were running late. We drove up to the hotel and carried in our little suitcases and checked in.

"How long will you two ladies be staying?" asked the guy behind the counter. Oh, about fifteen or twenty minutes, we said. On the elevator, we almost collapsed, laughing, when I pointed out what that man must have thought we were.

After we freshened up, we went to the Commonwealth Club. That was when I saw my first heckler. The Commonwealth Club is a lovely group of people, and most were very supportive. But there's always somebody who thinks, no matter how carefully you explain your position, that you're planning to take everybody's guns away. I got yelled at that evening by that gentleman. But it didn't scare me. I mostly found it amusing.

After the speech, we rushed to the airport to catch a late plane to L.A. Barbara, who was fifteen years younger and considerably faster, got well ahead of me and went through the security checkpoint first, racing for the plane. As I put my things down on the conveyor belt, a small woman ran up and put a gun in my pocketbook. I grabbed the purse before it went through the magnetometer, and I pulled out the gun and gave it back to her. "You can't do that!" I said. She didn't seem to speak any English, and just jabbered at me. So I put my pocketbook back on the belt, and lo and behold she put that gun in again, right in front of my eyes. I grabbed it back, and got the guard's attention. He came over and told me not to worry. It was not a real gun, but a child's cap gun. By this time, the plane was getting ready to leave, so I went through security and hopped right on.

To this day, I don't know what was going on there. Was someone running a test to see if you would notice if anyone tried to use you to sneak a gun on board? Or trying to find out whether the gun would be noticed by the security people? I have no idea. Whatever it was, imagine how different the reaction of the security guards would be today to any remotely similar incident—how entirely changed the atmosphere is, especially since the horrific events of September 11, 2001.

We boarded the plane for the short flight from San Francisco to L.A about 10 P.M. We had almost landed, were very nearly on the ground, when the plane suddenly shot straight back up into the air. "Sorry about that, folks, but the plane ahead of us dropped an anchor," the pilot said. Later, I found out that meant another airplane had stopped on the runway; if we had landed we would have come down right on top of it. That was my first scary moment on an airplane—and the start of my fear of flying, which has been with me pretty much ever since.

It was 1 in the morning before we got to our hotel—4 A.M., Washington time. We were absolutely exhausted. Even so, the next day, we somehow managed to get through one of the first big television appearances I ever did, plus a few other interviews, before flying home. I can't imagine how we found the energy.

Each of these early trips proved to be a real learning experience. Not long after that visit to California, I was invited to address a town meeting near Lake Winnipesaukee, New Hampshire, the heart of gun country, very proud of its militant slogan, "Live Free or Die." I was looking forward to that trip. I had been to Lake Winnipesaukee as a child, and although this was winter, I thought how charming it would be. The organizers had booked me at a place called the Inn of All Seasons, and I had visions of a cozy New England evening right out of the picture books.

I flew to Boston from Washington. Along the way, someone in the cockpit announced that there was trouble with the tail rudder, so we would fly at a somewhat lower altitude than usual. The thought of something being wrong with the rudder made me extremely nervous. I kept thinking the rudder is what makes the plane turn, and I knew that Boston's Logan Airport was not an easy landing, since the plane has to bank into it over the water. That was one of the most tense hours I ever spent.

We landed safely enough, and I went to rent a car. I had rushed off to the airport without a bite to eat, and I thought maybe I could grab something at the airport before driving to New Hampshire, so I asked whether I could wait a half hour or so to pick up the car. The folks at the rental agency strongly advised me not to wait. "Look out there—the snow has already started," they said. Just my luck: I had to drive to New Hampshire through what turned out to be a horrendous snowstorm. I was on the interstate most of the way, and no one was going faster than ten miles an hour. It was a horrible ride. About halfway there I did stop to get a cup of coffee, but I thought I'd wait to eat until I got to my cute little inn on Lake Winnipesaukee.

It stopped snowing just before I got to New Hampshire, and although there had been tons of snow, the roads were fairly clear on the big highways. But the town on Lake Winnipesaukee was a disaster. I managed to plow my way through to the hotel—and what a disappointment! This quaint inn I had envisioned was actually a four-story yellow brick monstrosity, an undistinguished motel built in the 1950s or 1960s. As I checked in, I asked where the dining room was. The guy behind the counter said, "Oh, right over there, but it's been closed for two years."

It was about 5:30. I'd flown with a bad rudder and driven through a horrendous snowstorm. I had to give a speech in a little over an hour, and I hadn't had a thing to eat all day. The man told me there was a Coke machine on the second floor and a cracker machine on the fourth, so I raced from floor to floor to get a little fortified for the speech.

When the people who had organized the town meeting came to pick me up, they said they really should have canceled the speech; they thought the storm would keep everyone away. Sure enough, when we arrived at the civic auditorium, there were two people inside. I felt incredibly guilty at the idea of taking any money when only two people had come, and I also wondered how on earth you could give a real speech to a crowd of only two. I was awfully new at this game.

Before long, the doors to the auditorium opened and in marched
two complete busloads of men—maybe 150 in all. There was not one
woman in the group. And every single one of them was wearing a National Rifle Association hat. So I proceeded to give my speech to two
townspeople, the two organizers of the event, and 150 or so NRA
members. But they turned out to be very polite. We had a question-
and-answer period, and it was not at all confrontational. They never
smiled at me or gave me much encouragement, but at the same time,
no one screamed or picketed angrily, as dissenters often would over
the years ahead.

When that speech was over, I was completely drained. But the organizers, who knew I'd only had crackers and Coke all day, said they
had a great place to eat. We drove up, and there it was: the darling little
country inn I had imagined I'd be staying in. I was so happy—I'd have
my charming New England evening after all. When we got inside, I was
astonished to see that it was a Mexican dance place. Lots of Mexican
music, good margaritas, and wonderful Mexican food. I hadn't enjoyed
a meal so much in years.

I had found it a little intimidating to look out at that Lake Winnipesaukee crowd, knowing that none of them—or very few—agreed
with a word I said. But there were a couple of things that made me
much more nervous in those early days than members of the NRA.
One of them was testifying before a congressional committee.

During one of Congress's recesses, the House Judiciary Committee
held a field hearing in New York City and invited me to testify. Although I almost always wrote my own speeches, Charlie Orasin usually
wrote my testimony, which has to be much more formal than regular
public speaking and also has to be turned in ahead of time. Charlie was
just wonderful at any kind of political thinking, and he always got the
words just right.

When you're testifying, you sit before a microphone facing the members of the committee. All you have to worry about is sticking to the text and reading correctly, with some sense of decorum. I got through the testimony all right, but as the committee members were about to start asking questions, I realized that I had been so tense all along that my jaw was quivering uncontrollably. All I could think of was Howdy Doody—how the bottom of his mouth used to kind of flap up and down. It was the most peculiar feeling.

I was very fortunate that first time—there were no hostile questions of any kind. That's always a worry when you testify, that someone will ask a question you don't know how to answer. You want your testimony to be compelling, you want to know exactly what you're saying, and you want to be extremely accurate and factual, never emotional. So I had studied long and hard to make sure I understood all the facts about the issue and could answer almost any questions. As well-prepared as I was, though, there was always that fear that someone might trip me up.

There was one other public appearance that terrified me. When I first started speaking for Handgun Control, I agreed to participate in quite a few debates, and one of the schools at Harvard University invited me to defend gun laws at one such event in Cambridge, Massachusetts. Just the thought of appearing at Harvard made me feel incredibly inadequate, and I was extremely nervous as I prepared for that event. In the end, I think it went very well.

But it was not long before I decided I should not be taking part in debates. I certainly didn't mind defending my position against challengers in question-and-answer sessions after speeches, for example, but appearing with gun lobby spokesmen as relative equals in staged debates felt as if I was dignifying the other side; it suggested that their position and mine were opposing views competing on equal footing in the public arena. And frankly, I didn't consider the two arguments to be equal. According to the polling, I represented what 95 percent of the American public believed. The gun lobby spoke for only 5 percent. As the Brady bill began to make real progress, and as both Handgun Control and I became better known across the country, my presence at some event could draw press attention it wouldn't otherwise attract. To tell the truth, I didn't particularly want to lend credence and publicity to my opponents.

It is worth noting, incidentally, that the Reagan administration didn't do much for them, either. The National Rifle Association's leaders had thought that Ronald Reagan's election paved the way for them to get almost everything they wanted from Washington. They made much of the fact that the President was one of their own—a card-carrying life member of their organization. But I don't think President Reagan cared one bit about their agenda. He never fought for any of the gun lobby's legislation. And in a conversation a few years later, he told me that he had never actually joined the NRA, despite its public gloating about his life membership. Clearly somewhat amused by the whole subject, he said, "They just gave me a card."

When I first decided to get involved with Handgun Control, I wanted to make sure the White House knew. President Reagan had just been re-elected, and I did not want to be disrespectful in any way. Donald Regan was White House chief of staff at the time, so I called him and explained my decision. He thanked me for letting him know, and said his wife, Ann, would be right there in my corner, fighting.

That was it. I never heard anything negative from anyone in the administration from that point on. As Jim got better, we were included more and more in White House activities. The Reagans always saw to it that we were an integral part of things. They have never been anything but wonderful to us.

Which reminds me: Jim just got a birthday letter from Nancy. They never forget his birthday.

CHAPTER ELEVEN

Cowardly Lions
and Brainless Scarecrows

Toward the end of 1987, Handgun Control lost two of its most valued team members. Barbara Lautman, our communications director—a human whirlwind who had astonished me with her energy and knowledge—left to become executive director of our embryonic sister organization, the Center to Prevent Handgun Violence, which had been set up to pursue educational ventures distinct from our lobbying activities. Mary Louise Westmoreland, our wonderful legislative director, went to work on the staff of Senator Howard Metzenbaum of Ohio, the Brady bill's Senate sponsor; from there, she would continue to be very helpful to us.

Susan Whitmore, who had started at Handgun Control the same day I did as an assistant to Barbara Lautman, succeeded Barbara as communications director. As our new legislative director, Charlie Orasin hired Gail Hoffman, who had been chief of staff to a state senator in Massachusetts. Gail, Susan, and I came together just as the effort to pass the Brady bill was beginning to take off, and during what I think of as our Glory Years, we worked incredibly well as a team. Remembering those terrific adventure stories I had loved so as a child, I always thought of our little threesome as the Bobbsey Twins Plus One. What adventures we had together!

Gail, who had considerable experience in statewide campaigns, immediately started to organize the legislative work ahead. She examined the voting records of all members of Congress—looking, for instance, at how each one had voted on issues such as the McClure-Volkmer attempt to roll back the 1968 gun law and the ban on cop-killer bullets—and developed a rating system for every incumbent. Someone ranked number one was solidly on our side; a two was leaning toward our position; a three was undecided; a four was leaning against us, and a five was totally opposed. More broadly, Gail was responsible for planning the overall strategy to get the Brady bill enacted into law. She helped develop the agenda and the marching orders for folks in the other divisions of Handgun Control, so that everybody involved in the effort knew precisely what part he or she was to play. Perhaps most important of all, Gail had an incredible winning attitude from her very first day on the job. "We can do it—I don't care what anybody says," she'd insist. "This is winnable."

One example of her can-do approach that I remember especially fondly took place after Ed Feighan of Ohio agreed to be Brady's main sponsor in the House of Representatives. When Feighan first introduced Brady in 1987, the bill was a real long shot. The National Rifle Association was such a threatening presence in the halls of Congress that even a potentially powerful friend of gun control like Barney Frank of Massachusetts was urging fellow Democrats to abandon the issue as a losing cause. Feighan's legislative assistant was George Stephanopoulos, who later went on to fame in the Clinton administration, and even George said to us, "Too bad—this is a wonderful bill, but it's not going to pass." Gail never missed a beat. "No, George, that's the wrong spin," she told him. "It *is* going to pass." When she said it, it was hard not to believe her. And it was not long before she had Barney Frank on board as well.

Susan Whitmore turned out to be a natural as communications director. She understood the press, got to know the individual reporters well, and instinctively understood how to put together a good media campaign. She was a great leader and had a terrific staff—loyal and tireless. The press conferences she arranged drew cameras and reporters galore. She was constantly preparing op-ed page articles for us and our supporters and getting them placed in newspapers around the country. Whenever we traveled, for speeches or on other business, she would set up meetings so that we could explain Brady to the editorial boards of local newspapers. She made sure the press got weekly, if not daily, updates on the latest polling and research—anything they needed to keep up with the issue.

And two or three times a week she'd be in my office with stationery and a pen, making sure I kept in touch with press people who had done outstanding reporting on the gun-control issue or who had simply been good to me and to Jim over the years. In the latter category were folks like Steve Neal, the Chicago columnist who had helped arranged for Jim to throw out the ball for the Cubs, and Ann Landers, who always was writing approvingly about us and the gun effort. Susan never missed a chance to keep those relationships open and our valuable ties strong.

It was obvious that to win anything, we needed the support of law enforcement. This became one of our biggest priorities. We were not trying to enact a law that simply made people feel good about themselves; we wanted one that police truly felt would be helpful, one they would support with genuine enthusiasm. So Handgun Control set up a law-enforcement division, designed to coordinate with and build support among law enforcement groups across the country. One of its most critical members was a woman named Jane Clarenbach, who had been working with law enforcement for years and knew all of the organizations well.

I incorporated this mission into my other lobbying duties, and over the next few years, I attended law enforcement conventions all over the United States, presenting our thinking first to the organizations' boards of directors, then to entire membership groups. I remember quite vividly my first big speech to one of these groups, the Fraternal Order of Police—the largest rank-and-file organization in the country. One of our contacts, a former policeman from Oklahoma named Richard Boyd, arranged for me to speak at the FOP's national convention in Mobile, Alabama. Jane went with me, and the night before the speech, an incredibly sultry evening, we had a wonderful time eating seafood and drinking beer with all the cops down by the waterfront.

The next day, I spoke to 7,000 police officers. I told them, of course, about my father's career in law enforcement. I told them about that bulletproof vest Jody Powell had bequeathed to Jim. And I told them about the Brady bill, and our conviction that it would make life safer for civilians and police alike. Jane recalls "the standing ovation for a woman who they knew had a honest respect for law enforcement." When it was over, the Fraternal Order of Police polled its members, who almost unanimously endorsed the Brady bill. That was a special thrill, since the NRA had been putting it about that rank-and-file police officers did not support us.

Meanwhile, a separate group at Handgun Control concentrated on winning the support of other kinds of organizations—groups representing sectors of society that had a deep interest in public safety. They were disparate organizations: the National League of Cities and the National Council of Churches, the U.S. Conference of Mayors and the AFL-CIO, the National Association of Counties and the American

Medical Association, the PTA and the American Bar Association, the National Education Association and the International Ladies Garment Workers Union. It wasn't really a formal slogan, but our message about the waiting-period legislation to all these groups was the same: "It's seven days in order to keep guns out of the wrong hands."

We also started a state legislative division, which both battled the gun lobby on state initiatives we opposed and worked with sponsors of state laws that we supported. This was a critical area because what happened on the state level sent a loud national message. When a state votes for something, it becomes much easier for its representatives to support the same position in Washington. It gives them cover.

Often, over the next years, we found ourselves fighting the gun lobby's attempts to enact "preemption" in various states—laws mandating that that no locality can pass a piece of legislation unless it's approved by the state legislature. The NRA loved preemption bills because in almost every state, the large urban areas most favor stricter gun control; in states with preemption, a single city can't crack down without the approval of the whole state legislature, where rural areas tend to have more influence. Increasingly, we also fought the gun lobby's state initiatives to allow civilians to carry concealed weapons.

The state efforts we supported varied widely. One state might be trying to enact a waiting period and background check; another might be working on a ban on assault-style weapons. One of the earliest efforts we backed was in Maryland, which wanted to ban sales and ownership of Saturday-night specials. Handgun Control worked very hard to get out the vote on the 1988 referendum. It passed easily.

That victory inspired Jim Brady's first public statement on the gun issue. We were doing a publicity tour for *Thumbs Up*, Mollie Dickenson's book about Jim.* Members of the press were there, and because

---

Thumbs Up: The Life and Courageous Comeback of White House Press Secretary Jim Brady was published in 1987 by William Morrow and Company.

Maryland's ban on Saturday-night specials—the first in the nation—had just passed, one of the reporters asked Jim for his reaction. "Thumbs up for Maryland!" said Jim, accompanying his words with his trademark gesture. That was his first foray into the gun battle, and he never retreated from that day on.

All told, we were just unbelievably busy—and would be for the next five years. We constantly updated our "target areas"—parts of the country we thought were crucial to our success. We did our best to make speeches in those areas and were always on the lookout for what else we could do to help the cause while we were there. Could we speak to editorial boards? Could we do a press conference? Was there a like-minded local group that we could help to raise money? All this was part of the strategy, and carefully planned.

Apart from all the traveling and speaking I was beginning to do, my main work in 1988 consisted of heavy-duty lobbying on Capitol Hill—going from office to office trying to win members of the House and Senate to our side. We deliberately kept our approach extremely factual, never using emotional appeals. Usually, Gail and I went to the Hill together. We began by paying calls on all our supporters, thanking them for their help. Then we started down Gail's rankings, paying special attention to the twos and threes. Eventually, we even visited most of the recalcitrant fours and fives, always hoping that we might win over a few of them.

There were times, given all our hard work, when we'd be exhausted to the point of giddiness. One of my favorite memories is of a late evening after we'd spent hours upon hours lobbying up on the Hill. Gail, Susan, and I were walking through the subway that connects the Capitol and one of the House office buildings when suddenly, it struck us that the floor resembled the yellow brick road in *The Wizard of Oz*. It wasn't long before—amid much laughter—we were comparing our congressional opponents to the familiar characters in that movie.

Some reminded us of the Scarecrow: If so-and-so only had a brain, we reasoned, he'd support us. Someone else was obviously a Cowardly Lion—simply didn't have the courage to do the right thing. And then there was the occasional Tin Man: "He doesn't have a heart, just cares about getting himself re-elected." This became an ongoing theme for the three of us—sort of our private version of Gail's ranking system.

The work could get very intense, but it was often great fun. The best thing, of course, was to go into an office and actually get a member of Congress to change his or her mind. It was also great to see all our work elsewhere in the country starting to pay off. Our extensive meetings with local editorial boards and press conferences out in the states were generating a lot of good press. Editorials almost everywhere were endorsing the Brady bill, and the word, inevitably, was getting back to Washington.

Brady wasn't our only focus in 1988. We were also in the early stages of seeking a ban on assault-style weapons, work that would continue over the next few years. And despite ferocious opposition from the gun lobby, we were still trying to outlaw handguns that cannot be detected by magnetometers at airports, and 1988 was the year we won.

The main reason was Nancy Kassebaum, then the Republican junior senator from Kansas. Her office really took the lead on plastic guns, and from that point on, Handgun Control worked closely with Senator Kassebaum on every piece of legislation we supported. She was a true statesman, as distinguished from a mere politician. She knew and understood the Senate. She knew and understood the strengths and weaknesses of her fellow members, and she liked and respected every one of them. And she had an unerring instinct for how to get things done: whom to go to and what tactics to pursue. She was—is—simply wonderful, always willing to do anything she could to help if she believed that the cause was right.

Another senator I grew to like enormously was Edward Kennedy.

He had long been active in the gun control movement, so he was one of the first people I visited in the Senate. At first, I was absolutely awestruck. But even though he seems bigger than life, he is incredibly humble. Through every fight we waged over the years, Senator Kennedy was always working behind the scenes, lobbying his colleagues on our behalf and helping us with direct-mail solicitations, yet he never wanted any credit for his efforts.

In the House, our margin of victory on plastic guns was a spectacular 413 to four. It is worth noting that one of the four who voted against the measure was Dick Cheney, then a congressman from Wyoming and an extremist on gun issues all through his tenure in the House. With hindsight, that particular vote seems very ironic. Cheney, of course, went on to become vice president in an administration that declared war on terrorism. The law he opposed, which made certain that every gun manufactured contained enough metal to be detected at checkpoints, helped keep skyjacking and terrorist activities at bay for more than a decade and has played a critical role in the Bush-Cheney administration's attempts to tighten airport security.

But throughout everything, the Brady bill was our primary mission. By the spring of 1988, the momentum was beginning to build. In June, Ed Feighan introduced Brady as an amendment to the Omnibus Drug Initiative Act, which was being considered in the House Judiciary Committee. That committee approved the amendment on a voice vote and sent it on to the full House.

We knew we had enough votes lined up to at least come close to winning, and with victory almost in sight, we redoubled our lobbying efforts. It got to the point where we had talked to all the people who were even remotely likely to support us, and were visiting those we were pretty sure would not. But we wanted to touch all the bases.

Finally, I decided I should talk to Dick Cheney. Jim knew him from his days working for Donald Rumsfeld, a Cheney friend, and socially, we had seen Dick and Lynne Cheney several times at the house of our friend Ken Adelman. I felt I knew him well enough to at least touch base before the House vote.

To put this in context, I had been talking all along with Cheney's colleague Alan Simpson, the Republican senator from Wyoming. Senator Simpson was wonderful. He always asked how Jim was and gave me a joke to relay to him, and he was entirely straightforward with us. He could understand our view, he said, but he was not going to be supporting the Brady bill. Wyoming just wasn't behind it. He was always friendly, honest, and upfront—never afraid to explain just where he stood. He was one of my favorite opponents.

What a contrast Dick Cheney turned out to be. I placed two or three calls to his office over three or four days. He never returned one of them. All he had to do was get on the phone and say, "Hi, Sarah—I appreciate what you're working for, but I just can't be with you on this issue." He never even bothered, and that, to me, was unconscionable.

Going into the vote on the Brady bill, it was so close we didn't know how it would turn out. In the end, we were foiled by a delaying tactic supported by the National Rifle Association. Before Brady came up for a vote, Representative Bill McCollum of Florida—the ranking Republican on the crime subcommittee of the Judiciary Committee, and an avowed opponent of the Brady bill—introduced an amendment asking the Justice Department to study the feasibility of an instant background check on would-be gun buyers; the idea was that an instant-check system would make any waiting period (and thus the Brady bill itself) unnecessary. Members of Congress who had been wavering on the issue saw this as a way out: Why not study the matter for a year or so, and delay having to vote yea or nay on Brady itself? As the NRA had hoped, on September 15, 1988, the "McCollum substitute" prevailed. We lost our first vote on the Brady bill by a vote of 228 to 182.

I hadn't realized how hard it would be to lose that vote. I took it very personally. As it happened, we had been invited to the Adelmans' for dinner the night after the vote. I knew the Cheneys were going to be there. And I have to admit that I just couldn't face going. I was afraid of what I might say to Dick Cheney because I was so furious that he hadn't taken the time or effort to return my calls. I never quite forgave him for that.

Once we at HCI got over our initial disappointment, we realized that we had actually done phenomenally well, considering the fact that we'd been pushing hard for Brady for only one year. We emerged from that loss more convinced than ever that we could win.

So for the next couple of years, we worked even harder—lobbying, traveling, speaking, meeting with editorial boards, cultivating support and spreading the word in every way we could. Our momentum continued to build. Before long, our backing from law enforcement groups was overwhelming. Ours was the first piece of gun legislation that won the support of every one of the major law enforcement organizations, from those representing the rank and file to those representing the chiefs of police.

We put together a Law Enforcement Steering Committee, made up of one member from each of the twelve top organizations that supported us,* and pretty soon, all twelve were lobbying hard for the Brady Bill, the first time they had ever worked together on an issue.

During 1988, I had finally gone on Handgun Control's payroll as a regular employee. Scott was in school fulltime by then, so I could spare more time away from home. And I knew Jim would be leaving his posi-

*The Federal Law Enforcement Officers Association, the Fraternal Order of Police, the International Association of Chiefs of Police, the International Brotherhood of Police Officers, the Major Cities Chiefs' Association, the National Association of Police Organizations, the National Sheriffs' Association, the National Organization of Black Law Enforcement Executives, the National Troopers Coalition, the Police Executive Research Foundation, the Police Foundation, and the Police Management Association.

tion at the White House at the end of the Reagan administration, so I was going to be the family breadwinner. I had been a member of Handgun Control's board of directors since a year or two after I started working for HCI, and in 1989, board chairman Pete Shields asked me to become its chair. Pete, who had prostate cancer, was eager to retire, and he thought I was the obvious person to replace him since my face and name had become so firmly connected with Handgun Control. Although I didn't consider myself your typical chairman of the board—thought I could be useful more as a figurehead—Pete finally talked me into it.

On a personal level, 1989 became very difficult. My mother had a very severe stroke and had to have fulltime nursing care from that time on. Jim's mother had needed some home care for a year or two already, and at almost exactly the time of my mother's stroke, we were told that Dorothy Brady had to be put in a nursing home. We found a lovely place, and Dorothy didn't seem unhappy about it—in fact, I don't think she really understood where she was. But that was very hard on Jim and me because we couldn't get out to see her very often. That was the year I really began to understand the concept of the "sandwich generation." I had ten-year-old Scott at home, of course—and Jim—and now had to worry about our ailing mothers. It was a lot of extra responsibility.

There were challenges galore on the Brady bill front as well. In 1989, of course, we faced a new Congress—the 101st—and a whole new cast of characters. One of the congressional subcommittees critical to the Brady bill's fate was the House Judiciary Committee's subcommittee on crime. Brady had to get passed there in order to go to Judiciary for hearings and from there to a vote by the full House. There was a new chairman of the crime subcommittee: Democrat Chuck Schumer of New York, who is now his state's senior senator. We had worked extremely hard to get New Jersey's Bill Hughes, Schumer's predecessor as chairman, on board with the Brady bill. Fortunately, Schumer was a much easier sell. He became one of the bill's strongest supporters—and eventually, a chief sponsor.

The Judiciary Committee itself was a different story. It, too, had a new chairman—Democrat Jack Brooks of Texas—and he was very much against us. We knew that was a big problem: As Judiciary chairman, he could simply refuse to hold hearings on the bill, and thus block its introduction for a vote of the full House.

Jack Brooks wasn't the only stumbling block. The House had a new Speaker, Democrat Tom Foley of Washington state, who had replaced the retiring Thomas P. "Tip" O'Neill. Like Brooks, Foley was a staunch ally of the National Rifle Association. So we faced formidable opposition not just from the chairman of the committee from which our bill had to emerge, but from the Speaker himself, who controlled the legislative agenda for the House of Representatives. We had no intention of letting that stop us, of course. We kept right on lobbying the new Congress, talking to all the new members, lining up our support once again.

Finally, there was the new President, George Herbert Walker Bush. A year earlier, in January 1988, we had been invited to the White House for a Super Bowl party—the last of Ronald Reagan's administration. At the party, Vice President Bush, who was running for the Republican presidential nomination, came over to Jim and me and said, "I just admire what you're doing. Keep up the good work—it's so important."

I was thrilled. I thought, *How wonderful! He's on our side!* As a result, we did not take any stand in the presidential contest of 1988, George Bush versus Michael Dukakis. Handgun Control never had taken sides in a presidential election, but we definitely stayed out of that fight, believing that no matter which man won—whether it was Bush or Dukakis—he would be with us, in favor of common-sense gun laws.

Jim and I were invited to the Republican National Convention in New Orleans that year. We were there when Bush announced that Dan

Quayle would be his running mate. We knew Quayle's background and didn't think he'd be on our side, but we thought it didn't matter. Bush would be with us, we figured, and that was what counted.

Bush, of course, did win that election. And it's a sign of how far we had come on the Brady issue that Barney Frank, who a year before had been arguing that gun control was a lost cause, later chewed us out roundly for staying out of the campaign. By now, our cause was well-known and important enough so that he thought a Dukakis endorsement from us might have made a real difference.

The Bushes—Barbara, especially—had always been very good to us. And shortly after George H. W. Bush took office, they invited Jim and me to a party at the White House. There was a buffet, and people sat around the living room eating with their plates on their laps or at little tables. President Bush sat down with Jim and me. It occurred to me to bring up the Brady bill, but I thought—no—this is a private dinner, and they were lovely to invite us. I'm not going to bring up the gun issue now.

So I didn't. In retrospect, I'm very sorry. Maybe things would have turned out differently if I had started working on him then and there.

CHAPTER TWELVE

Party Politics and Brass Knuckles

PEOPLE HAVE OFTEN asked me whether it was difficult to find myself on the opposite side of my own Republican Party. The answer is that in those early years, we didn't see the Brady bill as a partisan issue in the least. The Reagan White House didn't oppose it. It certainly wasn't a party platform issue at the time. Right from the start we had many good, strong Republicans on our side in Congress. In the Senate, they included stalwarts like Kansas's Nancy Kassebaum, Rhode Island's John Chafee, and Virginia's John Warner. In the House, we were backed by highly respected conservatives like James Sensenbrenner of Wisconsin and Henry Hyde of Illinois. Conversely, there were plenty of Democrats against us, starting with the Speaker of the House himself, Tom Foley.

If anything, where members of Congress stood on the issue was dictated by where they were from. Those who represented rural districts tended to be more against us than those with big-city constituencies. Midwesterners and Northeasterners were more likely to be on our side than those from the West or the South.

That said, my personal relationship to the party I had grown up with had been uneasy for some time. Before Scott was born, when I was working at the Republican National Committee, Pete Teeley joined us as our head of communications. Pete was also chairman of the Arlington County Republican Committee in Virginia and, knowing we lived in Arlington, he asked if I'd be interested in serving on the committee. I was.

This was the mid-1970s, and in those days, there was a constant battle between the two wings of the party. On one side were the Republican moderates like Pete and me, who believed in limited government power and spending, but tended to be more "liberal"—or at least not rigidly ideological—on social issues, gun control among them. We also believed that compromise is a necessary part of politics. You might disagree, even heatedly, with your opponents, but the discourse was most always civil, and the objective was to accomplish the business of the people. On the other side were the growing ranks of hard-core conservatives, whom we fondly called the bomb-throwers. Many of them had grown up in the Young Republicans, and they took party politics and partisan ideology very seriously indeed. I always envisioned them carrying *Robert's Rules of Order* in their briefcases, constantly on the lookout for some way to ambush the other side.

Our committee was dominated by the moderate wing, and Pete wanted to keep it that way. We had our share of bomb-throwers, though, and the Republican-versus-Republican battles in those county committee meetings were every bit as fierce and sometimes even more so than those between Republicans and Democrats. In the state at large, the wars were even worse. There were many ultra-conservatives from southern Virginia. People who had been southern Democrats before the Democrats embraced the civil-rights movement had come flocking into the party. And while the moderates still dominated in the mid-1970s—certainly through Gerald Ford's administration—that was beginning to change, just as it was in other states.

During the Carter years, I was less actively involved in party politics than I had been, since that was when I discovered the joys of staying home with Scott. But when Jim first signed on with Ronald Reagan's campaign, I felt a twinge of worry. Jim kept assuring me that although Reagan was fiscally conservative and favored a strong national defense, he was not a social conservative—not one of the "bomb-throwers" I disliked. As the 1980 campaign progressed, it became clear to me that Reagan appealed to a broader base than did most conservatives. I liked him immediately once I met him and developed a kind of blind faith: Even though I knew the conservatives would try to use his victory to push their social agenda, I believed Reagan himself would rise above it.

My first real anger at the party's new course came in 1985, when Congress passed the Gramm-Rudman-Hollings bill, named after Senators Phil Gramm of Texas and Warren Rudman of New Hampshire—both Republicans—and Ernest F. "Fritz" Hollings of South Carolina, a southern Democrat. Congress was unable to cut the budget because members did not want to give up their own pet projects. Republicans were always calling for budget cuts, but the reality was they wanted cuts only in the Democrats' programs—and to be fair, the Democrats acted much the same way. Gramm-Rudman-Hollings was an effort, later declared unconstitutional, to force spending cuts by mandating across-the-board reductions in the budget. That meant that programs like workman's compensation for the sick and disabled—the segment of society that most needed help—were cut equally along with some of the rampant, silly programs members of Congress protected as their own.

That law struck very close to home. Jim's medical bills had been exorbitant, and if he had not been eligible for workman's compensation, since he was injured in the line of duty, I don't know how we would have managed.* I thought back to all those people I had seen in the hospital, people whose regular insurance wouldn't even help them through rehabilitation. Surely there must be better ways to cut a budget than to shortchange programs that help to bring people back to being productive members of society. I was furious. It seemed to me that the face of my party was drastically changing, being taken over by ideologues who were nothing like the Republicans I had grown up with.

They also were nothing like the Reagans. Oh, they had glommed on to Ronald Reagan, sort of hitching their wagons to his star, and after his election, they became more powerful than ever before. But deep down, President Reagan himself was never a social conservative. He was a much more compassionate, caring person than so many of these others who stood in his shadow.

But in the big push for the Brady bill in the late 1980s, party politics simply wasn't the point. After we lost the vote in '88, Gail Hoffman and I resumed our trips from office to office on Capitol Hill, looking to both sides of the aisle for support. What a thrill it was when we won someone over! Dan Lungren, a Republican from California, was an important early convert, a key member of the House Judiciary Committee. Wisconsin's Jim Sensenbrenner had once yelled at me on the telephone that he would never vote for any gun control measure. But the NRA had crossed him in the intervening years—mischaracterized him in one of its mailings—and he changed his mind. Ultimately, he became the primary Republican sponsor of the Brady bill. Among the im-

---

*Not long after Jim was hurt, Senator Bill Roth, his old boss, got Congress to pass a bill giving Jim three-fourths of his salary as workman's comp, rather than the usual two-thirds, since he had been injured in an assassination attempt.

portant Democrats we succeeded in winning over were Representatives Mike Synar of Oklahoma, Rom Mazzoli of Kentucky, Charlie Stenholm of Texas, and Les AuCoin of Oregon. Once they came over to our side, they were incredibly helpful in bringing others along with them.

Although Gail and I were the point people in Congress, our lobbying effort got a great deal of help from the outside. Our allies among the law enforcement community were incredibly influential, underscoring our message that the Brady bill would be extremely helpful to police. Figures like Evy Dubrow of the International Ladies Garment Workers Union and Mayor Raymond Flynn of Boston also worked hard on our behalf—Dubrow among union members and Flynn from his position as head of the U.S. Conference of Mayors. Another great ally was Coretta Scott King. One year early in our push for the Brady bill, she had invited me to Atlanta to speak at the King Center on the anniversary of Dr. King's death. That day began our personal friendship, and over the years, she was always available to do anything she could on behalf of the Brady bill.

In March 1989, the Bush administration gave us new reason to think it was going to be with us. In an executive order, the president banned imports of assault weapons. We were very pleased, and it gave us an opportunity to renew our press for a ban on sales of domestic assault weapons as well. It may have been that executive order, which infuriated the National Rifle Association and brought ferocious new pressure on its Republican allies in Congress, that ultimately ensured that President Bush never lifted a finger to help with the Brady bill—the work he had told us he so admired.

Meanwhile, ever since his "thumbs up for Maryland," Jim had whole-heartedly joined the push for the Brady bill. When Reagan left office and Bush came in, Jim's life changed drastically. For one thing, of course, we had to give up the White House drivers. Early on, four of

Me, at age 3, with my beloved lambie pie.

Enjoying an outing in one of the infamous Buffalo snows with my mom and dad, Stan and Frances Kemp.

Proudly holding my William and Mary diploma. It took a while to get it but now I was on my way.

Stan Kemp as a young FBI agent always stressed firearm safety and locked up his own service revolver the minute he came home each evening.

Jim (far left) in 1970 as a young advertising executive. You can see why he swept me off my feet that year.

Missy, Jim, me, Mom, and my brother, Bill, at a family get together in the summer of 1972. Notice the polyester.

Toasting our marriage and future—we never dreamed of the magnificent highs and devastating lows ahead of us.

The uniting of the Brady clan with the Kemps. Stan and Frances Kemp on the left, Dorothy and Big Jim Brady on the right. Missy is in front.

Jim sailing with Bill Greener and Admiral Staser Holcomb. This was on the infamous Hawaiian trip with Secretary of Defense Don Rumsfeld in 1976. I was home pawning the silver.

Scott, Jim, and an agonized cat at Dennis Thomas's annual crab feast, 1980.

I was the proudest Mom in the world and never enjoyed anything as much as staying home taking care of my wonderful Scott.

Jim taking Scott on his first sled ride down our hill in Arlington, December 1980.

Celebrating with a glass of champagne moments after Ronald Reagan called to offer Jim the job of White House Press Secretary.

Leaving for one of the many Presidential Inaugural events (notice me in that old gray coat with fur balls). January, 1981.

With President Reagan at Jim's swearing-in ceremony: my aunt Helen Dehner (left) and mother, Frances Kemp. It's official— he's Press Secretary to the President.

Taking a press inquiry as President Reagan's new Press Secretary.

Photo © Bernie Boston

The new White House Press Secretary peers out his West Wing windows. Looking for Helen Thomas, no doubt.

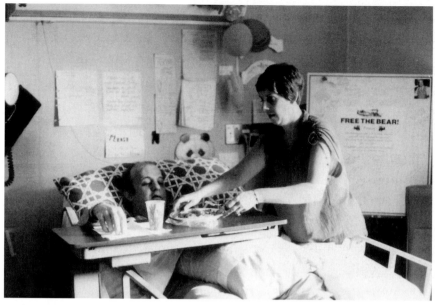

Helping Jim with dinner at George Washington Hospital. Note the "Free the Bear" petition in the background. Summer, 1981.

Jim and Scott share a special moment at the White House's Fourth of July celebration. This was Jim's first outing from the hospital.

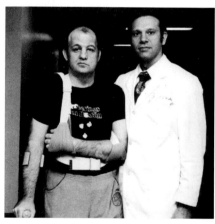

Jim and Dr. Kobrine after one of Jim's PT sessions. PT stands for physical therapy, but Jim always called it pain and torture.

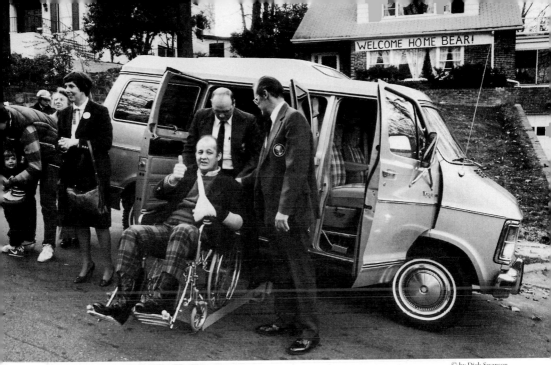

*The Bear is free and comes home for good. What a wonderful day that
was. We were to start a new chapter of our lives. November, 1981.*

*Back to family traditions like
barbequing in the backyard—
Missy, me, Jim, and Scott. 1982.*

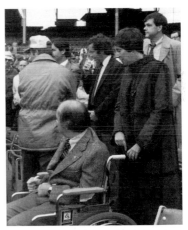

*Jim and me at Wrigley Field in
Chicago. This was Jim's first out-of-
town trip. He threw out the first ball
for his beloved Cubs. 1982.*

*Scott gives Jim a goodnight kiss
in Pooh Corner. All of us are
adjusting to our new life. 1984.*

Dear Sarah -
We bent thru' something that will bind us together forever - and you'll always have my admiration for your courage - and my love
Nancy

Nancy Reagan and I, both thankful our ordeal is over, but knowing life will never be the same.

Testifying before the Senate Judiciary Committee's Constitution Subcommitee. Jim's testimony that day had the room in tears and was the essence of what the fight was all about. He dominated the network news that night and the country began to rally around our cause. November 1989.

The last press party of the Reagan Administration in Santa Barbara. We rode out in Air Force One and the President and First Lady helped us celebrate Jim's birthday. August, 1988.

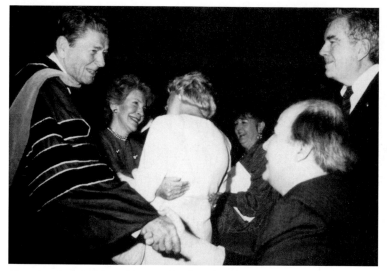

*Jim thanks President Reagan for formally endorsing the Brady
Bill at a ceremony dedicating the Ronald Reagan Pavilion at the
George Washington University Medical Center. We know now
we're headed for victory.*

*The Brady Bill passes the Senate for the first time, another hurdle out of the way.
With Senators Joe Biden, Bob Dole, Howard Metzenbaum, and George Mitchell at
a press conference in the Senate swamp. June, 1991.*

With Susan Whitmore and Gail Hoffman, the Bobbsey Twins plus one— what fun we had in our long years of work to pass the Brady Bill.

Holding forth in one of our hundreds of press conferences designed to keep Congress and the nation focused on the need for the Brady Bill. September 1992.

Photo by Dorothy Andrake

And yet another press conference with some of our myriad allies in the fight.

"Did we take a wrong turn, Jim? This doesn't look like San Diego." A proud but nervous moment for Jim and me as we address the Democratic Convention in Chicago. 1996.

Celebrating in the Oval Office just after the final passage of the Brady Bill are Attorney General Janet Reno, Vice President Al Gore, Gail Hoffman, Sheila Anthony, President Bill Clinton, Jim, and me. Seven hard years finally produced the Brady Law. November 30, 1993.

*Jim and I join President Clinton at a law enforce-
ment ceremony in the Rose Garden commemorating
the anniversary of the Brady Bill in 1998. Violent
crime rates have begun to plummet.*

*Jim, Scott, and I chatting with President Clinton following the
dedication of the James S. Brady Press Briefing Room. What
an honor! Several years earlier President Clinton honored Jim
with the Presidential Medal of Freedom.*

*What a day for giving thanks. My little family and Scott's friend
April Parker, together* **and** *at the beach in our new home.*

*Scott carves the turkey for our
family Thanksgiving celebration.*

*How could life get any better? Setting
up my office at the beach just a stone's
throw from our new home.*

five of them wanted to make some extra money, so we hired them when they were off duty and they took turns driving Jim; eventually, we hired one retired White House driver, Ross Giacomo, who worked for us fulltime.

After leaving the White House, Jim went to work at the National Organization on Disabilities. He soon also got involved with the Brain Injury Association. Along the way, he spent more and more time on the handgun issue. He was especially well-known for "dialing for dollars." Jim could get through to people no one else could reach—rich and famous heads of corporations and foundations—and talk them into contributing. The better he got physically, the more active he became. Soon, the Brady bill was as big a project for him as it was for me.

In November 1989, Jim testified at a hearing before the Senate Judiciary Committee's subcommittee on the Constitution, which was chaired by Democrat Paul Simon of Illinois, Jim's home-state senator and one of the Brady bill's great supporters. Although people on Capitol Hill were well aware that Jim had been increasingly involved with the push for Brady, this appearance was in some ways his real public debut on the issue—and the first time most Americans had a chance to see how he was faring eight years after the shooting. Gail and I spent most of the weekend before the hearing working on Jim's testimony.

In it, he spoke bluntly about how his life had changed—"Damn it, I even need help to go to the bathroom"—and juxtaposed the slight inconvenience a seven-day waiting period might cause a gun buyer against the extraordinary inconvenience he now experienced every day of his life. "And I'm one of the lucky ones," he added. He reminded the senators that "there was a day when I walked the halls of this Senate" right along with them. He told them that there were "too many Cowardly Lions" in Congress, all of them terrified of the gun lobby. Being Jim, he couldn't resist ad-libbing, making his unquenchable spirit apparent to all present. There were a lot of tear-filled eyes in that room.

Gail remembers his testimony as the very essence of what our fight was all about.

Through the speakers' bureau and then through Handgun Control itself, Jim and I started appearing all over the country. We called our speeches "dog-and-pony shows," and when I'd mention that, Jim would point to himself and say "Pony, Pony." He was just charming. You never knew what he was going to say. I played the straight man.

At the beginning and end of our appearances, Jim would read a short prepared text, and in between I would talk, usually about our background and what brought us there, then about our beliefs about why people should support waiting periods and background checks. As I'd be talking away, Jim, who always had a little hand-held microphone, would chime in whenever he felt like it. I never knew what to expect. But he was absolutely wonderful. And the more he did it, the better he got.

Throughout 1989, we kept up our Brady efforts on all fronts. A look at my calendar from September of that year gives a flavor of how hard we worked. On September 7, I met with Roger Porter, the chief domestic policy adviser at the White House, and also had an interview with the *Journal of Emergency Medicine*. The next day I visited Lee Atwater, then chairman of the Republican National Committee, trying to convince him that Brady deserved the RNC's support. (In later years—largely because of the huge donations to the party from the National Rifle Association—the RNC took a strong position against gun control. But Lee, who liked to win, felt that if Republican members of Congress wanted to vote for Brady, he wasn't going to make it a partisan issue.)

On September 12, I was in New York City for a meeting with the National Academy of TV Arts and Sciences. On September 15, I had a breakfast meeting with *Ms.* magazine's "Women of the Year"; I had been shocked and honored to be named one of them. On the eighteenth and nineteenth of September, there was a Handgun Control board meeting. On the twenty-first, Jim and I took Scott with us to Buffalo, New York, for a speech—a fundraiser for Our Lady of Victory Hospital. On September 25 I met with Senator Kassebaum, and on the twenty-seventh with Arizona's Democratic Senator Dennis DeConcini, who eventually introduced an assault weapons bill. The next day, Jim and I spoke at Vanderbilt University in Nashville.

The traveling was relentless during those years. I took many trips to Ohio, which was always a key state for us. I also spent a lot of time in New Jersey and California, which were long at the forefront of sensible gun legislation. I did lots of work in Connecticut, too, and in Georgia, where the city of Atlanta was trying to pass its own ban on assault weapons and a local version of the Brady bill. I also visited New York quite often. That gave me a chance to meet Governor Mario Cuomo, who remains one of the people I most admire—a brilliant, sincere, incredibly hard-working man.

Amid all the trips, of course, the lobbying continued. Just as in the run-up to the 1988 vote, I found our visits to the Hill mostly interesting and fun. There are only two meetings I remember with real distaste.

One was with Phil Gramm of Texas. Gail, Jim, and I went to see him together. Although I don't think we held out much hope for his support, there was just a chance that Gramm, a very smart man, would actually see our side of the issue and that he might be the kind of senator who would vote his conscience rather than the National Rifle Association line. But in the event, he was breathtakingly arrogant and condescending. No wonder we felt as we did, since poor Jim had been hurt, he said. But we just weren't looking at the issue the way it ought to be looked at. It was very understandable that we'd have such a benighted view, but he, Senator Gramm, knew better. It left me with a very bad taste in my mouth.

The other unpleasant meeting was almost funny, looking back on it.

It was with a new Democratic congresswoman named Jolene Unsoeld. A former legislator in Washington state, she was an ultra-liberal. But the congressional district she ran for was not quite the same as the one she had represented in the state legislature, and to appease its pro-gun voters she had done an about-face and come out against gun control. She was now the NRA's darling, the gun lobby's token House liberal.

We decided to appeal to her conscience, since as a true liberal, she should have been with us. It turned out to be one of the wildest meetings I have ever attended. Once again, it was Jim, Gail, and me—plus Representative Unsoeld, who was completely defensive from the moment we stepped in that door. Almost immediately, she started pointing her finger at me and screaming questions about where I stood on abortion, which of course had nothing whatsoever to do with what we were there to discuss. We hardly got a word in edgewise, nor did we want to after witnessing her decidedly peculiar performance. She ran around the office fumbling with things and screeching, her voice extremely high-pitched. She reminded me of a bird flitting from limb to limb in a tree. Finally, I said I didn't think this was going to do us any good, that it was time for us to leave, that she had made her feelings quite clear. But she wouldn't let us go—just wanted to continue her tirade. I think poor Jim wanted to put his hands over his ears because her voice was so shrill and she was so emotionally whipped up. When she was defeated, after her third term, I was one of the first to cheer.

As support for the Brady bill grew, our office began to get a lot of hate mail. When Jim and I traveled, there were often demonstrators, and there were times when I was extremely nervous about security. We faced some touchy situations.

The first scary occasion took place in Las Vegas. The students and the University of Nevada at Las Vegas had asked Jim and me to come out. They had planned well in advance and advertised our speech widely. They wanted a big crowd, and they got one. Not only were there lots of university people on hand, an NRA organizer had helped to make sure that there would be plenty of anti-Brady people there as well, and they had come by the busload from California and other nearby states. Some were members of extremist groups like Posse Comitatus. Before the speech, we ate dinner with some of the students, who were just great, and they told us there were two or three hundred demonstrators present. That didn't bother us much—we'd had them before, and it hadn't been horrible.

The speech took place in a gigantic gymnasium. The lights were on us, and out where the audience sat, it was quite dark. That's always a little disconcerting, because as you look out, you can't see much past the first row. There were nearly two thousand people present, so three hundred demonstrators didn't seem overwhelming. But the protesters had done a very clever thing: They had spread themselves out, taking seats in little pockets all over the auditorium.

Jim and I started the dog-and-pony show, in which he would speak first, then I'd take over and he'd kibbitz, using his hand-held mike. Out of respect for him, I guess, there was pretty much dead silence when Jim led off, and he got a nice round of applause. But as soon as I rose to speak, I could get through only a sentence or two before shouts of "LIAR! LIAR!" broke out all over the place. Every time one pocket of protesters yelled something, all of them started hollering. I tried to ask them to respect my First Amendment rights, but it was no use—they just wouldn't let me speak.

A big group from Sigma Chi, Jim's college fraternity, had come to hear us. We'd met them before the speech and had our picture taken with them, and they had all sat together in the audience. When the heckling started, the Sigma Chis—along with a number of UNLV faculty members—tried to take on the protesters, saying, "Sit down, be quiet—we came to hear the Bradys." But the demonstrators were so awful that pretty soon even the audience was scared. It was an explosive situation, and everyone knew it.

I didn't want to let them run me off the stage, but I had no idea how to handle such a loud, large-scale attack—no notion of how to disarm them. I turned to Jim and asked what I should do, and he was clearly terrified. He said, "Just talk. Get it over with. We've got to get off the stage. Finish up." So I did. It took me much longer than usual to get through the speech, since I had to keep stopping to let them calm down. This was all, by the way, caught on videotape by CNN, which covered the event.

When I finished, I was shaking like a leaf. The second I stopped talking, the curtain closed and we were surrounded by policemen with guns, and not just normal guns—several of them carried semi-automatic weapons. They scooted us offstage and into a back room. We didn't realize it at the time, but the university's security force had called in the Las Vegas police. I guess everyone had realized that the intensity of the heckling was such that there was a potential for physical violence.

We had to stay back there for almost an hour while the police cleared the area. At one point, a young piano tuner arrived at the back door and must have been extremely startled when he walked in to find those police aiming an array of impressive weapons at him. When an all-clear was issued, the police escorted us back to our hotel, taking a highly circuitous route to make sure we weren't followed. Before long, thirty or forty Sigma Chis arrived, bringing plenty of beer, and we all settled down in our nice suite and watched the events of the evening on the late-evening news.

There were more frightening incidents over the next few years. Some places where we were to speak set up metal detectors to ensure our safety. Once, when I appeared in Oklahoma, officials caught someone trying to sneak in a gun. Jim ran into several similar situations. Once it became clear that there really was some danger out there, we began to take some precautions. But contrary to what the National Rifle Association always claimed, we did not have Secret Service protection, nor did we ever have private bodyguards. We simply tried to make sure that the organizations that sponsored our appearances took adequate security precautions.

The need for such ground rules had been driven home to me not long after that Las Vegas appearance. I had been invited to speak at Miami University of Ohio, on one of its campuses near Dayton. Often, organizers used our appearances as fundraisers. They would charge people to get in and make sure the occasion was well advertised to ensure a good turnout. For this Miami of Ohio event, fliers went out in advance, and some of them turned up at a knife and gun show in Dayton. As it turned out, the majority of people who came to my speech—in droves—had heard about it at that show.

This time, it wasn't a huge, darkened gymnasium. I could see all the faces in the audience, and it was about the scariest looking group I could imagine. A man in the front row wore a long black raincoat and a black hat right out of an old cowboy movie, and he had what looked like brass knuckles and other hardware hanging from his belt. I was nervous, not at all sure that there weren't some serious weapons in that room.

The school had warned me that there would be some demonstrators, but the fellow who organized the event said the university believed in free speech, and both sides had to be able to speak out. So the university did not pay much attention to security, apart from stationing a couple of campus guards in the back of the room. I realized that I was going to have to handle this on my own.

I started out by saying that I knew there were many present who didn't agree with me but some at least wanted to hear what I had to say. I asked the audience to hold all comments until the question-and-answer period at the end, and promised that everyone would get a chance to express his views.

It didn't work. Every time I said something my opponents didn't agree with, one of them would yell out something and they'd all start booing and screaming. I'd try to restore order, and for a while it would be all right. But there was an elderly man over to my right, about halfway toward the back of the room, who got more and more worked up as the speech went on. A few minutes before I finished, I noticed that the guards were carrying him out. For a minute, I thought the university had finally decided to do something about the heckling.

As I left the stage, someone told me I would have to wait back there for a few minutes because the paramedics were working on that man. It turned out that he had collapsed, and he subsequently died of a heart attack. My first reaction was terrible guilt. Afterward, I went out with the guy who had organized the speech—we were both quite shaken up by all that had happened—and I told him how guilty I felt. All of a sudden both of us did a double-take. Why should we feel guilty? If he wanted to come and scream and work himself into a coronary, that was his problem. I'm sorry he died, but it was his own fault.

As time went on, I grew more confident about handling hecklers. I was determined not to be shouted down, not to be silenced by a group of extremist thugs. They are a tiny minority, that group that is obsessed by its hatred of any kind of controls on guns, and I wasn't going to let them get the best of us.

There was something else. It became clear, with experience, that the extreme hecklers ended up actually helping our cause. They always looked bullying, intolerant, and crude, and in most cases clearly didn't even know what they were talking about. In truth, our worst opponents provided some of the best public relations we could have hoped for.

CHAPTER THIRTEEN

"Just Tell Howard It's the Devil Herself"

B Y THE SPRING OF 1990, we had lined up Brady sponsors and co-sponsors and we were close to having enough votes to get the bill passed. But Speaker Tom Foley, from the start, was very contrary. He was just not going to put that bill on the House floor. It was a very difficult period. There was never any animus between us and the Speaker—just unending frustration.

Of course, the harder we fought to get a vote on the Brady bill, the more we looked like David to the NRA's Goliath—and the more the press loved the story. We got terrific coverage. Susan Whitmore's press conferences attracted all the top broadcast and print media—a far cry from the first one I'd attended after joining Handgun Control, which had drawn only two reporters. We ran advertisements all over the country explaining that the Speaker was holding up the Brady bill and urging Americans to write or call and tell Foley that the bill needed a hearing on the House floor and should be brought up for a vote. Mayor David Dinkins of New York saw one of those ads and called Foley from a car—then phoned me to say he had just yelled at the Speaker. So we knew the pressure was building, but still, Foley didn't budge. Of course he was also getting a lot of heat from fellow pro-gun members of Congress who did not want Brady to come to a vote. This lasted all through that year.

True to form for the Brady family, we had more excitement on the home front as well. In 1989, I had realized that our beloved old house, where we had lived for sixteen years, just wasn't what we needed; its elevator went only to the second floor, for instance, so Jim couldn't get to the third floor and never even saw Scott's room. Eventually, I found a newly built townhouse nearby that had an elevator to all three floors, and late that year, we had moved in. It was fun furnishing the new house, and it was very pretty.

The day before Easter 1990, I went out to buy food for a brunch we were giving on Easter morning. When I got home, Jim and Dee Hardy, his nurse, were watching television, and Scott had gone upstairs to play his guitar. I hadn't even put the food away when I noticed that there was smoke coming from the recreation room. I ran in and saw that a small pile of papers had caught on fire, and the smoke was positively billowing. Dee and I both got water to throw on it, but we could see it was spreading so fast that there was no way we'd be able to put it out.

We called 911. I got Scott downstairs and we wheeled Jim outside. By this time, it was really smoky, and words from *Uncle Tom's Cabin* came to my mind: "It felt like those dirty dogs were nipping at our heels." We had to go through the garage, and it occurred to me that if the fire got that far, the car might blow up. So after we got Jim out, I backed the car out, too—then went back into the house to get our yellow Labrador, Mollie.

The fire trucks came, and eventually, they put out the fire. Even though it had been pretty much contained to that one room, the smoke damage was tremendous all through the house. Everything was ruined. On the first floor where Jim had been sitting, the television had melted. Everything made of plastic had melted. It was a disaster.

A neighbor very kindly offered to take care of Mollie for the next few days, and I called a White House driver to come get us. He took us to my mother's house to reconnoiter. We didn't have a stitch of clothes or even a toothbrush—just my waterlogged pocketbook, which the firemen had rescued from the house. Finally, I called a nearby Marriott Hotel, and we got a room. I remember getting Jim and Scott to bed that night, then lying down myself and thinking, *Oh my God, we're home-less! What are we going to do?* But then I looked at where I actually was, in a Marriott, in a lovely warm room, and came to my senses. There were plenty of people who were far worse off than we were.

The next day proved the point. First, the Marriott had to bring big coat racks into our room because so many friends arrived with dona-tions of clothes for the three of us. Then there was another little mira-cle. Since the damage to our house had been so great, it was apparent that we were going to have to live somewhere else for the next couple of months. Out of the blue, we got a call from Brian Lamb, the founder of C-Span. Brian lived in a townhouse in our complex, and he had just bought a second one, where he planned to move as soon as he sold the first. Why didn't we stay in the new one as long as we needed to? He had no intention of taking rent, but I insisted, and we had a contract drawn up. So we moved to Brian's townhouse with rented furniture and borrowed clothes, and we were there for two or three months while our own house was cleaned up. All our furniture had to be taken away and refurbished. Our clothes had to go to a cleaner that special-ized in smoke removal. Sadly, we lost many treasured photographs from the Reagan years, a lot of mementos and personal items.

But that experience gave me new insight. There is just nothing material that's of any import. There is nothing as important as having your lives. That was a destructive, difficult episode, one of many, but we made it through. We still had each other, and once our townhouse was restored—looking pretty much as it had before the fire—boy, were we glad to be home.

In January 1991, we once again had a new Congress. And once again, Ed Feighan introduced the Brady bill in the House. This time, Tom Foley had promised that he wouldn't stand in our way. He had no intention of helping the bill along, but he was committed not to block it. He had been bombarded by criticism for his previous intransigence, and he wanted the issue to go away.

In March, we got a huge—and unexpected—thrill, a great boost to our spirits and to the cause itself. Ronald Reagan's office called to say that he planned to endorse the Brady bill at the dedication of the new Ronald Reagan Institute of Emergency Medicine at the George Washington University Medical Center. And on March 29, in an op-ed piece in the *New York Times,* President Reagan explained his support for Brady to the whole world.

While the bill was still in the Judiciary Committee, one of its members, Democrat Harley Staggers of West Virginia, tried an anti-Brady tactic much like the "McCollum Substitute" of 1988. Instead of a seven-day waiting period for handgun sales, the Staggers proposal would have required gun dealers to call a national hotline for an instant computer check on would-be buyers.

On the face of it, an instant check system seemed appealing. But in the early 1990s, the data base necessary to make such a check effective simply did not exist. The individual states kept most criminal record histories. Only a few states had their records up to date and ready to be fed into a nationally accessible computer system. Most states had no computerized records; many were in files, on microfilm, or stowed away in shoe boxes. The best estimate was that it would take six to eight years to get a national system up and going. That was the point of the Brady waiting period: It would give each state the time it truly needed to do a thorough check.

The Judiciary Committee rejected the Staggers amendment. And in April, the Brady bill went to the full House, where it was scheduled for a vote on May 8.

Because Speaker Foley did not offer any help from the Majority Whip's office, the usual mechanism for getting the troops in line behind a piece of legislation, we had to set up our own whipping operation. New York's Chuck Schumer, chairman of Judiciary's crime subcommittee, took on the job. He was superb. One of his best ideas was called "Operation St. Joseph" (I don't remember why, but perhaps it was because Joseph is the patron saint of doubters!). Schumer enlisted Marty Russo, a Democrat from Illinois, to go after members of Congress who were definitely not going to vote for the Brady bill; Russo's assignment was to persuade them not to vote for the Staggers amendment, either, since it, too, was a form of gun control. This tactic worked very well among gun control's most hard-core opponents.

In the days leading up to that vote, the tension was enormous. The newspapers and airwaves were filled with ads on both sides of the issue, and lobbyists of all stripes crowded Capitol Hill. Then, on May 8, 1991, the House of Representatives passed the Brady bill by a vote of 239 to 186.

That was probably the single most exhilarating moment of my life. The first thing I did was call President Reagan to let him know what had happened and to thank him, again, for his support. Then we had a press conference on the House side of the Capitol and a wonderful party at a nearby hotel, where we were joined by dozens of our supporters, including many of the members of Congress who had been on our side.

The next day, a picture of Gail Hoffman and me was on the front page of the *New York Times*, and we made headlines in almost every newspaper in the country. From nothing, the Brady bill had become a household word, something most of the country was rooting for. It was really something to see. I find it hard to express how incredibly gratifying it was.

There's an amusing postscript to that House vote. One of the members Gail and I had lobbied hard was Howard Coble, a Republican from North Carolina who sat on the Judiciary Committee, as nice a fellow as you could want to meet. Before the Judiciary Committee vote in 1990, I had talked and talked to him, and to my astonishment, I convinced that man to vote with us. But sometime between that vote and the next year, somebody—maybe the NRA—got to Howard Coble, and he was against us when the bill came up in 1991. Later, he was interviewed about his change of heart, and he goodnaturedly explained that he had been swept away by me—and said he'd rather talk to the Devil himself than to Sarah Brady. Only later, he said, had he come to his senses. He meant it as a compliment, and we always laughed about that. In fact, once when I called him up on other business, his office asked who was calling and I said just tell Howard it's the Devil herself.

Our next challenge, of course, was the Senate. Early on, Democrat George Mitchell of Maine, who was the Majority Leader, had been somewhat dubious about the Brady bill. He was asked about it during an appearance on one of the Sunday morning talk shows, and he explained that he thought the Brady bill did not go far enough. Originally, and as passed by the House, the bill just called for a waiting period; it did not require a background check on a gun buyer. In Senator Mitchell's opinion, a background check should be included. At that point, Gail and I began spending many an hour with the Majority Leader, whose help was critical to the fate of the bill.

Over the next several weeks, Senator Mitchell met not only with us, but also with the National Rifle Association. He's a great dealmaker. I suspect he thought he could come up with a piece of legislation that would make both sides happy, and if anyone could have done it, he was the one. But as he went back and forth between us and the NRA, it became obvious to him that while we were willing to negotiate, the gun lobby was not.

Ultimately, a new Brady bill was introduced by George Mitchell, Herb Kohl of Wisconsin, and Al Gore, then the junior senator from Tennessee. The new bill made the waiting period five working days, added a required background check by local law enforcement, and gave federal money to the states to upgrade criminal record histories so that, eventually, the kind of instant-check system the NRA wanted might actually prove effective. That last point was very important, and Senator Mitchell had worked very hard on it as a compromise between the NRA's position and ours. He had also worked very hard to get Minority Leader Bob Dole on board. Unlike his Kansas colleague, Nancy Kassebaum, Dole was no friend of Brady; all along, he had been meeting with the NRA, but never agreed to see us. But the issue had been a thorn in his side for a long time, and he was eager to get it resolved. He was happy with Mitchell's version of the bill, and even though the NRA never did approve of it, Dole worked with Mitchell to get it passed in the Senate.

On June 28 1991, I put Scott on a plane to fly to New York, where he would be picked up by camp counselors. He would be away at camp for two months, his first time away from us, and it was a very emotional morning. I felt this was good for both of us; at twelve, you probably need to be away from mom for a while and also to pick up some of the skills camp tends to teach. But it was very hard to let him go. The camp had told us ahead of time that kids were not allowed to call home for the first week or so. They tended to be homesick, and contact with their parents just prolonged the adjustment.

After I put Scott on the plane, I went into the office. There was news: Brady might very well get scheduled for a vote that same day. Our sponsor in the Senate was Ohio's Howard Metzenbaum, who was devoted to the legislation and had worked day in and day out to get it passed. We had done a great deal of lobbying, but we still had many last-minute calls to make to make sure our supporters were in line, available to vote. So Gail Hoffman, Susan Whitmore, and I—our gang of three—went up to the Hill.

All the ranking senators have offices in the Capitol itself, small, private places they can use when business is heavy, precluding the need to go back and forth between the Capitol and the Senate office buildings. Senator Metzenbaum had offered to let us use his own Capitol hideaway as a headquarters for our last-minute negotiations and calls.

Because of his rank, he had a particularly lovely office—beautifully furnished and filled with fine art he had collected. And it was directly across the hall from the office of the Minority Leader. In those days, smoking was allowed in the Capitol. But I would never have smoked in Senator Metzenbaum's office, so every time I wanted a cigarette, I'd go out into the hall, where there was a big ashtray. Senator Dole's door was wide open, and from my vantage point at the ashtray, I could see everyone who was going in and out of his office.

Brady was *the* big piece of legislation that was coming up, so you can imagine who Senator Dole's visitors tended to be that afternoon and evening. They were, in short, the pro-gun, anti-Brady faction—the NRA's in-house lobbyists and representatives of its outside lobbying firm. The most important of the latter was a very prominent force in Washington, Tom Korologos, who stood out like a beacon from all the other politicians in their somber coats and ties; Korologos was wearing green-and-blue plaid pants and a green sweater.

I'd watch the Dole doings for a while, then return to Senator Metzenbaum's hideaway. Unlike the Minority Leader, we kept the door to the hall closed, and I noticed that there was an enormous key in it. One of us took it out, revealing a huge keyhole. You could peer through it and see right into Dole's suite—through the reception room in the front, on through the staff office in the middle, and right into where the senator himself sat at his desk. We took turns on our hands and knees, keeping an eye on what was going on. Because of the vantage point, of course, you could only see people from the waist down. And because of his plaid pants, it was very easy to keep tabs on Tom Korologos.

By this point, I think we were just giddy. We'd worked so hard for so long on this bill. There were still many delaying tactics in the works, since everyone knew how close the vote was likely to be. All of a sudden, things quieted down, and I was sure we weren't going to get our vote that day. I was exhausted. So at about 9:30 that night, I went home.

When I got there, Emmy told me Scott's camp had called. My heart sank. I grabbed a beer, then called back. The counselor said everything was now all right, but that earlier he'd felt he had to call: Scott was so homesick, he was convinced that his grandma was going to die. She'd had her stroke, and she had moments when she wasn't doing so well, and the minute he'd gotten away from home, he had started worrying. But ultimately, the counselor said, Scott had calmed down.

I finished my beer and was just about ready to eat something when the phone rang. It was Gail. I had to come back immediately, she said—the Senate was going to vote. I said oh, no, I can't come, I just had a beer. I was so tired, so emotionally strung out from all the work and sending Scott away for two months. But Gail said I had to get to the Capitol right away. So I made a quick pot of coffee, drank some, and went back to the Hill.

By this time it was close to 11. The lights were all down low, and the members of the Senate all inside, all anxious to get out. I was nervous as could be. There were still a few undecided senators, and every time you saw one going by, you'd grab him and implore him to vote on your side. It was very tense and exciting. We thought we might have it, but you could never be certain until the votes were actually in.

Finally, late at night, the vote came. The Senate adopted Brady—a slightly different version from the House bill—as an amendment to the crime bill by a vote of sixty-seven to thirty-two. Oh my God, we were thrilled. But it was too late to do much of anything about it. This time, there was no celebratory party.

We had won. We were in seventh heaven. I remember going home that night and wondering what I would do with the rest of my life. All in one day, Scott had gone away and we had passed the Brady bill. I was thinking life in the future would just be a piece of cake—that I'd have two months with no work. How wrong I was.

Several weeks later, on July 11, the Senate passed the entire crime bill, seventy-one to twenty-six. It seemed as if the Brady bill was actually on its way to becoming the law of the land. It went to conference, so that the differences between the House and Senate versions of Brady could be resolved, and in November, the House adopted the conference report. But the Senate failed, by a vote of forty-nine to thirty-eight, to invoke cloture—to end debate and get to a vote.

For almost the entire next year, this stalemate continued, as Senate Democrats and Republicans battled over their differing versions of the omnibus crime bill. They just could not come to terms. In March 1992, a second attempt to invoke cloture failed, fifty-four to forty-three. In September, Senator Mitchell introduced a freestanding Brady bill, despite the fact that President Bush had made it quite clear that he would not sign the Brady bill into law unless it was attached to the crime bill. This time, Senate Republicans threatened a filibuster, so Mitchell was unable to schedule a vote. Finally, in October, Senator Mitchell sought unanimous consent to limit debate. Republican Senator Larry Craig of Idaho, one of our biggest foes, objected. With that, our last hope of having the Brady bill pass in the 102nd Congress abruptly ended.

During that last fall, I had been willing to try almost anything to get the crime bill passed. We didn't particularly care about the rest of the bill—it was just that Brady was attached to it and President Bush had said he wouldn't sign the Brady bill into law independently. I even got to the point where I was working as kind of a go-between between Senator Joe Biden of Delaware, who was the author of the Democrats' version of the crime bill, and Attorney General William Barr, who was working the bill from the Republican side. At one point, the attorney general said the president would not sign the crime bill unless the Republicans got their way on habeus corpus reform, and Biden and Barr couldn't agree on the issue. Up to that point I hadn't known a damn thing about habeus corpus, but I learned pretty fast, and tried as hard as I could to nudge them toward agreement. Biden would say, well, if you can talk Barr into so and so, I might give on such and such. So I'd go to Barr and make the case—then carry his words back to Joe Biden. Each side was hoping the other would give just enough to get that bill passed—and so was I. But it wasn't to be. The administration did not want to accept Biden's crime bill.

That marked a turning point for me. Had it not been for President Bush, the Brady bill would have become law that year. It would have started to save lives. In October 1992, a presidential election year, I realized that this time, we were going to have to take a stand. And it was not going to be in favor of George Herbert Walker Bush.

CHAPTER FOURTEEN

"If You Send Me the Brady Bill, I Will Sign It"

To my dismay, Gail Hoffman had left Handgun Control in the spring of 1992. She went to work for the Clinton presidential campaign. She was co-chairing the campaign's Crime and Drug Policy Task Force, and in that capacity was still working closely with law enforcement. And she was very eager to have me endorse Bill Clinton.

I let our board know that I was planning to do it, and that I would be speaking only for myself, not for Handgun Control. The date of that endorsement was October 17, only three weeks before election day. Susan Whitmore, Gail, and I—the Bobbsey Twins Plus One together again—flew to Detroit, where a law enforcement conference was taking place, accompanied by some key supporters, including members of the National Association of Police Officers. At a press conference there, I endorsed Bill Clinton for president of the United States. I acknowledged, of course, that I was a lifelong Republican, but added,

"The issue of public safety is not political—it does not belong to one party or the other." I said that the Brady bill had been "blocked in the final days of the 102nd Congress by a president fearful of crossing the special interest gun lobby," contrasting him with Bill Clinton, who "has spoken out because he knows it's the right thing to do." I was speaking out for Clinton, I said, because that, too, was the right thing to do.

About a week before the election, I got a call from the Clinton-Gore campaign asking me to do a press conference on Brady in Florida. They were very concerned about winning the state, and thought the gun issue was very good for them, especially in the Miami area. I flew down the evening before the press conference was scheduled and was picked up at the airport by two volunteers—a lovely couple, senior citizens who took me to my hotel and then picked me up the next day for the press conference.

It turned out to be one of the most unusual press conferences I've ever attended. On the way to the courthouse where it was to take place, the volunteers told me that I would be joined by a local prosecutor, a very popular woman named Janet Reno; the couple just raved about her. A police chief, Gil Kerlikowske of Fort Pierce, Florida, would be there as well, and all three of us would speak about the Brady bill in an effort to get some good press for Bill Clinton.

When we got to the courthouse, I waited on the steps for a few minutes, and then along came Janet Reno, all by herself. Soon Gil Kerlikowske showed up too. So here we were, the three primary folks for the press conference, but there was no one there from the Clinton-Gore campaign—nobody to help set up the conference and tell us what to do or how they wanted it handled. So the three of us talked among ourselves, and pretty soon, we began wondering whether any members of the media would actually show up. Ten minutes before the press conference was scheduled to start, no one was there.

Suddenly, a car pulled up and a woman got out. She was running for a seat in the Florida state legislature, and she was going to be part of our press conference. She said not to worry—she'd just come from another press conference, and the press would be right behind her. Sure enough, in another minute or two lots of cars and vans appeared, and out popped loads of cameras and reporters.

Still, there was no one there to organize everything. So Janet, Gil, and I just did our thing. Each of us talked about the Brady bill and the importance of getting it passed. We praised Bill Clinton for his campaigning on the issue and for being a friend to sensible gun laws. Then, when we had finished, the press jumped back into their vehicles and off they went, leaving the three of us standing, astonished, on the courthouse steps. We laughed about it, congratulating each other on the fact that clearly we had no need of press secretaries and campaign organizers; we had handled that quite well on our own. At the time, I had no idea how soon I would meet Janet Reno again. But I remembered her very fondly from that day. She was so down to earth, so committed to the Brady bill, such a very nice person.

When Bill Clinton beat George Bush, I was ecstatic. We knew now that the Brady bill was one huge step closer to reality. Clinton had campaigned on the Brady bill, had spoken often about its importance, and truly believed in the need to keep guns out of the wrong hands. It was our hope that this time, Brady would be enacted on its own, free of an overall crime bill.

To replace Gail, Handgun Control had hired Bob Walker as legislative director. He arrived in early 1993, shortly after President Clinton's inauguration, and was immediately immersed in the job of getting Brady passed. First we had to find out what the new administration had in mind—who would be deciding what legislation they would push. So we met with Howard Pastor, the director of congressional relations for the White House. He was sympathetic and supportive, but he would not commit to a specific timetable. Then, in his first State of the Union address that year, Clinton made clear his own feelings about our bill. "If you send me the Brady bill, I will sign it," he declared.

Back in October, after I endorsed Clinton, a bunch of us had wandered into a back room to talk. The Clinton campaign staffers were absolutely exhausted at that point, and kept saying they couldn't wait for the election to be over so they could get some rest. I commiserated with them because I could remember when Jim went through the same thing, but I gave them a warning: If you think you're busy now, wait until the election is over—the transition begins immediately, and you will not have one moment to rest. I think they thought I was crazy. They were new to this business. But it wasn't long before they found out how right I was.

At the time of the State of the Union, Clinton was still trying to put together his Cabinet. After several disappointments in trying to name an attorney general, he settled on Janet Reno. I was elated at the news. I knew she would be a huge help in getting Brady passed. Our own Gail Hoffman became part of the Reno confirmation team. Early on, I met with Janet and Gail, and I came away feeling confident that we had an ally in place who would be pushing for us all the way.

Meanwhile, the Clinton administration was working with Joe Biden, chairman of the Senate Judiciary Committee, to put together a comprehensive crime bill. Early in May, I met once again with Janet Reno and told her how much we hoped the Brady bill could be separated from the crime bill; that way, it would be easier to keep it on a fast track, free of the complexities of drafting the bigger bill. As usual, General Reno gave us her absolute support. For her, she said, Brady was a top priority. She would back whatever strategy we chose to pursue.

Despite all the work we had done to put together support for our bill over the previous six years, there remained some potential roadblocks in Congress. Speaker of the House Tom Foley was still smarting from the pressure we had put on him for holding up Brady back in

1990. The last thing he wanted was more trouble like that, so he promised that we would get a floor vote. But he didn't set any timetable, and he certainly had no intention of helping us get Brady through. Neither did Jack Brooks, chairman of the House Judiciary Committee, which would have to send the bill to the House floor.

The biggest problem was simply getting the Brady ball rolling, and I am quite certain that it was only the administration's efforts on our behalf that allowed us to make any progress. All during the summer and early fall, Janet Reno spoke out loudly and clearly on the need to give Brady a fair hearing as a separate bill. She made personal visits all over Capitol Hill, she made phone calls, she wrote letters. She was a tireless worker.

Meanwhile, we had to re-energize our supporters and recruit new allies among the freshman members of Congress. Ronald Reagan, Jimmy Carter, Gerald Ford, and Richard Nixon—all the living presidents except George Bush—signed a letter pushing for the bill. "It is not often that the four of us agree on a major issue of the day," they wrote. "But we share common ground on the desperate need to pass the Brady Bill." It was time, the presidents urged, "to put aside partisan politics and do what is right for the American people." Presidents Reagan and Ford even wrote personal letters and made phone calls to their fellow Republicans on our behalf.

In September, Bob Walker, HCI's legislative director, came up with a gimmick designed to get public attention and put even greater pressure on Congress. He had cardboard figures made that looked like the chalk outlines police draw around murder victims; on the back of each figure—we lovingly called them "Bud the Bod"—was a long list of people who had been killed by guns since the Brady bill had first been introduced, people whose lives might have been saved by a waiting period and background check. The message was simple: Too many lives have been lost already—pass the Brady bill now. We hand-delivered a

Bud the Bod to every member of Congress, and the gimmick worked just as Bob Walker had planned. We made a lot of press on that one.

Finally, in October, Speaker Foley threw the decision on how to handle a Brady vote to Jack Brooks of Judiciary. Brooks had to craft a rule for the Rules Committee, which determines when and in what form a bill will be considered by the House. Since the Speaker had no intention of putting the force of the Majority Whip behind the bill, we had to set up our own whip operation, just as we had in 1991. Once again, Chuck Schumer—now Brady's chief sponsor in the House, since Ed Feighan had not run for re-election—whipped up a storm.

By 1993, Jim was beginning to take an awful lot of pressure off me. After all the years of my being in charge, the only one who could do certain things, all of a sudden it was both of us. He was traveling on his own with a nurse, doing fundraising events, speeches, and press conferences for state legislative races. It was wonderful to see him get so much more active. He was terrific at that work, because he always brought his special wit to the job. And oh, did he love it!

But that didn't mean I gave up traveling and speaking—far from it. And there were two events that year that I remember especially fondly. The first was at the end of March, the twenty-fifth anniversary of the shooting of Dr. Martin Luther King Jr. Coretta King invited me to come for the services at the King Center in Atlanta, and I took Scott with me. It was a very moving, historic occasion, and he learned a lot about the history of his country.

Then, on the twenty-fifth anniversary of Robert Kennedy's death, I was invited by Ethel Kennedy to speak at an official commemoration in Arlington Cemetery. Members of the Kennedy family read Bible verses at the ceremony, and then eight of us who had known Kennedy or who worked in fields related to his concerns were assigned readings from his own words. My excerpt was about violence. I worked for weeks and weeks memorizing and practicing it. I was so honored to be part of that occasion.

But almost all of my energy that year was devoted to the Brady bill. Finally, all our years of hard work paid off. On November 10, the House passed the Brady bill by a vote of 238 to 189. Ten days later, the Senate passed its version by 63 to 36 and requested a conference. On November 22—the thirtieth anniversary of the assassination of John F. Kennedy—the conference convened, and the House and Senate agreed to the conference report. On November 23, the final version of the Brady bill passed the House by 238 to 187, and the next day, on a voice vote, the Senate passed it.

On November 30, 1993, President Clinton signed the Brady bill— or, as it was now officially named, Public Law 103-159.* What a day that was. Since the Clinton administration had taken office, we had been to the White House a few times for meetings. But our first official visit was for the signing of the Brady bill. It took place in the East Room, and the White House had allowed Handgun Control to put together a huge guest list. People were just jammed in. The staff was there, of course, and so were former members of our team like Gail Hoffman, Jane Clarenbach, and Charlie Orasin, who had left HCI after Brady first passed in 1991. There were representatives from all the law enforcement groups and other organizations that had backed us for so long. And there were victims of gun violence who had testified at many of the congressional hearings over the years.

The signing ceremony was scheduled for 10 or 11 in the morning. Jim and I and Scott and my brother, Bill, and a few others were supposed to be there about forty-five minutes ahead of time to meet with

*The Brady law went into effect on February 28, 1994.

the President; other guests were also asked to arrive early so they could be seated in time for the signing.

When we got to the White House, we were escorted to a private holding area. Everyone in the administration who would be involved in implementing the Brady law was there—Janet Reno, for instance, and Treasury Secretary Lloyd Bentsen, since the Bureau of Alcohol, Tobacco, and Firearms was under his jurisdiction. Then came my first real experience with "Clinton time," his chronic tardiness. The Clintons arrived, and the President chatted with everybody, just taking his time and seeming to enjoy every single person there. As I remember, we were at least an hour and a half late when we went into the East Room, where the guests had been jam-packed for all that time.

But no one minded. It was a wonderful occasion, a celebration, the moment for which we had labored for seven long years. When the White House ceremony was over, Handgun Control held a huge party at the Capitol Hilton.

The next week, with all the pressure finally off, Jim and I went to New Orleans with our dear friends Jerry and Debbie File. We had known the Files since right after Scott was born. Since I wasn't working at the time, I had joined the Alexandria Hospital auxiliary as a volunteer, and there I met Debbie, who lived across the street and one house down from my mother. After Jim was hurt, during that first month when I was always at the hospital and Scott was at Mother's house, Debbie organized the hospital volunteers so that every night one of them would bring dinner to Mother and Scott. It was a godsend. Afterward, Debbie and Jerry often invited Scott to their house to give my mother a break. We quickly became very good friends, and have remained so. Nothing in the world means more to me than what they did for my family.

And I've always had a fond place in my heart for New Orleans. I had visited quite a lot, because Louisiana's gun laws are not good and the city's mayor and police chief were always trying to bring attention to the fact. Besides, it's certainly the most fun American city I know. The spring before the Brady law was signed, Susan Whitmore and I had been in Baton Rouge for a press conference about the Japanese student, Yoshi Hatori, who was shot and killed while trick-or-treating on Halloween. When we were finished, we drove to New Orleans for the night. As we were leaving our hotel for dinner, we stopped to hear a street musician who happened to be playing "Do You Know What It Means to Leave New Orleans?" My father, a big Dixieland fan, always loved that song, and so do I. We listened until he finished, and then, as we walked away, the musician yelled "SARAH BRADY!" I turned, and he said, "Thumbs up—how's Jim?" I was so surprised and so touched that he recognized me, and that encounter reinforced my affection for the city.

Visiting such a beloved city with dear friends like the Files was almost guaranteed to be wonderful—and it was. We all stayed downtown in the French Quarter, at the St. Louis Hotel, our favorite. It's very accessible for the handicapped, as is all of the Quarter. You don't have to take cabs or rent a wheelchair van or anything. We could just wheel out and go anywhere with ease. Of course, since it was New Orleans, everything revolved around eating, from beignets in the morning to glorious gumbos at night.

One evening we had reservations at Armand's, an easy four-block walk from our hotel. When dinner was over, we decided to come back down Bourbon Street, which is lined with houses and bars and storefronts, almost all of which have little second-story balconies. That particular night, all the balconies seemed to be filled with people, as was Bourbon Street itself—the whole neighborhood was just teeming. As we turned the corner, somebody up on a balcony recognized Jim and shouted, "Jim Brady—Thumbs Up—Way to Go! Congratulations on the Brady bill!"

It was like a wave. All the people on the balconies and on the street went berserk. People hovered around us and shook our hands and congratulated us and cheered and took our pictures. There were hundreds upon hundreds of them, from all over the country, all over the world. There wasn't one boo, not one single person who was against us. It took us almost two hours to travel those four short blocks back to our hotel. It was the most spontaneous thing I've ever seen. That was truly a night to remember.

CHAPTER FIFTEEN

The End of the Glory Years

O UR NEXT LINE of business was the assault weapons ban. We had been working on it for several years, and by 1994, when the Brady law went into effect, we had put together a good coalition. For the most part, the folks who had supported Brady could be counted on to back a ban on assault weapons as well.

But we didn't take anyone for granted. Once again, we lobbied hard, visiting friends and foes alike. One of the most interesting encounters was with South Carolina's Strom Thurmond, who was a member of the Senate Judiciary Committee and had always been very kind to Jim and me.

We had visited him several times over the years. He was in his early nineties by 1994—the Senate's oldest member—and often it was quite difficult to discern where he would come down on a particular issue. Usually, in our meetings, he seemed fairly eager to help us. But he was very carefully watched by his aides, who were always in close contact with the Republican leadership. In fact, one of his primary assistants sat in the same office with him. They never let him meet with us by himself.

When we spoke with Senator Thurmond about assault weapons, he was appalled to learn that they were actually sold to civilians and said he wanted to help us in any way he could. But about two days later, we received a letter from him—obviously drafted by one of his staff members—which said that on the contrary, Senator Thurmond would not support any ban on assault weapons. That was always a difficult office to deal with.

On assault weapons, as with the Brady bill, we had lots of outside help from law enforcement groups and others. One person who was extremely effective during the congressional hearings on the issue was a New Yorker named Carolyn McCarthy. On December 7, 1993, her husband had been killed and her son injured when a crazed gunman, carrying an assault-style weapon, opened fire at rush hour on a Long Island Rail Road commuter train. The next spring, Carolyn McCarthy arrived on Capitol Hill, a powerhouse one-woman lobby on the subject of assault weapons. The U.S. representative from the New York district where she lived eventually voted against the ban. And when the Democrats approached McCarthy, a lifelong Republican, and asked whether she'd be willing to run against him in 1996, she agreed to do it. She beat him, and has been in the House ever since.

Over the years, there had been many versions of assault weapons bills. Howard Metzenbaum had worked on one for ages, as had his Democratic colleague from Arizona, Dennis DeConcini. Metzenbaum's approach had been to define the physical characteristics of weapons that would be banned, while DeConcini's bill named specific weapons that would be outlawed for civilian purchase.

The real lead on the law that finally passed was Democratic Senator

Dianne Feinstein of California, who essentially forged a compromise. Because so many people were worried that hunting guns might fall under the ban, her bill—at our urging—specifically exempted more than six hundred kinds of guns. In the end, it banned by name nineteen weapons and copies or duplicates of those weapons. It also stipulated, for pistols, rifles, and shotguns, the array of features that would fall under the ban. For instance, if a rifle had more than one of the following characteristics of assault weapons, it would be outlawed: a folding, telescoping stock, a protruding pistol grip, a bayonet mount, a threaded muzzle, a flash suppressor, or a grenade launcher. In addition, manufacturers would be prohibited from producing for civilian use magazines or ammunition-feeding devices capable of holding more than ten rounds. Any such devices produced before the date of enactment were still perfectly legal; only future manufacturing and sales were affected.

Unlike Brady, the assault weapon ban moved along as part of President Clinton's comprehensive crime bill. It passed with relative ease. On September 13, 1994, President Clinton signed the crime bill into law.* The ban on assault-style weapons went into effect the very next day.

Without doubt, 1994 was a banner year. First the Brady law went into effect; then we passed the assault weapons ban. It was interesting to see the effects on Handgun Control. By this time, the staff had swelled to seventy—from just a dozen when I had first started. But many of the people like Charlie Orasin and Gail Hoffman, who had campaigned so hard for the Brady bill during the glory years, had de-

---

*The crime bill contained several other elements of interest to Handgun Control: It banned juvenile possession of handguns or handgun ammunition and made it a crime to give or sell a handgun to anyone eighteen years old or younger. It also toughened requirements for licensing firearms dealers and outlawed firearms possession by anyone subject to a restraining order because of threats of domestic violence.

cided that it was time to move on to something else. By 1995, Susan Whitmore—the last of our threesome—had moved on as well.

Meanwhile, during 1993 and 1994, a lot of new people had come on board. They had not been there during the big push for Brady, and thus had not witnessed the extraordinary effort it had taken to win. None truly understood that we had fought to victory from nothing—from a time when no one took us seriously and hardly anyone was eager to help. I don't think those who came later ever appreciated how difficult it had been to build our coalition group by group, to win co-sponsors in Congress, to keep the issue constantly in the public eye. Many seemed to think, *Wow! I've been here just a year, and we've won the Brady bill and the assault weapons ban, and we can do anything, just take over the world!* They had inherited these victories, but didn't know how they had been won.

Perhaps because of that rather naïve euphoria, we made a big mistake, and I am certainly guilty of going along with it at the time. What happened was that Handgun Control set out a mammoth agenda to pass national laws requiring the licensing and registration of guns. We should have remembered the lessons we had learned so painfully during the push for Brady. There is no way you can win and maintain the support of Congress and the American people unless your agenda is focused on something for which they see a real need. You have to do your homework.

We didn't. We put out an agenda that was not realistic. At the same time, the political atmosphere was changing drastically. The 1994 midterm elections, when Republicans took control of the House of Representatives for the first time in forty years, marked the start of Newt Gingrich's Republican "revolution," the start of a much more partisan period on Capitol Hill. On the gun issue, among others, there was suddenly almost no chance for progress. For us to be pushing anything as ambitious as registration and licensing at that point was unrealistic, to say the least.

In planning our new agenda, we should have begun afresh, working to keep all our old coalition members in the fold and running everything by our allies in Congress, in law enforcement, and in other groups that had supported us. But there was a cockiness there, especially among the new folks, who didn't really know what it takes to put together a campaign. Many of our old allies had enjoyed the great publicity that came out of the Brady and assault weapons campaigns, and their constituents were happy with the new laws. But those deals were done. And very few of our old coalition members were anxious to take giant steps in the future.

The demand for Jim's and my time was still very heavy. We were doing lots of speaking, a great deal of campaigning in local and state elections, and more and more work helping state legislatures pass good gun laws. Meanwhile, our sister organization, the Center to Prevent Handgun Violence, was expanding its educational programs and research and trying to develop new constituencies, and we played a part in that as well.

Jim, who improved physically with every year that went by, was devoting more time to fundraising, dialing for dollars with a success no one else could match. As for me, I was frankly tired—and a bit dispirited. At the national level, we no longer had that focus we'd had with Brady and assault weapons, and I missed it.

But I continued to enjoy our work on state legislation and referendums. The issues in question were usually tightly focused, and it was fun to be part of putting together a campaign plan and making it work.

The National Rifle Association's push to make it legal for people to carry concealed weapons was one of the most important battles we faced. In most states, you had to obtain a permit to carry a concealed weapon, and you couldn't get the permit unless law enforcement signed off on it. The new laws the NRA was pushing permitted anyone who passed a background check to carry a concealed weapon. Virginia passed such a law very quickly—right at the beginning of the state's legislative session, before anybody had a chance to lobby against it. That put us on notice that if we weren't careful, this was going to be happening all over the country.

There were quite a few fights on concealed weapons. Texas was a prime example. Polling showed that nearly two-thirds of the state's residents did not want people to be carrying concealed weapons. Even so, year after year the gun lobby would fight hard in the state legislature, and year after year the legislature would pass a law permitting concealed weapons. When Ann Richards was the governor, she'd simply veto it, and the law's supporters didn't have the votes to override her. But in 1994, George W. Bush defeated Ann Richards and took over as governor of Texas. Once again, the legislature voted for a concealed weapons law, and this time the governor happily signed it, even though that law was against the will of the people.

In addition to concealed weapons, we were doing a lot of work on Child Accident Prevention laws. In Florida, a young mother who had lost her son to gunfire at the hand of a friend started the movement for a CAP law, and her state was the first to pass one. It made parents responsible if a child is able to get hold of a gun and misuse it. Soon after Florida's CAP law passed, we found ourselves working in many other states for similar measures. Ultimately, at least fourteen states passed CAP laws of their own.

Meanwhile, the National Rifle Association was still trying to enact preemption laws all over the country, prohibiting localities from passing gun laws unless the state legislature approved. In California, always on the cutting edge of gun control, every legislative session brought another piece of legislation that we endorsed and for which we were more than happy to campaign.

In November 1995, as part of our ongoing efforts to build support for sensible gun laws, I took a trip to Birmingham, Alabama. Our outreach department was involved in a conference called "Preventing Handgun Violence: Strategies for Community-Based Change." It was being sponsored by the mayor of Birmingham, the civic association, and the city government, and it was held at the Birmingham Civil Rights Institute, a museum dedicated to all that went on in that crucial city during the civil-rights movement.

The Reverend Joseph Lowry was president of the Southern Christian Leadership Conference at that time, and he and Mrs. Lowry—who keeps a national victims' quilt for SCLC—were there. There was a candlelight vigil in the city park where many of the civil-rights marches had been coordinated back in the 1960s—and where the infamous Bull Connor, Birmingham's commissioner of public safety, turned water hoses and police dogs against the peaceful marchers. There were also commemorations for the four African-American girls who died when a member of the Ku Klux Klan bombed Birmingham's Sixteenth Street Baptist Church. The conference was designed both to remember past victims of violence and to discuss strategies for preventing violence in the future.

I flew down one evening, and after landing, headed down to pick up my luggage. It never appeared. Someone went to check on it and returned to say it had been found, but that unfortunately it had gotten caught and dragged underneath one of the baggage carts. The suitcase itself was totally destroyed—torn open. My clothes were mostly fine, but all my makeup was gone. And first thing in the morning, I had to make an important public appearance.

Two staff members, Natalie Durham and Alicia Horton, had met me at the airport, and I told them I simply had to get some makeup for the speech. Natalie mentioned that they had been accompanied to the airport by some Birmingham police officers, and she ran out to ask them whether any mall might still be open. They said yes, but that it closed at 8 P.M. and we'd really have to hurry.

Natalie had rented a sub-compact car, the teeniest little vehicle you ever saw. We rushed out and hopped in, and the policemen—there were six of them, I think—said they would escort us on their motorcycles. Later, they told us they hadn't had a chance to practice their presidential motorcade skills for ages, because no sitting president had been to town; they were thrilled to use us as an excuse. Four of them led us and two followed behind. They got us out of the airport and up on the highway, doing all sorts of fancy maneuvers, clearing all the other cars off the highway and going at breakneck speed. Here we were in this little tiny car, trying to keep up. We were scared to death. Natalie was just gripping the steering wheel, and Alicia and I were holding on to each other in terror as we sped like maniacs to the mall.

The policemen screeched to a stop in front of the mall, hopped off their motorcycles and told us to leave our car right where it was. We ran into the department store—Alicia, Natalie, me, and six uniformed cops flanking us. Everybody just stopped what they were doing to watch. I asked where the Lancôme counter was, and someone pointed upstairs, so we all raced up the escalator, Alicia talking on her cell phone the whole way to the people at the hotel who were expecting us for dinner. The woman behind the Lancôme counter gaped at us. I told her what I needed, naming off the products. As I was paying, she was still staring at us, wide-eyed, so I explained what had happened and why we were in such a rush. It turned out that the Lancôme lady had been convinced that Alicia and Natalie were FBI officers, that I was in the witness protection program, and that the policemen were protecting me.

The conference was incredibly interesting. I was privileged to sit with several older members of Birmingham's African-American community, who talked about their experiences going back to the 1920s.

And when it was time to return to the airport, Natalie and Alicia said they would take me—and that the police wanted to escort us once again, just for practice. So we did it again, racing pell-mell down the highway in that teeny car. This time, Natalie was feeling confident—driving as if she was Mario Andretti. But Alicia and I were still scared to death. To this day, the three of us still laugh about that experience.

After Labor Day in 1995, Jim and I went to New York, where we were to accept an award. We took a train up on a Sunday evening, accompanied by our nurse, Dee Hardy. We ate dinner at our hotel, then retired to our little suite. Dee took Jim back to the bedroom, and I turned on the television in the living room.

All of a sudden I heard the most awful scream and then a crash, and I knew Jim had fallen. When he walks, he likes to follow the wall, which gives him some extra stability. Without knowing it was there, he had leaned on one of those closet doors that fold inward when you push on them. It folded, he lost his balance, and he went straight over on his face. He was covered with blood, and his face was already so swollen it looked as if he'd been in a prize fight.

I dialed 911, and an ambulance responded immediately. We were at the hospital all night long. Hospital workers X-rayed Jim, even gave him brain scans, but it turned out that other than knocking out a bunch of teeth, he hadn't done much damage. He hadn't broken a single bone or hurt his neck or head. But he looked like the devil, mainly because of the blood-thinner he takes, which makes you bleed and bruise much more easily than normal.

As we were about to leave the emergency room, someone noticed that my foot was all swollen. Two days before, I had stubbed my toe, and it turned out that I had broken a little bone. So here we'd spent the entire night at the hospital with Jim, who looked so pathetic, and I was the one with a broken bone.

In the morning, I quickly changed clothes and went to accept the award. When we got back to Washington, Jim went to see his own doctor, just to make sure everything was fine. I was worried about all those missing teeth—and he had to have even more taken out because they had been knocked loose in the fall. I knew something needed to be done. So we began going to a top-notch dentist to see if implants might do the trick.

During that period—twice, if I remember correctly—right around bedtime Jim would say he was hot, and didn't feel very well, and it turned out that his temperature had spiked as high as 104. Both times, I called Mike Newman, Jim's doctor, who prescribed antibiotics over the phone. On both occasions—they were maybe a month apart—the fever quickly broke and disappeared.

Finally, Jim's temperature seemed to have settled down, and at last he was scheduled to get his tooth implants. On the appointed day, I took him to the dentist's office, where there was a little surgical suite. I had brought a book and a tuna fish sandwich with me, and since the implants, under general anesthesia, would take at least two hours, I settled down with my sandwich to read.

Suddenly, someone rushed out of the surgical suite. Jim had gone into cardiac arrest.

CHAPTER SIXTEEN

"You'll Be Seen by Millions"

SOMEONE HAD ALREADY called 911, and while we waited for the ambulance to arrive, the dentist and the anesthesiologist performed CPR on Jim. I couldn't ride with him to the hospital because the paramedics had to work on him all the way. I found out later that they used the defibrillator on him, and it took nine or ten zaps before his heart started beating again.

We went to Fairfax County Hospital, which is known for its cardiac work. As it happened, the head of the emergency room had been at the George Washington University Hospital when Jim was shot, so he was somewhat familiar with Jim's case. An electrocardiogram showed that there was no heart damage, so they were a little unsure about what had caused the cardiac arrest. Jim didn't seem to have had an allergic reaction to the anesthesia. The emergency room chief said that he suspected it might have had something to do with Jim's head injury.

Perhaps Jim had over-reacted to the shot of anesthesia—the brain sometimes does that after a head injury—and then, when he was given something to calm the reaction, he over-reacted in the opposite direction, causing his heart to stop.

The doctor said Jim had not yet awakened, but that wasn't surprising, since he'd had all that anesthesia. He was going to put Jim in the cardiac care unit, where he could be monitored, and the doctor thought he would soon wake up. I felt pretty good about things at that point. Scott, who had wanted to go to boarding school starting in ninth grade, was at Little Keswick near Charlottesville, Virginia, and I asked the doctor whether he thought I ought to have him come home. "Immediately," was his response. That was when I realized how very serious this might be.

So our driver, Ross Giacoma, took off to get Scott. At that point, friends started arriving at the hospital. Jim didn't regain consciousness until early evening, and the anesthesiologist and the dentist were incredibly upset. I had to keep calming them down—especially the anesthesiologist. After all, they had done everything they could, and actually had saved Jim's life until the ambulance got there. As far as I was concerned, they were superheroes.

Finally, Jim began to wake up, which was very good news. When I went in to see him, I noticed that his arm was incredibly swollen and purple. I pointed it out to the people in cardiac care, and they said that's where he had received injections during the cardiac arrest; it was probably just a result of all the drugs that had been shot into him. But I was terrified that it would turn out to be a blood clot, so they gave him a Doppler ultrasound to make sure it was not.

That was an awfully difficult day and night. All told, Jim had to stay in the hospital for nearly two weeks to make sure there was no further trouble. But he had no heart damage of any kind. Although he still refers to that episode as his heart attack, that is not what it was. Something else caused the cardiac arrest. But there is no denying that once again, he had come perilously close to dying.

Jim came home from the hospital about a week before Christmas, and he hadn't been there for twenty-four hours when he spiked that high temperature again. Dr. Newman told me to give him Tylenol—no antibiotics—and said he wanted to see him first thing in the morning. This time, the blood tests showed that he had an infection in his bloodstream. Obviously, that was what had caused the earlier fevers in the fall, but because he had immediately started antibiotics on both occasions, Dr. Newman had never been able to detect the underlying cause of the problem. I wonder whether that infection didn't contribute to the cardiac arrest, as well, perhaps by weakening his system overall.

Jim immediately went into GW Hospital and was started on two intravenous antibiotics, which he would have to take for a full month. After three or four days he came home, where I was to be responsible for administering the IV medication. To make it easier, the doctors had put a central line in his neck that contained four ports. And we were prescribed an IV nurse who would stop by once a day to make sure everything was fine.

A medical supply outfit delivered everything I would need—IV pole, syringes, medications, rubber gloves—and the nurse showed me how to administer the antibiotics. Every four hours, I had to flush an open port with saline solution, then hook in the medication. After thirty minutes, when all the medicine had gone into Jim's system, I would unhook it and flush the port again, this time with saline and heparin, to make sure it didn't clot up. And then every twelve hours, I would have to give Jim the second antibiotic. It was a little like having a new baby and having to do regular feedings round the clock.

Apart from that, life went on pretty much as usual. We even had company for Christmas dinner, and while everyone else was having a drink, Jim sat there with his IV pole having his medication. The doctors stopped the medication a couple of days short of the full month, because he developed a slight rash, suggesting an allergic reaction to the drugs. But after that, he was just fine.

As usual, when August rolled around, I could hardly wait to get to the beach. In the mid-1980s, when Scott was four or five years old, we had started going to Dewey Beach in Delaware with Debbie and Jerry File and their children, Jocelyn and Jay. We always went in August, when Congress was in recess, and for several years, we rented a townhouse condominium. Our family took the first floor, so Jim could easily get in and out, and the Files had the third floor. The common areas—kitchen and living room—were in between. Once a day, for exercise, Jim would walk up to the second floor, where he'd spend the day; then, at night, he'd walk back down.

We had such fun. Those trips allowed me to relax totally, to forget all the pressure back in Washington. One of my favorite memories is of Jim's showers. There wasn't a good handicapped shower at the condo—just one shower stall outside the house. We'd get Jim into his bathing suit, and Debbie, Emmy, and I would wheel him into that shower and soap him down. He hated it because it was prickly and made him cold. And he was still at the stage when any unhappiness made him wail uncontrollably. So Debbie, Emmy, and I would all sing as loudly as we could to cover up the wailing.

In the early 1990s, Jim and I finally bought a little two-bedroom townhouse on New Orleans Street in Dewey Beach. It had a wonderful view of the ocean, and we adored it. We'd spend weekends there in the spring, summer, and fall, and in August, we'd try to stay for several weeks. Those years of relentless work and travel were taking a toll, and every year, I found I was looking forward more and more to our beach trips, even though they always seemed to be interrupted by a committee meeting or a trip or a speech.

In 1996, I thought we might just be able to spend the entire month of August by the ocean. I was wrong. We'd just settled in at our beach house when we were told that the Democrats wanted us to speak at the Democratic National Convention. Of course, we were thrilled—who in the world could say no to an honor like that?—but still, it meant once again that we wouldn't have our month at the beach.

Courtney Gardner, the daughter of our friends Theresa and Mickey Gardner, was working as my assistant at Handgun Control, and I asked her to bring a computer to the beach so I could start working on a speech. I did map out a lot of the things I thought we should say, but Bob Walker, who was now the president of Handgun Control, drafted the final version. Then we were off to Chicago—along with Scott and his girlfriend—for the convention. We were always so happy to be in Chicago.

We arrived two days before we were to appear, since the day before the speech would be devoted to security matters and practice sessions. Not long after we got there, we learned that our appearance was to take place in prime time. Somebody said, "You know what that means—you'll be seen by millions around the world." Despite all the speech-making I had done over the years, that struck a chord of sheer terror in my heart.

The night before the speech, Jim was dying to have dinner at Gene & Georgetti, one of his favorite places on earth to eat. So he and a bunch of our staff people and friends all went out for steaks. I stayed behind at the Chicago Hilton, the official convention hotel. I was so nervous about that enormous prime-time audience that I didn't dare do anything but remain in our room to practice.

The next morning, I got some help. Convention organizers had assigned us a generous block of time with Michael Sheehan, an absolutely terrific media coach from Washington who was helping everyone who was to appear at the convention—teaching us, among other things, how to use the teleprompter. I worked with him for about an hour, right on the convention floor where the speech would take place. It's quite incredible how slick that operation is. The words of your speech are up on the teleprompter almost anywhere you happen to look, so from the audience, or on television, it appears that you're just reciting from memory, and looking here and there at people in the audience as you speak. The experience was just invaluable.

That evening, the convention folks sent a car to pick us up at the hotel. When we got to the convention center, I ran through the speech one more time. The organizers wanted to know whether Jim could walk on. He said yes, he wanted to try.

I'll never forget as long as I live how it felt to walk out and to see the convention floor filled with thousands of people. And I guess it was the smell of the greasepaint and the roar of the crowd—being out there, hearing their cheers, and absorbing their enthusiasm sort of revved me up. All of a sudden, my nervousness was entirely gone. Jim and I walked to the podium, and then Courtney brought out Jim's wheelchair and he sat down. Everybody seemed to love our opening line: "Gee, Jim, this doesn't look like San Diego"—where the Republican convention had taken place.

When it was over, I felt I'd done pretty darn well. It was a great, celebratory night. We went back to the hotel and had drinks, then enjoyed a mammoth buffet and were able to watch several reruns of our appearance. By the end, we were exhausted and very eager to get back to the beach. But the convention speech was a great honor.

That fall, Jim and I both did a lot of campaigning all over the country. One state election was of particular interest to us. When Paul Simon was first elected to the Senate in 1984, his seat in the House—representing Jim's hometown, Centralia, Illinois—had been taken by Richard Durbin. And when Senator Simon decided not to run again in '96, Dick Durbin decided to try for his Senate seat. Early on, he had asked us to come out and endorse him, and of course we agreed. He was running against a fellow named Al Salvi, and the gun issue was central to the race. Dick Durbin had worked hard for us in the House. Al Salvi had taken money from the National Rifle Association, and he was running pretty much on the NRA line. In Illinois, our position definitely had majority support, so the polls showed Al Salvi's stand was really hurting him. But he kind of dug in on the issue, nonetheless.

The week before the election, Jim was in California on a campaign trip. Al Salvi was in Chicago, where someone asked him about the gun issue. Salvi said—he must have picked this up from some of the crazy propaganda about us our opponents were always disseminating—that Jim Brady had once sold machine guns. Someone called me and asked whether that was so, and I said of course not.

Jim was flying back from California the Friday before election day, and our office arranged for him to stop in Chicago on the way and to hold a press conference at the airport. I've seen clips of that conference. It looks as if every television camera and every print reporter in the entire state of Illinois was there. The audience was huge. Jim read a little prepared statement, but most of his comments were off the cuff. The most famous sound bite of the day was this: "You know, as a press secretary, I've been known to shoot off my mouth. But one thing I've never shot off is a machine gun, nor did I ever sell a machine gun." That weekend, the fracas dominated the papers and the TV news. And on election day, Dick Durbin won in a landslide.

About a week later, Al Salvi's wife called my office. I was out, but she left a message: "I just want to tell her my husband is not a mean man. He's not a bad man. He's not a gun-toting man." I guess he'd gotten such horrible press on the gun issue that she wanted to defend him. And damned if Al Salvi himself didn't turn around sometime in the next six months and announce that he'd been wrong about guns all along.*

*In 1998, Al Salvi ran for a state office, but lost. In 2002, he is running for the Illinois State Legislature.

Sometime in 1996, we got word that several sheriffs in the West were challenging the Brady law, even though the National Sheriffs Association had been a powerful force in passing it. They had filed suit, arguing that it was unconstitutional for the federal government to tell them they had to run background checks. They were not opposing the Brady waiting period, just the requirement for background checks. They strongly believed that Washington could not tell local law enforcement what to do. The Supreme Court agreed to hear the case.

Around Thanksgiving, Jim got a terrible pain on the right side of his abdomen. At first, I figured it was appendicitis, but it turned out that he had a kidney stone. The doctor gave him a little strainer and told him to drink all the water he could. We kept pumping in water, convinced that he would pass that kidney stone at any moment, but nothing happened. Eventually, the pain went away and Jim seemed fine. The doctor said it was probably just lodged somewhere, not moving, and he would keep an eye on it. He was hesitant to go in and try to blast the stone loose because it was very near the area where Jim's Greenfield umbrella had been inserted to prevent blood clots, and the doctors were afraid of dislodging the umbrella.

Then, very early in 1997, the pain started again. Jim had further tests and began drinking huge quantities of water again—and the pain, once more, disappeared. At this point, Jim's medical doctor and urologist were worried that since the stone was lodged somewhere, eventually it might interfere with his kidney functions. So periodically, they would check to see how he was doing.

In June, tests showed that his kidney function was diminishing, and the doctors decided that they had to remove that stone. I was very nervous about it, given Jim's last experience with anesthesia. But Mike Newman, his internist, consulted with Art Kobrine, who had operated on Jim so many times with no problems. Art mentioned that in all Jim's surgeries he had used a certain anesthesiologist, Dr. Don Lee, and so Dr. Lee was pressed into service for this kidney operation as well. The surgery was at Georgetown University Hospital, and it was scheduled for early morning on June 27. We had to get Jim there by 6 A.M.

As if that weren't enough to worry about, we had heard that the Supreme Court decision on the Brady law might come down that same day. I certainly didn't want to get dressed up and sit around the hospital all day in press conference clothes if the ruling didn't happen, so I stuck my good clothes and makeup in a bag and took them along with us.

Jim's kidney stone turned out to be much larger than the doctors had thought—so huge that he never could have passed it. In order to get it out, they had to break it apart. But he came through the surgery just fine, and in late morning, just about the time he awoke and I had a chance to see him, we found out what had happened at the Supreme Court. Handgun Control scheduled a press conference for around noon, and I got on my makeup and my clothes and scooted over to the Court.

In a five-to-four decision, the Supreme Court justices had struck down the mandatory background check of the Brady law, ruling that the federal government could not force local sheriffs to run checks. It was unfortunate; it would have been nice to have the entire Brady law upheld by the High Court. But to be perfectly frank, we did not consider this a serious setback. Apart from a few rural jurisdictions like those whose sheriffs had brought the suit, we had every indication that most local law enforcers wanted background checks and would continue to do them even if not forced to do so by federal law. And the background check had not even been a part of the original Brady bill. It had been added later by Senator George Mitchell.

The waiting period, the most important part of Brady, was still the law of the land.

CHAPTER SEVENTEEN

Growing Pains

.

THROUGH ALL THESE YEARS and all our adventures, of course, Scott was growing into the young man he is today. I know those years were anything but easy for him. To this day, I regret more than almost anything that he was unable to enjoy the kind of childhood I had—full of warmth, security, and peace. He has certainly had more than his share of excitement.

It never occurred to me that motherhood was going to be difficult. I wanted a child more than anything under the sun, and partly because I had been a good schoolteacher, I was convinced that I'd be a wonderful mother. I knew, for instance, how to set clear, consistent rules and enforce discipline. I thought it would be a piece of cake to raise a child of my own. Oh, how wrong I was.

From the very beginning, Scott was a wonderful little fellow. It wasn't long after he was born that Jim went off on the 1980 Presidential campaigns, so my son and I were alone for much of his first two years. Talk about bonding. Although early on I did try to go back to work part-time, I just couldn't bear to be away from him. I adored the simple daily routines—dressing and bathing and taking walks. As Scott got older, we went to the park every day, where we met neighbors with other little kids. He was such a happy little boy, very alert and bright, and he hardly ever cried.

He always hated to sleep. And he always loved music. Back when he was less than a year old, the *Washington Star*—now defunct—was running a television advertisement that featured a theme from Beethoven. Every time that ad for the newspaper came on, long before Scott could walk, he would stand up in his playpen and jump up and down and laugh and scream with pure joy. He loved that piece. Eventually, music became one of his major interests.

He learned to talk quite early, and spoke in complete sentences almost from the start. Somehow, he always struck me as being older than he actually was. Even when he was just two years old, you could discuss almost anything with him. The only word I recall him mispronouncing was "corduroys." When Scott said it, it always came out "cordurorities."

The older he got, the more devilish he became. When he was about two and a half, I started noticing that although he would listen carefully to things that interested him, it was very hard to get his attention if you wanted to give him directions or explain how he should do something. For example, when it came time for him to learn how to cross streets safely, I explained the rules, and he knew them. If you came to a corner and said, "Scott, what do we do now?" he would say, "You look both ways." But if, across the street, he spotted a motorcycle or something else of great interest, the rules went straight out the window. He would not even look. He would impulsively rush after whatever it was that caught his eye.

In the beginning, I thought this was normal. What little boy doesn't drop everything to look at a motorcycle? But as he got older, he didn't seem to outgrow this acting on impulse. Whatever Scott felt at any given moment was what he wanted to do, and I grew increasingly worried about his safety—especially after the time he explored our entire roof after climbing out one of his bedroom windows.

By the time he was four, I was worried enough to ask our pediatrician about the problem. He gave Scott a little test designed to measure skills such as how long he could pay attention to a single task. The test took about an hour and a half. When it was over, the pediatrician said, "We have a live one here." He was pretty sure that Scott had an attention deficit problem. The only way to be certain, he said, was to put him on Ritalin. If that worked, the diagnosis was almost certainly correct.

He sent us to a specialist, Dr. Joseph Balzarette, who gave Scott a full battery of psychological tests. On the IQ exam, Scott got to a certain point, then turned to the person administering the test and said, "I'm not going any further—I've done as much as I can do today—that's it." As it turned out, his IQ was sky-high.

I suppose most parents are thrilled to find out a child has a high IQ, but in a child with attention deficit, this is a real problem. It can cause performance to lag far behind ability. These kids know inside that they are smart, but they have such trouble settling down and mastering something—whether it's a rule, a safety process, or an academic procedure—that they can become totally frustrated. I hate to sound as if I'm parroting some politically correct nostrum, but this syndrome does hurt their self-esteem. Very early on, they see that they're different from the kids around them. A teacher gives directions and the student in the next seat catches on immediately, but the child with attention deficit hears only the first part, missing steps two and three.

Dr. Balzarette started Scott on a very low dose of Ritalin, and you could see the difference immediately. He could concentrate a bit better, but what really struck me was how much quieter he became. He seemed less spontaneous, much more serious. I worried about whether we were doing the right thing. And I often recalled the words of my friend Bobbie McGraw. I'd asked her, after the time I'd put a lock on Scott's bedroom door to keep him from escaping, whether I was doing the right thing. Bobbie, who had two boys of her own, said, "Sarah, you will *never* know if you are doing the right thing." Those were very wise words.

By the time Scott started kindergarten, he was doing well. But the teacher told me she thought he might have problems with "sensory integration," and she referred us to an occupational therapist named Jean Hanna. Sure enough, a battery of tests disclosed sensory integration problems, meaning that Scott's system sometimes found it hard to make sense of all the outside stimuli it was receiving. Too much noise, for instance, or excessive touching or jostling could be real problems for him. Jean Hanna compared it to watching television and having the channel change every thirty seconds. She said Scott was so bright that he would learn everything he needed to learn, but he would not do it the same way other kids did it. Most kids learn step by step and come to a conclusion; Scott would start from the conclusion and move the opposite way, to see how you arrived at it. This, she warned—quite correctly—meant schools would be a problem.

For the next several years, Scott went twice a week for therapy sessions with Jean Hanna. Around the time he started, I got a firsthand look at what his sensory integration problems meant to him. Some parents in our neighborhood were organizing a soccer team for little kids, and I asked if he'd like to participate. Sure, he said—so we went for the organizing meeting. It was a cold day. The session was incredibly chaotic. No one seemed to be in charge, kids were running in every direction, and it was extremely noisy. Even by my standards, there was altogether too much commotion, and the whole affair seemed painfully disjointed. We hadn't been there for more than twenty minutes when Scott said he wanted to go home. It was just too much, and he knew this was not for him.

The next year, armed with Ritalin and Jean Hanna's therapy, Scott started first grade. The very first day, at about 11 in the morning, I got a call from the principal, who said she thought I should come get him. Evidently, he had decided after an hour that he wanted to wait another year to start first grade. He was told that was not possible. So one by one, he started offering further excuses. He was homesick. He didn't feel well. The teacher had heard pretty much every story in the book and dismissed each one in turn. Finally, he approached her yet again. He was an alcoholic, he announced, and his mother always gave him a beer at 11, so he needed to get home. That one finally got their attention and led to the principal's call. Thankfully, on the second day of school Scott made some friends and forgot his imaginary addiction.

Although that elementary school was known as one of the best public schools in Arlington, there were things about it that I did not like from the beginning. Most important, I thought that the principal and teachers were far too concerned with test scores and that they spent far more energy on fostering competition among the students than on trying to help them learn.

During those years, I tried to take nothing longer than a day trip. But one evening bad weather grounded me in New York. I knew Scott had taken his first spelling test that day. We had worked on the words quite a bit before I left, and I could see that he was having a hard time. So when I called that night, I said, "Scott, how did you do on your spelling test?" And the poor little fellow said, "I lost."

My heart ached for him. He was trying, but memorization is among the hardest skills for kids with sensory integration troubles. When he'd been in school for about a month, his principal and teacher called me in for a consultation. They both felt that Scott was going to have a hard time in that classroom—and I had to agree. There was certainly no hint that anyone wanted to work with him to find different ways of getting to the same goals, something I had always tried to do when kids in my classrooms needed to find their own ways of learning. They said they could put him in a special class, but discouraged that, since he was so bright. The principal suggested a private school, where Scott could get more individual attention.

For the next couple of years, Scott went to a nice little private school in Alexandria. But in third grade, he ran into a teacher who insisted that everything must be done her way, and he was clearly having trouble. We transferred him to another school that specialized in learning disabilities, but that turned out to be not quite the right fit. Finally, he was admitted to the Lab School of Washington, which is famous for its creative teaching methods, and there he remained for the next several years.

By this time, Scott's personality was really coming into focus. He always had an uncanny sense of right and wrong, always sympathized with the underdog. He also was extraordinarily perceptive about people. By instinct, it seemed, he recognized the really true, good people—and also the ones he would rather avoid.

Jean Hanna got him involved in horseback riding. Much of her therapy was geared toward balance, which is related to sensory integration, and riding is a quintessential balance sport. So Scott took that up and did beautifully. He also learned to ski during those years and got to be top-notch at the sport.

But Scott's greatest extracurricular interest was definitely music. A neighbor's son had given him a ukulele when he was little, and from that, he moved on to the guitar. Even when he was little, he always looked up to the older kids who were a little off-beat—especially those involved in the music culture. Once we were in a grocery store where we saw a tattooed guy wearing patched jeans and motorcycle boots, with greasy hair down to his waist. Scott, with his blond hair and blue eyes and corduroys, walked over and said, "Nice hair, Man!" I could tell right then where he was headed.

By the time Scott was ten, he was begging us to let him get an earring. Although he was still in the lower school at the Lab School, the high school guys he thought were really cool all seemed to have them. I explained that he couldn't have his ear pierced without parental permission until he was sixteen, and said we should at least wait until he was a teenager. I hoped, of course, that he'd forget about it by then.

During a spring vacation, Handgun Control was holding a fundraiser and board meeting in Dallas, so Jim and I took Scott with us, along with our nurse, Mary Dickerson. To keep him busy while we were in the meeting, I gave Scott five dollars and he and Mary went off to a dime store. Suddenly, the doors to the room where the board had convened burst open. Scott rushed in, a panic-stricken Mary close behind him. "Look what I got!" he said with great excitement. His ear was pierced. In Texas, there were no laws about how old you had to be, so he had spent his five dollars on a piercing and a cheap earring. He could hardly wait to get back to school and show everyone.

The first school day after spring vacation, I went to pick him up, as usual, when he got out. My mother, whom Scott adored, was with me, sitting in the front seat. I saw him running toward us and watched as he spotted Mother and immediately slowed down. He got into the car with a very funny look on his face, said "Hi, Grandma," and kissed her from behind. I could tell he was trying to hide that earring.

We took Mother home, and it was one of the few times I ever saw Scott just furious with me. "How could you have brought Grandma over to see me with this earring?" I don't know how he'd thought he would hide it from her for the rest of his life, if he planned to keep it. But that night he took it out, and that was it.

These were the years when Jim and I were beginning to do our dog and pony shows, and whenever we had to perform on a weekend, we took Scott along. In September 1989, we had a Friday night appearance in Buffalo, New York, so the next day I decided to show Scott, Jim, and Mary Dickerson where I had lived as a child. After exploring Buffalo, we drove to Niagara Falls for lunch, then on to Toronto, where I had made reservations at a hotel with a five-star restaurant. At dinnertime, Jim and Scott decided they would rather order burgers and fries through room service and watch television. So Mary and I left them behind and had a divine meal at the restaurant.

When we returned, we heard gales of laughter coming from our room. When I opened the door, I was appalled to find that Jim and Scott were watching a pornographic movie. Scott's introduction to the genre came from his own father! A year later, we had a speech in Arizona, and Scott asked if I would bunk with Mary and let him stay with Jim. He needed some male bonding time, he said—and that promptly became the family euphemism for watching fare that was ordinarily forbidden.

For the next three years, Scott did quite well at the Lab School. He continued to have trouble with spelling and numbers, but was very good at subjects like English and social studies. I give the magazine *Rolling Stone* great credit for his English skills, since he always loved to read about the rock stars.

But at the end of eighth grade, to my astonishment, Scott said he did not want to go back to the Lab School. Instead, he had his heart set on boarding school. Many of our friends pointed out that some boarding schools specialized in learning disabilities and might well give him even more individualized care than the Lab School. So we sent for material, and finally settled on the Forman School in Litchfield, Connecticut. Off Scott went for his freshman year in high school.

I could tell the first time we visited him that the school was not going to work out. It was a wonderful school, but it did not provide enough structure for Scott. He just did not have enough self-discipline to flourish there, and while he still did fine at English and at anything that tapped his writing skills, he wasn't learning much of anything else.

Toward the end of that school year, I pulled Scott out of Forman and consulted an educational specialist named Ethna Hopper. I hadn't even known such people existed, or I would have gone to her long before—and I would advise any parent of a child with learning disabilities to seek out someone like her. She visited schools all over the country and was an expert in matching each child with the institution that would best suit him or her. She tested Scott and reviewed all his records and ultimately settled on Little Keswick near Charlottesville, Virginia.

Little Keswick wasn't accepting new students until summer. In the meantime, Ethna thought a program like Outward Bound might be very good for Scott. We found a program called Seuss, got him ready, and I flew out to Idaho with him. He was gone for about six weeks, during which the participants lived in the wilderness, trapping and foraging for food, cooking over fires, purifying stream water for drinking. At one point during the program each student had to spend a full twenty-four hours by himself, surviving entirely on his own.

I'll never forget picking Scott up. He did not know I was coming; I'd arranged with his counselors that I simply would show up, out there where they were camping. When I arrived, I hardly recognized Scott. He was darkly tanned, very thin, and muscular. He had grown a beard and his hair was long. He seemed very independent, suddenly, and there was a quiet simplicity about him that was quite new. He seemed confident that he could survive almost anything. He was in absolutely great shape, and he had loved being out there, but he was very happy to get home.

Little Keswick turned out to be one of the finest schools I've ever seen. It was small, located out in the country. It had horses, so that

Scott could keep up his riding. And the teachers, many of them graduates of the University of Virginia, were wonderful—young and extremely creative about working with kids.

The program was highly structured. Students had to earn points in order to do anything—even call home. It took Scott a while to settle in, but once he did, he began to shine. The structure and quiet and the stress on creative learning seemed to be what he had needed all along. In many areas, he became a school leader. He absolutely hated the food, for instance, and led a peaceful protest against it. The kids collected signatures on a petition, then went to the woman who ran the cafeteria and asked for—and won—some changes.

In January of his junior year, Scott decided he wanted to come home and finish high school at the Lab School. I think he felt he could handle more freedom now, although like many kids, he really did not yet have all the tools he needed to handle all his responsibilities. In some ways, the next few years were quite difficult. He loved to play the guitar, and he loved socializing with his friends outside school; studying was far from his number one concern. He was testing the limits, and it was very difficult for me to sit back and let him experiment.

I'll never forget waiting to see whether he would graduate on time. To graduate, he had to write a thesis, and because he had failed to get all his homework assignments in, he needed an A on that thesis. He also had to score well on his Spanish exam.

I hired a tutor for the Spanish, and that worked well: Scott aced the test. Finally, he buckled down to write his thesis. As a subject, he chose the Federal Aviation Administration, and he did an enormous amount of research to prove his theory: that the FAA was too cozy with the airline industry, and as a result, air travel was far less safe than it ought to be. Everything he wrote has turned out to be true. His thesis was really good, and he got an A plus.

*

Through all his early years, Scott was extremely close to my mother. As a little boy, he just loved to go to Grandma's and hear stories about her childhood and mine. He absorbed all the family lore and remembered everything she told him. She would take him to the Hot Shoppe for lunch, or she would make grilled cheese sandwiches that he simply adored—and that I've never been able to match. Mother's stroke, in 1989, was hard on him. But even though she never fully recovered, she got much better, and continued to live at home with some nursing help.

Scott went off to boarding school in Connecticut in the fall of 1993. About that time, I noticed a big difference in Mother. She had suffered a series of little strokes, and by Christmas, it was as if she had lost her will to live. Scott came home for the holidays, and I know it hurt him to see her. We took presents over to her house, but she didn't want to come for our big Christmas dinner. She wanted to sleep. She was beginning to talk a lot about her own mother and to say that it was time for her to go.

Scott went back to school, and I got back to work. In February 1994, I was in Boston when my brother called to say Mother was in the hospital and they did not think she would make it. I rushed home, and when I got there she had rallied a bit. For the next two days, Bill and I stayed at the hospital almost around the clock.

Finally, she was moved out of intensive care into a regular room. The hospital personnel could tell that she was going; her systems were beginning to shut down. But I guess I hadn't accepted the fact. On Friday night, I stayed with her until about eight in the evening. She hadn't awakened or recognized me, but she seemed to be breathing well, so I left to go home. I had no sooner walked in the door than the hospital called to tell me she had died. Bill picked me up, and we went to see her before the funeral home took her.

It is always hard to lose your mom. To this day, if I have to make a decision I always think what Mother would do or try to imagine what advice she'd offer. Of course, when you're young, you never want to listen to your mother, but I had learned to depend upon her even more than I realized.

The next morning we made arrangements for visitation on Monday night at the church, and for the funeral the next day. I got reservations for Scott to fly home on Monday. Then I made perhaps the single dumbest decision of all my years as a mother. I hated the thought of Scott's suffering before he absolutely had to, so I waited until that Monday morning even to tell him Mother had died.

Bill and I had had two full days, that entire weekend, to grieve. But Scott was pulled out of class, put on a plane, and rushed home just in time to attend the visitation at the church. Because I had wanted to spare him from a miserable weekend, he had no private time to come to terms with Mother's death. And he was just devastated. I don't think I had focused until then on how close he had been to his grandmother or how much she had meant to him. It was one of the hardest nights I can remember.

He did pretty well the next day at the funeral. But on our way to the cemetery, we passed the Hot Shoppe where he and Mother had eaten so often. At the very sight of that restaurant, he fell apart again.

I learned my lesson. When Dorothy Brady passed away later that same spring, I called Scott immediately. He was very upset. Even though Dorothy and Scott had not been together day in and day out over the years, as Mother and Scott had been, Dorothy had visited us often and Scott loved to go to Centralia.

I told him that he did not have to come all the way to Illinois for that funeral, and in the end, he decided not to go with us. He grieved for Dorothy on his own, not cheated, this time, by my misguided attempt to protect him.

CHAPTER EIGHTEEN

Back to Basics

B Y 1996, I had been at Handgun Control for eleven years—a long, hard eleven years. Jim was beginning to get tired of all the relentless traveling, and increasingly, I found myself thinking how wonderful it would be for us both to slow down, to change our lifestyle entirely and live at the beach fulltime. And fate seemed to be conspiring on my side.

In January, Scott came home to finish high school in Washington. Not long after he arrived, I got a phone call early one morning. "You don't know me, but my name is Sally Law and I think we ought to get to know each other," said the voice on the line. "My daughter's name is Heather, and I think Scott and Heather are becoming an item." We talked that first morning for more than an hour, hitting it off immediately. Over the weeks ahead, as it became clear that Scott and Heather, who were at school together, were becoming very close, Sally and I spoke many more times. We thought that if our kids were seeing each other, it was important for us to agree on the ground rules. We didn't meet in person until the end of that school year, but from that time on, Sally Law and I were the closest of friends. Although she's younger than I am, I call her "Aunt Sally," because Heather is actually her niece, whom she's raised since she was very little.

Our neighbor in Dewey Beach was a woman named Janet Judge, whose family had been one of the first in the community. Her son, Rick, owned a little spit of land between the ocean and Silver Lake, and he was planning to develop it. The original prices for the seven lots were completely out of our reach, but I'd sit and dream about that area all the time. It seemed so perfect to me—ocean on one side, lake on the other. The lots were laid out so that three houses would be right on the ocean, two on the lake and two in the middle. As the summer went on, I kept dreaming about that wonderful property. Meanwhile, the prices seemed to be going down. When one of the middle lots went on the market at a price that wasn't prohibitive, Jim and I decided to make an offer. Rick accepted it.

We hired an architect and got busy with plans to build our house, since we thought we'd like to move to the beach for good by the end of 1998. One weekend Aunt Sally and Heather came out to Dewey Beach for a visit, and I told Sally, who is a financial consultant, that we probably should sell our little place on New Orleans Street and use the money to build the new beach house. Out of the blue, Sally said she'd buy our old townhouse—and she did. She owns it to this day.

In the meantime, there were changes at Handgun Control that began to make it much easier for me to think about slowing down. I had been chairman of the board since 1989, and I disliked that part of the job. I never felt at home with the board, as I did with the staff. I felt out of place doing the kind of work a board must do: oversight, long-term planning, setting strategy. What I enjoyed and did best was more along the lines of public speaking and lobbying.

But every year, we were getting new members of the board, people like former White House press secretary Jerry ter Horst, who were extremely powerful and helpful. Nancy Kassebaum joined after retiring from the Senate, although she had to resign when she moved to Tokyo with her new husband, Howard Baker, the U.S. ambassador to Japan. By 1996, our new members were changing the character of the board, pushing it toward the kind of oversight a good board of directors should exercise. Phyllis Segal and Vicki Kennedy, in particular, were incredibly competent women who knew what they were doing and were willing to put everything into their work. I realized that I didn't need to worry about it any more, and that it was time to hand over my leadership responsibilities. I wanted to be always involved with passing responsible gun legislation, but I wanted to let others take the reins.

So I began planning our house and looking forward to moving to the beach. In the beginning of 1998, we submitted our plans to the builder. It was going to take almost a year to finish the house, and that was very disappointing. I didn't want to wait that long. But I went to Dewey to get the final contract, and the builder and I went out to our property. Suddenly Lucia Morrison, who had built a house on my favorite of the seven lots, right on the lake, stuck her head out the window. "Guess what," she said. "I'm selling the house and moving." We had been in her home, and just loved it. It had an elevator, and it was on a corner lot with a gorgeous view of both the lake and the ocean. That night another neighbor called. He had heard Lucia was selling her house, and thought we ought to buy it. He offered to buy our lot. Within two days, Jim and I made an offer on Lucia's house and she accepted it. We moved in right after Thanksgiving and were completely settled in by Christmas 1998.

I had wanted an entirely different look for our new life, so I sold much of our old furniture. But there were some pieces to which I was quite attached, largely because of family memories. I entrusted several antiques, including my mahogany dining room table and the bed I had slept in as a child, to a friend who will keep them for Scott in case he ever wants them. My friend Barbara Lautman, who had once worked with me at Handgun Control, was now working with antiques, and she painted some dark pieces creamy off-white so they would fit in at the beach. But almost everything else in our house is new—light and airy, wicker and calico.

We have two floors. On the second is a huge great room that stretches all the way across the south end of the house. From the east windows you see the ocean. The west windows look over the lake, where we built a little private dock, and right outside is a large screened-in porch and a deck. The kitchen is part of the great room itself, so everybody is there together. It's the most friendly setup—perfect for entertaining big parties and also for spending cozy nights by the fire, just the two of us.

There are three bedrooms on the second floor. I turned one into an office and another into what I call my sitting room, where I keep my clothes. The third is Jim's and my room. Downstairs, there are three spare bedrooms, one of which contains a sofa bed and a big television so that people who stay down there—usually Scott—can have a private sitting room in case they don't want to join us upstairs.

Being here is just what I've always wanted. There's a small-town atmosphere that I've loved ever since those family vacations as a child in Brookfield, Missouri. Even Alexandria, when I was growing up, had a small-town feel. But once Jim and I moved to Arlington, I felt as if I no longer lived in a community. I was just one of millions who lived in the suburbs of Washington, D.C.

There's quite an active social life down here, and yet there's peace and quiet when you need it. That's especially true where we live, since it's a little spit of land accessible only by a little road, and we're the last house on the road. You have the best of both worlds—you're a bit off by yourself, but close enough to other people that you don't feel alone or afraid. In the summer, of course, all the houses are teeming. But throughout the fall, winter, and spring, most of our neighbors are here mainly on weekends. We are the only people in our immediate neighborhood who live here year-round.

The first year we lived here, we went to Washington much more frequently than we do now. We'd taken a little one-bedroom apartment in a high-rise in Arlington. But we found the trips extremely difficult. For one thing, after living out here for several months, the traffic, construction, noise, and general hassle of the city bothered us more and more. I couldn't imagine how we had endured it for so many years. The apartment was difficult as well. Jim's van didn't fit in the building's underground garage, so we had to pull up in front and unload everything, then find a place to park—usually extremely difficult—and then haul everything inside. By the time we got in, we were so tired we never wanted to go anywhere at night. Meantime, I had to keep two places clean and remember which clothes were where. It wasn't long before I dreaded those trips. After one year of that, we gave up the apartment. So much work could be done on the computer and by phone that we really didn't have to go to Washington as much as we'd expected. When we do have to go to town, we now simply stay in a hotel.

In 1999, Phyllis Segal took over from me as chairman of Handgun Control's board—and what a godsend she is. She's so organized, so professional in her approach to making the board effective. Her sense of process is right on target. She knows what to do and how to do it. And after Bob Walker decided it was time for him to move on, we hired a new president, Mike Barnes, a former congressman from Maryland. He has done a miraculous job. He's a wonderful speaker, understands politics, works extremely well with the board, and has turned out to be a terrific fundraiser.

Ever since I had worked at Handgun Control, there had been discussions about changing its name. In June 2001, the board finally made it official. Handgun Control and its educational arm became, respectively, the Brady Campaign to Prevent Gun Violence and the Brady Center to Prevent Gun Violence. It was a great honor for Jim and me, and they marked it with a special tribute in Washington. Hundreds of the people who have worked so hard for us over the years were in attendance; it was a wonderful thing to see them all. And I feel very confident about the organization that now carries our name. Once again, it is focused closely on the kind of work I've thought we should do all along: making sure that every single gun sale, including all secondary sales, includes the very best possible background check.

When the Brady law passed, the waiting period it called for was set to "sunset"—Congress's term for "expire"—after five years, and the nation would then move to an "instant check" system. The thinking was that by then—1999—the necessary data would be available nationwide, allowing immediate background checks on anyone seeking to buy a gun. So when the expiration date arrived, the waiting period went out of effect in the twenty-five or so states that had not enacted waiting periods of their own. All the states that did have waiting periods continued to enforce them. But close to half the states in the country now have only the instant background check.

I always thought we should start preparing for the sunset of the Brady law so that we could make sure some waiting period continued to exist—perhaps seventy-two hours, rather than the full five days. We have worked hard for such measures in the states. But I would still like to see a short national waiting period as well. There are several good reasons for this. It's not just a cooling-off period, although that can be important. The problem is that the national instant check system does not examine all the records that I think need to be included in a check. Mental health records, for example, are seldom available to the instant system. And the national check system mainly tries to discover whether a would-be gun buyer is a felon; it does not pick up many people who are prohibited from purchasing a gun because of a misdemeanor for spouse or child abuse, or people who have restraining orders against them because they have threatened domestic violence. Many of these people slide through an instant check.

That's why I think we need a national requirement for a waiting period of two or three days between buying and taking possession of a gun. That gives local law enforcement the time to check further on their own, and local officials have access to a lot of information that isn't in the national system. That is what the Brady organization is now focusing on. It's back to basics: back to making certain that no gun is ever sold to the wrong person—including a terrorist.

So Jim and I continue to be the public spokespeople for the cause. We do, essentially, whatever Mike Barnes and the board think we need to be doing. In between occasional trips and speechmaking, we are blessedly free to live life the way we want to live it. For us, it has turned out to be the best of both worlds—still active in many areas, and yet mostly retired.

By our second Christmas on the beach, we were really ensconced. Come time for New Year's and the turn of the millennium, we had a big celebration. Aunt Sally came down, and so did my college roommate Sharon Hall McBay and another college friend, Judy Trelogan. Our neighbors planned a huge costume party for New Year's Eve. They don't have an elevator, so Jim and I didn't go to the party, but all the guests came over here and brought food, and we had people in and out of the house all evening long. It was great fun. As we entered the year 2000, we were enjoying life to the fullest.

CHAPTER NINETEEN

"This Is It, Then? My Life is Over?"

E ARLY IN 2000, I realized that Jim and I needed to get established with some local doctors, and I made appointments for complete physicals for both of us. We chose Dr. Charles Stanislav, a wonderful young physician who had taken over a practice from a woman who had treated Jim on one of our summer visits. His reputation was spectacular, and we loved his personality.

The physicals, of course, included loads of tests—blood tests, for instance, and for me, a mammogram—and Dr. Stanislav also said he thought I should have a chest X-ray. A year before, one of Jim's doctors who knew I was a heavy smoker had advised me to skip X-rays and get a lung scan, which could catch lung cancer very early, so I told Charlie that's what I wanted to do. I pointed out that I'd been smoking for a long time and that my father had died of lung cancer. If I did have anything, I said, let's catch it early. So he set up a lung scan for me at the

Beebe Medical Center in Lewes, Delaware—about seven miles from our house—on Monday, March 6, at 4 in the afternoon.

As it happened, Jim left for Colorado, accompanied by our wonderful companion, Emmy Bania, the day before my appointment. This was shortly after the school shootings in Columbine, and Jim had been asked to help rally public opinion behind legislation to close the legal loophole that permits people at gun shows to buy and take possession of guns without any waiting period. So they had flown out on Sunday, and I was home alone when I went in for the scan.

It was my first of those things, and it was quite uneventful. First they hooked me up to an IV and had me drink a barium solution. Then I went for a CT scan. They scanned me once, then injected an iodine dye, which helps enhance certain images, and scanned me a second time. The scanning took only about twenty minutes. When it was over, I went home and thought nothing of it for the rest of the day.

About 8 the next morning, the hospital called. They asked me to come back in as soon as possible because they needed to do another scan. I said sure—how about 11 o'clock? They suggested 10 o'clock instead.

I wasn't all that nervous on the way in, because I knew very well that X-rays and scans often don't come out clearly. That was probably the reason I'd been called back. However, as I was getting ready for the scan, I did notice a difference in attitude on the part of the woman who helped me—the same one who'd helped me the day before. She seemed much more solicitous and kind, and I had my first little chill of fear. When the scan was over, I asked why they had needed to repeat it. The fellow in charge said that two radiologists had a difference of opinion on whether or not there was anything there, and they thought they should take another look.

Once again, I went home. It must have been 11 or 11:30 by the time I got there, and by now, I was quite nervous. Maybe there was something there. I called Charlie Stanislav and explained what had happened. They must have looked at the new scan by now, I said; could he possibly call Beebe fairly soon and check to find out what it showed?

Bless his heart, he was back on the phone with me by noon. I was sitting on one of our kitchen stools when I took the call, and Charlie said, in a very matter-of-fact tone, "I hate to have to tell you, but the scan did show what looks to be a carcinoma—very small, but it's being read as a carcinoma—in the upper lobe of your right lung." I asked whether it could possibly be something else, scar tissue or something, and Charlie said that was possible, but it looked pretty definite. Since my father had died of lung cancer, and I had a good idea of how difficult it is to cure, I immediately asked, "This is it, then? My life is over?" But Charlie was very reassuring. Medicine had made great breakthroughs in recent years, he explained, and this was very small. Much could be done. He wanted to set me up immediately with Dr. Michael Salvatore, the leading lung specialist in our area, and he made an appointment for 11:45 the next morning.

I was stunned. I sat there for almost an hour, thinking this just couldn't be true. I felt a deep need to tell somebody about it. For me, talking things out is the most helpful thing on earth. But Jim wouldn't be back from Colorado until late that afternoon. Finally, I called my brother and shared the news with him. I spent the rest of the day swinging back and forth between thinking I was going to be fine, that I could fight this thing, and feeling somewhat blue and teary-eyed. I told two dear friends, Debbie File and Theresa Gardner, the mother of Courtney, my assistant at Handgun Control.

When Jim and Emmy got home, I first took Emmy aside for a private talk in our back bedroom. She says I was very upbeat, stressing how small the tumor was and how early it had been caught. When Emmy went home, I told Jim. For the life of me, I cannot remember anything about that conversation. I am sure he was upset, but being

Jim—he's very good at avoiding subjects he doesn't want to think about—I imagine he put it out of his mind as quickly as possible. I am sure he told me then, as he does every single time I light up a cigarette, "You don't need that."

Of course the person I most dreaded having to tell was Scott. He was living in Washington at the time, and I knew I could not do this by telephone; I would have to make a trip there and tell him in person. But it was a little premature to think about that. First, I needed to find out more from the doctors.

The next day, I went in for my appointment with Dr. Salvatore. He examined me, looked at the scans, gave me some preliminary tests, and then spent almost two hours just talking to me. He described, clearly and in great detail, the nature of the disease. There are two types of lung cancer. Small-cell lung cancer is the extremely virulent form my father had—so aggressive that sometimes it has already spread to the brain and other organs by the time it is first detected in the lungs. Non-small-cell lung cancer moves much more slowly, and he could tell by the shape of my tumor that it was of the non-small-cell variety.

At first, I was absolutely thrilled about that. But there is one problem with non-small-cell cancer: it doesn't seem to respond as well to chemotherapy. Dr. Salvatore said the very best thing would be to take out the entire upper lobe of my right lung, because in 99 percent of all cases, if the cancer hasn't spread beyond the original site, the surgery puts an end to it once and for all. I was incredibly heartened by that idea. Dr. Salvatore said there was a wonderful oncological surgeon on staff, Dr. James Spellman. He set up an appointment for me that Friday, March 10.

Meanwhile, my brother had done a lot of research on his own. Among other things, Bill had contacted one of our cousins, John Dehner, who lives in Richmond, Indiana, and he suggested that I talk to him. John is an oncological radiologist who works at a community hospital about the same size as Beebe. I asked him whether there were any questions I should ask the surgeon when I saw him, and he said yes: I should be sure to ask whether there seemed to be any involvement of the lymph nodes, whether they showed any swelling. I told John about Beebe—a really terrific regional hospital, but not a huge cancer center like Johns Hopkins in Baltimore or Sloan-Kettering in New York—and asked whether he thought I should be going to one of those places instead. He said the most important thing was that I must be happy with the team I was working with. He advised me to go ahead and meet Dr. Spellman. "You'll know after you meet him," John said. "You'll know whether you're going to be happy with his experience and with the relationship." He added that what I had been diagnosed with—technically, "speculated bronchogenic carcinoma," a tumor two centimeters in diameter in the right upper lobe—was not rare, nothing unusual, and community hospitals across the country dealt with it every day.

I was pretty well-armed with information by the time I met Jim Spellman that Friday. We had a long meeting, and I liked him very much. He was extremely thorough in explaining exactly what my condition was and how he would like to proceed. I asked about the lymph nodes, and he said it looked from the scan as if some of them were swollen. That didn't necessarily mean that the cancer had spread to them, he said; it might simply mean that they were overworking, or that there was a bit of infection because of the tumor itself. The only way to find out for certain was to test them.

Dr. Spellman described several different options, but suggested that the best course of action would be a procedure called a mediastinoscopy. I would be put under general anesthesia, and he would make an incision just below my neck, near the clavicle, allowing him to probe down into the area between the lungs and biopsy the lymph nodes. If the biopsy showed no cancer in the nodes, they would immediately go ahead and remove the entire upper right lobe of the lung.

He warned that removing the lobe was very difficult surgery. It would take at least five hours, he said, and he compared the effects of the operation to being hit by a Mack truck. Doctors would make a huge incision and break through several ribs, and it would take me a long time to recover. The good news, though, was they would not even proceed with the surgery unless the lymph node biopsy made them quite confident that I would come out of it entirely free of cancer.

I was extremely impressed with Dr. Spellman, as I had been with all the others at Beebe who would make up my team. I also liked the idea of staying near home, of being able to recuperate in my own house with my family and friends nearby. So I left that meeting convinced that Beebe was the right option and feeling extremely optimistic.

Now that I had a good idea of what was going to happen, I had to tell Scott. That same afternoon, I took off for Washington. On the way, I made a reservation at a motel near the house where Scott was living. I met him at the house—I hadn't yet seen it, and he wanted to show it off—and then we went to dinner at a little Korean place in the neighborhood.

We ordered dinner, and then I had to tell him. It was one of the hardest things I have ever done. He is my only child, my baby, and we have been kindred souls for so long, through so much. I broke down, and of course he did, too. After the initial sadness, he began to get angry—angry that yet another problem had cropped up in our lives. This was just unfair, he felt, another example of things not going right for us. I reminded him that everyone has a cross to bear, even if some of them weren't quite as obvious as ours. Eventually, I bounced back a little and said we had to be optimistic. It was early, and everything looked good. Hopefully, I could have this long operation, and although it would be painful, that would be the end of the cancer. And even if the surgery didn't work, there were other things that could be done. Scott is resilient, and he recognized the hope. He was eager to come home and be with me before the surgery and help take care of me afterward. We ended the evening feeling pretty cheery, and the next morning, at breakfast, Scott seemed fine.

Dr. Spellman scheduled the surgery for Friday, March 17. The entire week before was filled with tests of various sorts, since they have to make absolutely sure you can withstand this kind of surgery. I went through it all with a combination of excitement and apprehension—excitement at the prospect of getting rid of the cancer and apprehension about the surgery itself. But there was so much to do that I couldn't dwell too hard on what was ahead. Among other things, we had to make arrangements for additional help and relief for Emmy in the event that I was not able to do much for quite a while. After the big surgery, Dr. Spellman had warned, I would have to be in intensive care for several days and in the hospital for close to a week. Then I'd be pretty much out of commission for three months. It would be fully six months to a year before I'd feel back to normal.

On Wednesday of that week it occurred to me that Jim and I did not have a real will. So I made an appointment with Brandy Jones, an attorney we had used in the past, and the three of us discussed what we wanted in our wills and also drew up a living will for me, specifying that no heroic measures should be taken if they simply served to prolong life needlessly. I was very relieved to get those legal affairs out of the way.

By Thursday, everything was done. I had passed all my tests with flying colors. Scott and my brother, Bill, had arrived, and Theresa and Mickey Gardner came down, too. Thursday night, we all went out to one of our favorite restaurants, the Blue Moon, to eat and enjoy ourselves. We had a wonderful time.

The surgery was scheduled for 8 A.M., and I had to be there by 6. Bill drove me over, then went home to pick up Jim, Scott, and Emmy and bring them all to the hospital. Mickey and Theresa came on their own and looked in to say hello while hospital personnel were getting me ready for surgery. I was nervous, but there was so much going on that I was more or less distracted. They were going to put me on a respirator and get me ready for the full-blown, five-hour operation.

Of course, from the moment they start the anesthesia, you don't remember a thing. But I do remember waking up. The moment I did, I realized that I was more or less free of pain. And immediately, I knew that I had not been able to have the full operation—that they had stopped after the lymph node biopsy. That meant the cancer had spread.

Dr. Spellman was there. "I didn't get the big one, did I?" I asked. No, he said. I asked whether my family knew, and he said they did. I asked how Scott had taken the news. Pretty hard, he said, but they were all doing fine.

After Dr. Spellman left, they kept me in the recovery room to allow the anesthesia to wear off a bit more before I was sent to intensive care overnight. I napped for a while, then came to when they were getting ready to move me out of there. I'm a strange bird under anesthesia— always wake up pretty quickly, in a good mood. This time was no exception, but I was so thirsty I could hardly stand it. It must have been the effect of having that respirator tube down my throat. It was a horrible feeling, and I said to the nurse that I'd give the world for a Starbucks Frappuccino. By the luck of the Irish, one of them had a bottled Frappuccino, and she handed it to me. I downed it immediately. It was absolutely divine.

In intensive care, they hooked me up to all the monitors and gradually I became aware of the incision, just below my neck. It had a drain in it, a tube to carry out all the blood and other fluids that accumulated in the wound, and there was a kind of ball hanging out of the tube. It was uncomfortable enough so that I was given morphine. It was kind of scary. They wanted me to lie on my left side, and when I did, I was convinced that I would lie on that ball that hung from the tube, and I also got the distinct feeling that my head was going to fall off.

Jim, Scott, Bill, Emmy, and the Gardners came to see me soon after I was settled in the ICU. I was so glad to see them. They didn't seem desolate, and I certainly didn't feel that way. But I was sleepy, so they stayed only a few minutes and said they would come back later.

I slept through most of the afternoon, and when I woke up, I was absolutely ravenous. The hospital brought dinner very early, and I ate every bit of it. Not long afterward, in came Scott, bringing me a mammoth steak and cheese sandwich. I ate all of that, too. It tasted just wonderful. Then, not too much later, the Gardners arrived. Mickey had spoken to Dr. Spellman in the morning and gotten permission—Dr. Spellman had actually written it into his orders—to bring me martinis. He brought two huge ones, and they were delicious.

No one stayed too long that evening, and when they had all left, I decided to watch some basketball. It was time for the second round of the National Collegiate Athletic Association's basketball tournament, and I'm always a sucker for March madness. I had brought in my sheet showing who was playing whom and when the games were on television. But I was too tired to pay close attention, and eventually I decided to sleep. Despite my fear of rolling over on that drain and having my head fall off, it was not a difficult night. By the next morning, I felt much better, and Dr. Spellman, after removing the drain, said I could go home.

Before I left, the nurses said they'd never seen a patient quite like me. They said most people just want to sleep after having heavy anesthesia and being on a respirator. Very few have any desire to eat, and those who do want only mild liquids. I, by contrast, had consumed a Frappuccino, a regular hospital dinner, a steak and cheese sandwich, and two martinis—although I confess, I didn't actually finish the second one; on top of all the medication, it kind of did me in.

Jim should have been proud. It was definitely a performance worthy of a raccoon.

CHAPTER TWENTY

Fighting Back

I HAD DECIDED before I went in for the surgery that I had to quit smoking, and I disposed of all the cigarettes in our house except for one pack. So when I left the hospital, I was ready—determined to face a new life without smoking.

Bill and Scott picked me up at the hospital, and when we got home, the Gardners were there, including Courtney, who had arrived that morning. Although I tried not to show it, that first hour or two were absolutely awful. I sat down to talk with everyone, and all the time, I was feeling as if all the fun had been drained out of my life. I couldn't imagine what to do with myself because I wasn't smoking a cigarette. I was bored. I couldn't believe that I had been so addicted. It wasn't as if I was having any real physical symptoms of withdrawal from nicotine; it was entirely psychological. Without a cigarette, I was desolate. I was actually more unhappy about the smoking than I was about anything else—including the cancer.

Oh, how ashamed I am of this, but it's the truth: I remembered that last pack of cigarettes, the only one I hadn't thrown away. I had hidden it in my underwear drawer. Now keep in mind, I was a mature, fifty-eight-year-old woman. But the thought of that last pack gave me unbelievable pleasure. I rationalized. From now on, I thought, I would smoke one cigarette a day. At cocktail hour, I would sneak off and have a couple of puffs along with my drink, and nobody would know. That kept me going all day long, looking forward to that cigarette.

Without my knowing, Scott had invited Debbie File to come up from Washington. The Gardners were leaving, and he felt I needed some more support. Debbie arrived that afternoon, and we had a good visit. Then, just before dinner, I did my trick: I took my drink and sneaked into the back bedroom for a cigarette. Scott, who has always loved to cook, made dinner that night. He baked a chicken and served mashed potatoes and gravy, and I swear it's the best meal I ever remember putting in my mouth.

Bill and Scott stayed for several days. In the beginning, I moved around kind of slowly. I wasn't in pain; it was just that I felt very vulnerable with that huge incision near my throat. I was scheduled to go back to the doctor the next Thursday for a follow-up visit, where I would find out a lot more about the future. In the interim, I mostly rested and tried to come to grips with my condition.

I was not feeling depressed. It was still early, and there was a lot that could be done, and on the whole, I felt quite confident. My brother did a lot of research for me on the Internet. And I began reading a book that has probably helped me more than anything else—*From This Moment On: A Guide for Those Recently Diagnosed With Cancer*, by Arlene Cotter. Each page carries only ten or fifteen words. It helps you sort through and process your feelings, teaches you what kinds of decisions you need to make, and gives you an idea of what your life is going to be like. It explains how tired you will be, for instance, and how all the people you know will tell you what they think you ought to be doing. It warns that you're going to have ups and downs, highs and lows, and emphasizes that you need to make time just for yourself for rest and contemplation. The book helped me tremendously.

From that point on, I had very few blue moments. I knew that deciding on a course of action was up to me, and I planned to take my time. It was too early to begin chemotherapy or radiation, so I had time to kind of put myself mentally in charge, the single most important thing you can do.

That week went pretty quickly. I talked with friends a lot. Well-wishers brought cookies and flowers. Everyone was supportive and helpful, and nobody was in my way.

On Thursday, I went to Beebe for my follow-up with Dr. Spellman. He took off the tape that had covered my incision, which scared me to death because I couldn't get rid of the notion that my head was going to fall off.

Dr. Spellman had set up appointments for me to see Dr. Srihari Peri, an oncologist, and Dr. Andrejs Strauss, a radiation oncologist, at Beebe's Tunnell Cancer Center. Meanwhile, he told me to get plenty of rest and eat well and do whatever exercise I could tolerate, to get myself into the best condition possible. He talked about the great strides researchers were making in chemotherapy and radiation and said my life was not over—this was not a death sentence. He was very encouraging.

Long before I had even been diagnosed with cancer, I had heard on our local radio station that there was going to be a sock hop down at our convention center with songs from the '50s and early '60s—my era—and I thought it would be fun. The proceeds were going to the Tunnell Cancer Center for the breast cancer awareness program. So I'd invited friends to come. They were dubious, and kept checking with me all week to see if I still wanted them, but I just knew I would feel like going.

Scott came, and Bill, and Otto and Jan Wolff. Susan Whitmore, our communications director at Handgun Control, and her husband, Gary Frisch, came too, and some local friends, Ann Graham and Lucia Morrison, joined the party. No one stayed with us; they didn't want to impose. But that Saturday night, we all went to the sock hop, and I danced all evening. When it was over, several people came back to the house. My brother and I were dancing to some '50s tunes, and I noticed that Scott was fighting back tears. I knew exactly what he was thinking, and it touched me very deeply.

I was anxious to find out from the oncologist and the radiation oncologist just what was ahead for me. My cousin John, the radiation oncologist, had told me that I should make up my mind about whether to be treated at Tunnell after meeting with the doctors and looking over the facility to get a sense of whether it was up to date and in touch with the most modern treatment techniques.

That Thursday, I went in for the appointments, and I was incredibly impressed with both doctors. I first met Dr. Strauss, who said he would not begin radiation until I had two or three rounds of chemotherapy. That is the only way they can determine the effectiveness of the type of chemo they give you. The radiation destroys the tumor and any cancer in the remaining lymph nodes; if you did that first, they would have no way to judge whether the chemo was working. And once the cancer has spread, as it had in my case, the chemo is—for the long run—the most important thing. That's what will be working throughout your entire body, chasing down any wandering cancer cells, and they have to be sure it is effective.

Dr. Peri spent a long time explaining my condition and what could be done. There are three common types of non-small-cell cancer: adenocarcinoma, bronchoalveolar carcinoma, and squamous cell cancer. Although I didn't have one of those, mine was definitely non-small-cell, and it had been diagnosed as being Stage IIIA. When the disease is discovered and treated at this point, there is a 15 to 30 percent chance of surviving five years. While those odds are not great, they are not overwhelmingly bad, and Dr. Peri explained that many people respond beautifully to the chemo and radiation. Once you reach the five-year point, you can breathe a huge sigh of relief and begin to think of yourself as a survivor.

Dr. Peri also explained the type of chemo he would start me on: taxol plus a drug called carboplatinum. He said some people have an allergic reaction to taxol, usually within an hour and a half of its first being administered, so during your first treatment, the specialists monitor you very closely; if you do react badly, they stop it immediately and try a different drug. He also said they took every precaution to make sure that patients didn't experience nausea, but that I would definitely lose my hair. And he encouraged me to keep up my general health while I was going through the chemo.

While I was at Tunnell, I had a chance to look over the facilities, which were lovely. I sensed that I would feel comfortable there, or at least as comfortable as anyone could be under the circumstances.

As I looked around at all the people getting chemo, I realized that no one looked sick, nobody seemed to be in pain. Some were knitting, some were reading, some were watching television; a few were even napping. There are a couple of rooms off the main chemotherapy room for people who are very sick and need more privacy, but I rarely saw anyone in them. The general atmosphere was cheery and hopeful—not at all what I had imagined. So I left feeling eager to get started with my treatment. My first chemotherapy would be on April 6, one month to the day after the lung scan that discovered the cancer.

I was nervous, as everybody is at first. Scott, Bill, and Theresa and Courtney Gardner all came down for the occasion and sat with me while I had the chemotherapy. Before you actually begin the chemo, they give you "pre-drugs" intravenously—half an hour's worth of sugar water, to make sure you're hydrated, then anti-nausea medication, and finally a steroid, which helps in case of allergic reactions. Then you begin the real thing. I was there pretty much all day long, since they go very slowly at first, taking care that you don't have an allergic reaction to the taxol. I was lucky enough not to. When that finished dripping into my vein, they switched me to the carboplatinum, which took only about an hour. It was a pretty easy day—almost a festive occasion in some ways. Courtney went out at lunchtime and got us all wonderful sandwiches. When it was all over, I felt fine, as if nothing out of the ordinary had happened.

The third day after the chemo I did get some minor pains around my hip bones, but other than that, nothing. I didn't even feel tired. My treatment was set up so that I'd have a round of chemo every third week. Dr. Peri had said I'd start losing my hair between the second and the third week, and sure enough, it happened right on schedule. The first indication was some discomfort—an achy feeling—in my scalp. I'd reach up to rub it, and a clump of hair would fall out. After four or five days of that, I could see that my hairline was receding quite a bit, and the hair was coming out so fast that it was threatening to clog up the drains. So my hairdresser, Clint Vance, came over to our house to shave it all off, so I wouldn't have to have that done in public.

The first time you see yourself bald, it comes as quite a shock. I looked like a refugee from a concentration camp. My face is long and narrow, and I knew I had big ears, but without my hair, they seemed much bigger than I had realized. When I looked in the mirror, all I could see was ears. It was a little embarrassing—certainly nothing I wanted anyone outside the family to see. But it didn't really bother me or Jim. The person who suffered was Emmy, who cried at the very thought of my being bald.

When Clint came to shave my head, he brought along a hilarious purple wig. I wore that around for a while, and then Jim started wearing it. We still have that wig—kept it as a memento—and it definitely made me feel better about looking so horrible.

Before the chemo had begun, I had bought a nice wig to wear when I was out in public. But it really didn't bother me not to have any hair. In fact, I came to really appreciate not having to wash it and blow it dry every morning—I could just sponge off my bald head. I don't know how people wear wigs for any length of time, however. They're very uncomfortable, very itchy, and you're always aware that there's something on your head and if you move the wrong way, it could get off kilter.

But there was a great solution, at least for me. The American Cancer Society publishes a booklet called *TLC*, which offers all sorts of products that are useful or comforting to cancer patients, including alternatives to wigs like turbans and kerchiefs. Because this was spring and summer, the weather was lovely and I wore casual clothes most of the time. So I took to wearing plaid kerchiefs with little fake bangs under them and saved the wig for occasions when we had to dress up.

Meanwhile, I felt very well. And that lifted my spirits considerably. I was beginning to be convinced that I was Superwoman, that there was no way on earth that this drug combination wasn't working.

A week after a round of chemo, you have to have a blood test to make sure neither your red or white blood cell count has gone out of whack. Mine was always fine. After three weeks, I had my second dose, and again, the side effects were almost nonexistent, just a few aches and pains on the third or fourth day. I felt so well that one weekend when Scott and Missy were both visiting, we went out and bought a treadmill. I started spending at least thirty minutes each morning on it, trying to build up endurance and speed.

My next chemo was scheduled for May. But before I had it, Dr. Peri ordered a CT scan, and when he got the results, I could tell he was disappointed. There had been very little change in the tumor; he had expected far more dramatic results. He decided at that point to try a different type of chemotherapy. So I got an extra week between treatments while Dr. Peri did some research on what kind of chemo I should have next.

Meanwhile, it was time to begin the radiation. Before it starts, you have to go through a rather long measuring process. They put you on the table and figure out exactly where they're going to aim the radiation and mark you up accordingly. In my case, they would be aiming at the tumor itself and at the median section between the lungs where the affected lymph nodes were. Once all the measuring was finished, the radiation itself was pretty simple. It took only about five minutes a session, every day. All told, I think I had thirty-seven treatments. They tell you ahead of time that you won't feel any effects until the radiation is nearly over.

Just as I was beginning radiation, it was also time to start the new chemotherapy. Dr. Peri had settled on a combination of cisplatinum and navebene. Cisplatinum is a very strong drug in use for quite a few years; it is so strong that in the early days, patients had to be hospitalized to get it. But doctors had found they could give half a dose one day and the other half the next, allowing them to administer it on an outpatient basis. So every third week, I was to get cisplatinum for two days. I would get navebene once a week, and I was having the radiation every day. Needless to say, starting at the end of May, I was at the hospital an awful lot. I even had some minor surgery to remove some uterine polyps. It was a simple procedure, and they turned out to be benign.

Just once that month I took a trip away from home. Jim and I went back to Washington to attend the "Million Mom March," a demonstration designed to highlight the fact that sensible gun laws save kids' lives. The march was an overwhelming success. In fact, it was one of the largest ever—an estimated 750,000 women, men, and children. The stage was fairly near the Capitol, and from it, looking down the Mall, there were people lined up all the way to the Lincoln Memorial.

It was a very emotional experience for me. It was such overwhelming evidence of how our movement had grown. People from all over the country had come to Washington to support this issue, which was so important. It was just a joy to see.

I wore my kerchief that day, and I don't think anyone really knew why. If they thought about it at all, they probably just figured I'd adopted a new fashion trend that somehow hadn't caught on with many other women.

The second week in June, my cousin John Dehner and his wife, Maribelle, came to visit. By this time, my skin was beginning to look a little bit sunburned in the radiated area—nothing major. I had been warned that in very late stages of radiation there would be some internal burning, as well, around the esophagus.

One night, we all went out to eat at one of our favorite places—Espuma, a Mediterranean restaurant—and I ordered gazpacho, which I love. I took one bite and suddenly felt as if I was swallowing fire. But once the burning subsided, I went right ahead and finished the whole bowl. Each time I swallowed, it burned—but it tasted just wonderful. John told me to be sure to ask Dr. Strauss for a remedy for that esophagitis. He did, and it turned out to be exactly the same one John used in his own radiology practice: a combination of antacid and lidocaine called "swish and swallow."

In June, I had to have another minor surgery. Because I was getting so much chemo and having to give blood so often, my veins, which are tiny to begin with, were beginning to go to pot. Nurses and technicians were having trouble finding veins from which they could draw blood, and even worse difficulty giving me chemotherapy through an IV. At that point, I went back to Dr. Spellman, who told me I could have a port embedded beneath my skin, just below my sternum, feeding into a vein; that port could be used both to draw blood and to administer chemotherapy. The surgery took only an hour, and I came through it easily. For the first week or two, there were stitches all around it, and it was scary looking and felt peculiar. But it was not painful, and I soon got used to it.

Both the chemo and the radiation extended into July. At the beginning of one week I suddenly felt absolutely exhausted—so tired I could hardly move. I went in that Friday for the regular blood test that preceded each round of chemo, and it turned out that my red blood count was extremely low. I had to come in and have a transfusion. They gave me two pints of blood, and I had to skip chemo for that one week.

By August, I had finished both the chemotherapy and the radiation. The doctors wanted to wait two or three weeks before they gave me another scan because even though the treatments had stopped, both the radiation and the chemo would still be having some effect, and they wanted to wait until it was complete. On August 18, I had a CT scan, and the result was wonderful: the tumor was gone and the lymph node area was clear.

I was just elated. I had been right all along. This procedure had worked, and the chemotherapy, I knew, had killed any little cancer cells that might have migrated into the lymphatic system. It was a wonderful feeling. I was cancer-free.

CHAPTER TWENTY ONE

Packing Heat

I STILL DIDN'T HAVE any hair, of course. But I felt strong and confident, and we planned a trip in August to Martha's Vineyard. Eli and Phyllis Segal were holding a fundraiser at their home there in conjunction with the author Richard North Patterson, who, like Phyllis, was a member of the HCI board.

We drove up in our van, spending one night on the way, then took the ferry over to Martha's Vineyard. Neither Jim nor I had ever been there, so it was a real treat. We had to rush that trip a bit because Jim's sixtieth birthday was on August 29, and I'd planned a surprise birthday party on Sunday, August 27. About a hundred people were coming to the party, which was going to be at the country club a few miles from our house, and I wanted to be sure to have time to rest before it.

Before we left for the Vineyard, I had started noticing that when I woke up at night, my left eye wouldn't open for about thirty seconds. It didn't seem to be stuck—it was just slow. It was like that through the whole Martha's Vineyard trip, and it went on through Jim's birthday party and into September. At first, I hadn't worried about it much. But as time passed, I began to wonder whether the cancer might have spread to my brain. That's one of the things I think every cancer patient lives with: with every ache or pain, any unusual health development of any kind, you tend to leap to the conclusion that it might be caused by the cancer. You try to hold that in check and not become neurotic. But finally, I was worried enough so that I mentioned the problem to Dr. Peri, the oncologist, and he scheduled a brain scan. It came out totally clear, which was a great relief.

So from that point on, I pretty much put the cancer out of my mind. I decided I was going to return to a normal life and start doing things again. It was time to get back to work. The year 2000 was, of course, an election year, and one of the things Jim and I love more than anything is campaigning for the members of Congress who have been helpful to us. There were a lot of races that year that we really wanted to be involved in.

Our first big trip was to Florida to campaign for Bill Nelson. He was running for the U.S. Senate against Bill McCollum, a Republican who had been a thorn in my side from the moment I started lobbying Congress. Back in 1988, when the Brady bill was first getting close to a vote in the House, he was the one who had come up with the stalling tactic—"the McCollum substitute"—approved by the National Rifle Association.

McCollum had decided to leave the House and run for the Florida Senate seat vacated by Connie Mack. So for us, it was great fun to go down there and campaign for Nelson, a Democrat and former member of Congress who was a member of Governor Lawton Chiles's state cabinet. I am very happy to report that Bill Nelson won the race, and he gives his straight-talking, common-sense stand on the gun issue a lot of the credit.

We also got very involved in Missouri. Through several sessions of the state legislature, there had been an ongoing battle over whether Missouri residents should be able to carry concealed weapons. The gun lobby had worked hard for a bill allowing concealed weapons, and one of its closest allies was the state's junior senator, Republican John Ashcroft. Missouri's Democratic governor, Mel Carnahan, had worked very hard against the concealed-weapons bill, and we had joined him in his fight, along with the state's law-enforcement community. Finally, in 1999, the issue was put to a statewide referendum. Jim made quite a few trips to Missouri that year to rally opposition to the measure. And even though the National Rifle Association devoted four million dollars to promoting the measure—outspending our side by five to one—the voters ultimately rejected it.

Over the years, Jim had visited the Missouri governor's mansion often and had become very fond of Governor Carnahan and his wife, Jean. So in 2000, when Mel Carnahan decided to run against John Ashcroft for the U.S. Senate, we could hardly wait to help. We considered Ashcroft one of the most extreme members of the Senate, and the very idea of him beating the thoughtful, moderate Mel Carnahan was just repulsive to both Jim and me. But on October 16, less than one month before the election, Mel and his son, Randy, tragically died in a plane crash on their way to a campaign rally.

Handgun Control had been running pro-Carnahan ads in the state, but we pulled them off the air after the crash. It was too late to remove Mel Carnahan's name from the ballot, however, and Roger Wilson, the new state governor, announced that if Carnahan won the election, he would ask Jean Carnahan to fill the Senate seat. When she agreed to do it, we began running ads that emphasized Ashcroft's extreme views and argued that he did not represent the mainstream of Missouri voters, who, after all, had defeated the concealed-weapons measure. In the end, Carnahan won the race posthumously, and Jean Carnahan went to the U.S. Senate. John Ashcroft ended up being named U.S. attorney general by President George W. Bush—a development, needless to say, that Jim and I did not applaud.

We didn't win all of our races. A third campaign we took on was that of Senator Chuck Robb in Virginia. Jim did a fundraiser with him and both of us appeared at a press conference to endorse him, emphasizing that we had always been able to count on him in helping to make America safer from gun violence. Handgun Control did radio and television ads, too. All told, we spent a great deal of money on Robb's campaign.

We knew it was going to be tough. Robb was facing a really strong challenge from the former governor of Virginia, George Allen. Allen was one of the growing breed of Republican ultra-conservatives—in our view, an extremist on social issues. As governor, he had supported and signed a 1995 law, backed by the National Rifle Association, which substantially weakened the state's rules on carrying concealed handguns, and he was quite public about his belief that people ought to be able to carry guns almost everywhere—including recreation centers and places where alcohol was served. We very badly wanted Robb to beat him. But that was a losing situation. On election day, Allen won the Senate seat and Chuck Robb, our old Senate ally, was out.

When the elections were over, we attended Handgun Control's annual gala in Washington and had a marvelous time. Then, almost before we knew it, it was Thanksgiving. I love Thanksgiving. It's my favorite meal of the year, and I always cook at home. The company always includes our immediate family and usually a few friends as well; that year, we invited Ann Graham, whom Jim and I have known for years and who now lives nearby. The dinner always includes turkey, sage dressing, mashed potatoes, gravy, scalloped oysters (which Scott, Bill, and I overdose on), turnips for Jim, creamed peas and onions for me (no one else in the family will touch them), and either a cranberry fruit Jell-O mold or curried fruit with cranberry sauce. That particular Thanksgiving was particularly nice, since I felt I had so much to be thankful for. We all talked about it, and felt truly celebratory.

Then we were into that incredibly hectic time between Thanksgiving and Christmas. It always seems to go so quickly as you try to get everything done. Maybe it was because I had a newfound appreciation for life, but I found I wanted a really old-fashioned Christmas that year. I decided to put more emphasis on making the house feel Christmassy, and less on shopping for fancy presents. The tree was absolutely beautiful—"the most symmetrical one we ever had," Jim said, quoting my father, who said that every single year when I was growing up. I put small wreaths with bows in all our windows and roping on the railings of our front porch.

For my men, I decided to get only toys. No clothes—just things they really wanted. I got Jim, my lifelong train-lover, a G gauge electric train set. I found a remote control sail boat for Bill. And you probably won't believe what I bought for Scott. I had thought he wanted some musical equipment for his guitar, but when I asked him for some details, he announced that what he really wanted for Christmas was a hunting rifle.

At first, I was inwardly horrified. A hunting rifle certainly didn't qualify as a "toy" in my eyes. But I knew that Scott had learned gun safety and that he knew how to shoot, and he certainly had grown up with a better than average knowledge of what guns can do. I also knew that my brother had given him Jim's shotgun, which Bill had been keeping at his house since Scott was a baby. Although I don't care for hunting, I no longer wanted to play judge and jury in Scott's life. After all, he is a grown man now. And I wasn't going to let my personal feelings get in the way of giving him what he wanted for Christmas. Of course the whole time, in the back of my mind, I kept thinking that this Christmas could be my last.

So I went to a local gun shop, a family-owned business outside of Lewes, Delaware. It was a very small store, which mainly sold hunting rifles and shotguns and related equipment. There were several hunters there when I arrived. I bought a Remington thirty-aught-six rifle, a safety lock, a carrying case and a scope. Of course they ran the Brady federal background check, which was approved immediately, and then they ran the Delaware state check. The system was working. But when the owner called in the checks, it seemed to me he spoke unnecessarily loudly, repeating and spelling my name over and over on the phone. It was probably my imagination, but I was certain I could feel the eyes of those hunters boring into my back. And I can't describe how I felt when I picked up that rifle, loaded it into my little car, and drove home. It seemed so incredibly strange: Sarah Brady, of all people, packing heat.

Sometime during December I was scheduled for another lung scan, and the Friday before Christmas, Dr. Peri called with the results. The scan, he said, had shown a little something. It could be anything, he said, and he wasn't particularly worried. He was going to think about it over the holidays. But at that point he thought the right course was probably to wait six weeks or two months and then to do another scan. He wasn't at all alarmist about it.

Even so, that was a bit on my mind over Christmas. I knew Dr. Peri was a little concerned, because I had gotten to know so intimately the personalities of the members of my cancer team. I can't emphasize enough how wonderful the people at Beebe and the Tunnell Cancer Center are. All of them are so attentive, so involved in their patients emotionally and intellectually, always on the lookout for the newest techniques. You just couldn't be in better hands.

Bill came down for the holiday, along with Scott's friend Dylan Magowen, Dylan's mother, Maricruz, and his girlfriend, Samantha. We had a grand time. Christmas Eve dinner was simple—ham—and for

Christmas itself, Bill had brought a wonderful prime rib roast from Washington. We always have beef for Christmas dinner.

Right after Christmas, Dr. Peri called again. After thinking it over, he had decided that he wanted me to go to Baltimore, to the Johns Hopkins Hospital, for a much more sophisticated test—a PET (positron emission tomography) scan. The December scan at Tunnell seemed to show several small spots in my lower right lung, perhaps some involvement in the lymph nodes, and a hint of something in the left lung. But all these spots were so minute that it was impossible to tell much about them from that scan alone. The PET scan would show considerably more.

A few days later, I went to Hopkins and had the PET scan. When the results came back, they confirmed that there were several spots in my lower right lung. The rest looked rather negative, except for one thing: They wondered whether that hint of something in the left lung, which had shown up on the regular scan, might mean that cancer had spread to some bones. I immediately had a bone scan, which—thank goodness came back clear. The only problem was in the lower right lung. But there were several spots.

With this diagnosis in hand, Dr. Peri said he would like me to meet with Dr. David Ettinger, a specialist in cancer at the Johns Hopkins Oncology Center. I had heard Dr. Ettinger's name many times in the past year. One of Jim's doctors had recommended him to me right after I was diagnosed with cancer, and my cousin, John Dehner, who had been most impressed when heard Dr. Ettinger speak at a convention in Chicago, had strongly recommended him if I needed a second opinion.

Sometime during the previous summer, I had heard, in television news reports, mention of a new drug that had not yet been approved by the Food and Drug Administration. At the time of those reports, the drug—Iressa—had been through only one set of field trials. Researchers had tested it on three or four different types of cancer, and the one for which it had shown the greatest promise was mine—non-small-cell lung cancer. I had mentioned the new drug to Dr. Peri, who was already aware of it, and he had been following its progress ever since. He had heard, among other things, that Dr. Ettinger—the associate director of clinical research at the Hopkins oncology center—was going to be heading up the second set of field trials on Iressa. Dr. Peri wanted me to meet Dr. Ettinger, to get to know him and get his opinion. At some point, I might be a candidate for those field trials.

So Dr. Peri set up an appointment for me. When they spoke, Dr. Ettinger told him what it would take for me to qualify for the field trials. First of all, my cancer had to be advanced. It was. It had metastasized, and those distant spots had shown up in the lower lobe. Second, I had to have gone through traditional chemotherapies without success. I had been through two so far. Dr. Ettinger thought there was one more I should try before I would be eligible for Iressa.

CHAPTER TWENTY-TWO

Good News, Bad News

I N January 2001, Dr. Peri started me on the new chemotherapy, which was called Taxotere. I knew that essentially I had to flunk this round of chemo in order to be accepted into the field trials for Iressa.

Like taxol, Taxotere was administered once every three weeks, combined with navebene, and in the beginning, its side effects were very mild. A couple of days after getting the chemo, I had a few aches and pains, very much like those you get with the flu. Three or four days after the treatment, my sinuses and my eyes dried up, my mouth became dry and sore, and I lost my voice for a couple of days. Then, gradually, I felt pretty much back to normal, although probably a bit more fatigued than I had felt during chemo the summer before.

Every week, my blood count was checked. After the first treatment, my white cell count had dropped so low that it was considered extremely dangerous, and I had to be isolated—stay at home with only family allowed near me. I was very glad I didn't have to be isolated in the hospital. But even being stuck in my house was a little difficult for me, because I like to be in control—do my own food shopping, for instance. Emmy did everything just as I would have done it, of course, but nonetheless, I longed to be wandering through the supermarket on my own.

A week later, my blood count had bounced back, and by the time I was scheduled for the second round of Taxotere, it was pretty much normal. After the second treatment, I started a series of seven shots—one a day—of a drug that helps sustain your white blood cell count. Because I'd given shots to Jim and to one of our cats, which has diabetes, I was proficient enough to give myself the injections at home instead of going in to the hospital every day. That drug worked very well; this time, my white blood count remained fine. So I did seven more shots after the third round of chemo.

But each round of the Taxotere got progressively harder. After the first treatment, I felt all dried out and lost my voice for only a couple of days. After the second round, the side effects lasted four or five days. After the third chemo, I was miserable for nearly three weeks. Now it wasn't just my sinuses, eyes, and mouth that were afflicted; my lungs and chest cavity were involved as well. I was constantly wheezing and feeling short of breath.

After the second round of this chemotherapy, I'd been given another scan. The little spots were still there, although Dr. Peri did think they might look a bit smaller. But in the meantime, he had asked the head chemotherapy nurse to get in touch with Dr. Ettinger, and when she did, she discovered that the field trials of Iressa were going to be ending the very week I was scheduled to begin my fourth round of chemo. It did look as if I was beginning to flunk the Taxotere, which was a necessary precondition for my being admitted to the Iressa trials; the side effects were so hard on me that I probably would not be able to withstand much more of it. When he heard the latest report, Dr. Ettinger said I should come to Johns Hopkins immediately to be tested to see if I could be accepted for the field trials.

That's just what I did. First, I had to have a CT scan of the lungs and abdomen. In preparation, as I had in the past, I had to drink several large glasses of barium and have an IV inserted for injection of the iodine dye. The scan itself took less than ten minutes and was entirely painless. I lay on a long, skinny table with restraints that kept me from moving, and the table moved into a tube, which took pictures of the chest and abdomen. Then the table moved back out, the iodine dye was injected, and I was scanned again.

I also had to have a complete eye test. One of the side effects of Iressa is apparently some temporary irritation to the eyelids and cornea, and doctors want to make sure you don't have some previously existing conditions that could make that worse. I passed that test.

Then came the hardest part: filling out a long questionnaire about my health and attitude. I was most anxious to get into this program, and I wanted to be honest and truthful, but some of the questions were very difficult to answer. "Do you have any pain?" That one was easy for me—none at all. But "Do you have difficulty breathing?" Well, yes. I'd had difficulty breathing for years, because of smoking and various allergies. I coughed a lot. But it was not really a new thing, a result of this lung cancer. Questions like that seemed simple on the face of it, but when I tried to answer, I found they were not. I knew that getting into the program depended on my passing the physical tests and also on how I filled out that questionnaire. It made me quite nervous, almost as if I was applying to college again.

When I'd completed all the tests, Dr. Ettinger's office told me I would hear the next week whether I had been accepted, and I was free to leave. It was a Friday, and I was not going straight home from Baltimore; instead, I was driving to Washington to meet Jim, who had left earlier that day. About 6:30 that evening we had planned to meet Art and Cindy Kobrine and our friends Jim and Mollie Dickenson for cocktails and dinner. It had become a kind of annual ritual for us to take the Kobrines out around this time of year. We always call it a day of celebration of the fact that Art had saved Jim's life after the shooting, and this was a particularly important occasion: March 30, 2001, would be the twentieth anniversary of the assassination attempt.

I wasn't finished at Hopkins until almost 5 that evening, and as I started the drive to Washington I found myself smack in the middle of rush hour. On top of that, my eyes had been dilated for the eye exam, and they had not yet returned to normal. I could hardly see a thing. To get over to Interstate 95, the main route between Baltimore and Washington, I had to drive due west, directly into the setting sun, and I could see so little that I had to pull into a hotel parking lot and sit for almost half an hour, waiting for the glare to subside.

By then I knew I would never make it to Washington in time to meet our friends at 6:30. But I really wanted to see everyone, so I gave it my best try. That trip was positively hair-raising. Once I turned south on I-95, I was no longer staring directly into the sun, but I was still half-blind, and here I was on a major interstate packed with rush-hour traffic. I called my brother on my cell phone to tell him what was going on and to ask him how to get into the city once I reached the Washington Beltway; it was not the way I usually approached Washington when I drove in from our house at the beach. Bill was so concerned about my trying to drive with my eyes in such bad shape that he stayed on the phone with me through the whole trip—until the valet parker at our hotel had taken my car.

It was almost 8 P.M. by the time I met everyone for dinner. We had a great time that night, as we always do with the Kobrines and Dickensons. And the next night was the Gridiron dinner. Jim and I had missed the Gridiron the previous year, because I had just come out of surgery. This year, we were looking forward to it.

It was odd, though: We didn't recognize as many people at the dinner as we usually do—didn't see as many friends as we had hoped. One we did see was Sam Donaldson of ABC News, whom both Jim and I have always adored. Sam stopped by our table to say hello, and we got to talking. He has battled melanoma in recent years, and I told him I, too, had cancer, and that I had seen a wonderful piece he'd done on a doctor he had worked with at the National Institutes of Health. At some point, I said, I might want to call him to find out more. Sam immediately said that he would have that doctor—Steve Rosenberg at the National Cancer Institute—call me the next week. He couldn't say enough about Dr. Rosenberg and all the great things being done at NIH to fight cancer. I kept trying to explain that I was fine for the moment, and hoping to get into this promising new program, but Sam was insistent. I just had to talk to Dr. Rosenberg, he said.

Hopkins had told me that I would hear that next week whether I had been accepted for the field trials. On Wednesday, I finally got nervous and called Dr. Ettinger's office to find out. They called back and said I was in. I was to come in two days later, on Friday, to begin the program.

Meanwhile, Sam was as good as his word. He called Dr. Rosenberg's office and Dr. Rosenberg called me. He missed me on that first try; Jim and I had gone back to Washington for a Handgun Control press conference timed to the twentieth anniversary of the shooting. But I called back the next morning and had a wonderful chat with him. I explained my entire background, the history of the cancer, and all the drugs I had taken, and told him that I had just been accepted in the Iressa program. He was delightful, a very interested listener, and he asked good questions. Right away, he said that everything I had done so far was just as it should have been. Everything was exactly right. He also said he thought Iressa was the best possible course at the moment. It had a lot of promise, and there was good reason to hope that it would work.

I was elated by that conversation. I had felt quite confident about my treatment so far, but it was good to hear such a distinguished and learned person confirm that it had all been just right. And that wasn't all. Dr. Rosenberg said that if I ran into trouble, if for some reason the Iressa didn't work or I had problems taking it, I should give him a call. He said they had lots of research in the pipeline, many new treatments they were working on. I should let him know, if necessary, and we'd see where to go from there.

That was such a good thing to hear. It gave me a great deal of additional hope at a time when I really needed it. Because it was now just over a year since my cancer had first been diagnosed. Of course, it's always a huge shock to find out that you have a potentially terminal disease, but despite that, I had started out with great optimism. First I thought I would certainly be able to have that big surgery, and the cancer would be excised and I would be cancer-free forever. When that didn't work, I thought the radiation would, and that the chemotherapy would kill off any other little cells that might be lurking somewhere in my system. For that entire year, I think I was pretty good at keeping a positive attitude. But step by step, as each treatment didn't seem to do the trick, there was no denying the fact that I was coming a little bit closer to an end point.

I had come to Iressa afraid, on some level, that it might be my last chance. And although I was still maintaining my optimism, I am also a realist, and I had to face the fact that there might come a time when there would be no hope left, nothing further to look forward to. So I was extremely glad to hear Dr. Rosenberg say that even if the Iressa failed, there were other treatments to try.

That Friday, I started the Iressa. It was quite an easy program: two pills in the morning and two pills at night. Every four weeks I would have a blood test and check-up, and every two months I had a scan. The field trial was designed to find out the optimum dosage of Iressa, and also to see whether larger doses produced worse side effects. All seven of us in the trial were given at least the therapeutic dosage, and some got twice that amount. I have no idea which group I fell into.

I had slight digestive problems, which caused me to lose three or four pounds. For a while, I tried eating rice and other palliative food, but I finally decided to eat whatever I wanted and just ignore the unpleasantness. It was never severe. Other than that, I felt a bit more tired than I had a year earlier. But I had been through a lot of chemo and radiation, and after all, I was a year older as well. So it's hard to tell whether the fatigue was from the Iressa. It's my guess it was not.

My blood tests each month were fine, and so were the bimonthly scans. I had a marvelous spring and summer, enjoying life, eating out, going places, seeing people. And toward the end of summer, someone suggested a Stufflebean family reunion. Most of our relatives on my mother's side of the family live in Indiana or fairly nearby, so we decided to have the reunion in Indianapolis. Scott drove out by himself, and I took Jim and Emmy in our van, bringing T-shirts for everybody. The husband of one of my second cousins is an artist, and he drew a caricature of my mother and her sister and brother, Frances, Helen, and John Stufflebean. That was on one side of the T-shirt. On the other side, I used a slogan provided by another cousin: "With a name like Stufflebean, you've got to be good." Forty-two of us attended, and we knew there was another on the way, so I took forty-five shirts. As it turned out, it's a good thing I did, because when we got out there we discovered yet another cousin was pregnant. The last T-shirt went to another second cousin's dog. There were just enough for everybody. We had a wonderful time. And a week after we got back, I went in for my next scan. Once again, it was fine, and I was thrilled.

During the fall, Jim and I did several campaign trips, plus a bit of traveling for the Brady Campaign. I also did some radio and telephone ads for the New Jersey governor's race, which was run predominantly on the gun issue. I was planning a trip to Dallas on September 25 for a fundraiser, but it turned out I couldn't get back in time for my next scan and check-up, so Jim did that trip on his own.

On September 24, I put Jim and Emmy on a plane in Baltimore. Then I drove to Virginia to do a press conference for the state attorney general, who was running on the gun issue. When it was over, I returned to Baltimore, and on the morning of September 26, I went in to Johns Hopkins. After the scan, I went to see Dr. Ettinger, who said, "The scan looks great—no change." What wonderful news that was. I'd gone close to a year with no change whatsoever in my scans. It was almost like a miracle. Dr. Ettinger tossed me a robe and said he'd be back in a minute for my examination.

He had scarcely begun the exam, starting at my neck, when he found a huge swollen lymph node between my collarbone and my neck. How I could have missed it, I will never know. It was actually visible. Dr. Ettinger turned to Paula Grouleff, his nurse, and said, "Now you know why we always have to do an exam."

So on September 26, at noon, I found out that the cancer had spread, although so far, it was contained to the chest and this one lymph node just above the right lung. "Does this mean it's gone to the brain?" I asked. Dr. Ettinger said, "No—it doesn't mean it's gone to the brain—you may just have straw up in your brain, anyway. Why do you think everything goes to the brain?" He added that there were other treatments to try, but that he wanted me to get this radiated immediately before starting any new program. He immediately took me off Iressa.

Paula had set up an appointment for me to see Dr. Strauss the next week. I started the radiation almost immediately. Since they were giving me a larger dose than they had a year earlier, I had to go in four days a week instead of five, and I was scheduled for eighteen radiation treatments in all.

After eight, the lymph node was substantially smaller than it had been at the start.

CHAPTER TWENTY-THREE

Thanksgiving

WHEN MY FATHER DIED of lung cancer in 1975, only sixty
years old, it was the first time I was forcefully struck by how
precious life is, how you have to savor every moment. I might have reacted by vowing to stop smoking—I certainly knew I should—and by
resolving to take care of my health so that what happened to my father
would never happen to me. I didn't. Instead, I reacted to his death by
vowing to live life the way I wanted to live it, since you never knew
when it might end. I felt much the same way—perhaps even more
so—after Jim was shot. And except for that period when I quit, from
when I had Scott until after Jim was hurt, I kept right on
smoking—even after I was diagnosed with lung cancer. Not long after I
sneaked that first cigarette after my surgery, I was back to smoking
full-time.

It is almost impossible to explain to someone who has never experienced the addiction. Here I was, neurotic about cars, airplanes, and all kinds of other things. The one big risk I took in my life was smoking. Even when all my friends had quit, I kept right on doing it. I knew I should stop. I knew I had the guts to do anything I wanted to do. But I always found some rationalization for not kicking the habit. When I was young, I thought I had years before I had to worry. After I had cancer, quitting seemed a bit like closing the barn door after the horse was long gone. Although I am terribly ashamed of it, I can only tell the truth: I love to smoke.

So when I was diagnosed, it never even occurred to me to think of myself as a victim or to spend any time wondering "Why me?" I knew perfectly well that I had brought it on myself—that I was stupid enough to have smoked all this time and perhaps to have caused my own eventual demise. There is no excuse. I have tried to face that squarely and move on from there.

There are moments, from time to time, when I have what Jim has always called "lurkies"—when I'm suddenly hit hard by fears or worries that ordinarily lurk somewhere below the surface. Usually it lasts just a second or two, just long enough to wonder how long I will live, how long I will be so lucky. But my main worries now are for my family.

The bonds between Scott and me are very strong. If I cannot beat this cancer, he will be devastated. But beyond that, there is so much I hope for him. After graduating from high school, he put off college, explaining that he didn't want to enroll until he was ready to go to a first-rate school. In 2000, with money he inherited from Jim's family, he bought a beautiful piece of property south of Charlottesville, Virginia. His plan was to build a log cabin there, then enroll in a community college in preparation for applying to the University of Virginia. He started construction in the spring of 2001, and the house is almost complete. The experience has been good for him: It has taught him much about how to be patient. He wants to finish that cabin as soon as possible, he says, so that he can get back to school. I hope he really will. He would make a fantastic writer. He'd be a marvelous lawyer. Or he'd make a superb counselor. He understands other people's problems and knows how to help them. He is a very loving young man.

And of course I worry tremendously about Jim. Financially, he will be fine. It's his emotional and intellectual needs that could be a problem. He is so smart, but his judgment is sometimes poor about matters like what kind of media exposure he should have, or how much he should travel. He needs to be reminded to do certain things—to call Scott and Missy, for instance. And most of all, he needs to be engaged in good, stimulating conversation about politics, about current events, about the world around him.

Scott and Missy can help a lot, but I want them to live their own lives as well. Meanwhile, Scott himself will need someone he can depend on for help and advice. Jim loves both his children deeply, but is sometimes unrealistic in dealing with them. Bill, my brother, will be a big help to both Scott and Jim, but I don't want him to be saddled with constant care and feeding. These are the kinds of things that worry me.

Over the years, I confess, we have not been the best churchgoers. Jim was raised Catholic, and I was raised Presbyterian; because Jim had been divorced, we could not be married in the Catholic Church, so we joined the Episcopal Church, and that is where Scott was baptized. But both Jim and Scott have always felt a great allegiance to their Irish heritage. After my cancer was diagnosed, I began to think about the emotional support they might need, and I suggested that Jim might want to reestablish his ties to the Catholic Church. He liked the idea. So I went to church several times with him, and ever since, he has been going alone to Saturday afternoon mass at Saint Edmonds, which is right down the street from our house.

People have sometimes asked how I found the courage to get through the hard times we have faced. The truth is that I don't think it was a matter of courage. After Jim was hurt, I simply faced the facts. Life was not going to be what it had been, and either I could complain about it or I could strive to make our new life as good as possible. Once I knew Jim was going to live, I was so thankful that I hardly ever looked back. I am my mother's daughter. She would have momentary lapses when things went bad, and she would be discouraged for a brief time, but it never lasted long. She was resilient, and she'd snap back because there was so much to be done.

I don't consider it courage to do something you have to do. That's simply a matter of accepting responsibility and moving ahead. Now Jim has been very courageous, in that he has had to fight pain and keep on going. But I've only had to pick myself up and do a few things I was a bit nervous about—like the time I spoke at the Democrats' convention.

I am proud that I've been able to keep my little family together. But I haven't done anything most other people don't do: simply get on with what needs to be done in life. I've made mistakes all along the way. And all along the way we have been blessed with the most extraordinary support system of family and friends. On the whole, I consider myself incredibly lucky.

Since I was diagnosed with cancer, I notice certain changes in my outlook. Little things don't get me down the way they once did. Take traffic, for instance. Everyone around here complains in the summer when it gets a little crowded out on the highways. That just doesn't bother me at all anymore. Life's little hassles seem insignificant.

I've learned to take things much easier. It seems to me that we spend too much of our lives looking forward to the future. When you're a little kid, you can't wait to be a teenager. Then you focus on getting your driver's license, graduating from high school, going to college, getting married, raising kids—you're always looking ahead, kind of wishing your life away.

That's something I don't want to do now. I am living in the present and rejoicing in all the beauty around us here. I find myself loving every season, enjoying the changes as I never have before.

I most especially love to sit on the beach and watch the ocean and the sand. Every day it's different. Depending on the weather and the waves, the beach itself grows and shrinks, and each day brings shapes and patterns, pools and gullies, that were not there before. Some days there are shells, and some days there are none. The water can be rough and wild or still and shining. It's always a wonder to behold.

We have a phenomenal number of critters and birds in this area. The lake draws geese and ducks, and we have two beautiful herons. We call them Henry and Henrietta, although we have no idea which is which. There's an otter in the lake, and on several occasions I have seen a beautiful fox out there. On the ocean side are the gulls, even a pelican every now and then. And although I have never seen a deer on the beach, I have spotted their tracks in the sand during the seasons when there aren't so many tourists.

I love the peace and stillness here. In fact, I find it very difficult to visit Washington or any other big city. It is so much harder there to see beauty, and that is increasingly important to me.

Our life is quite simple, on the whole. It seems like heaven on earth to me simply to sit outside and listen to a good mystery book on tape. And we love seeing our friends, of course. These days, I find myself noticing how each one has some different quality that I prize, something special to share. All of them provide so much support, and I could not be more thankful.

I don't know at this point what the future will bring, but I know the experts have some more rabbits in their hats. When I finish with these radiation treatments, I will be on a new regimen of some kind to attack the cancer systemically. In the meantime, I'm feeling well and looking forward to the holidays, especially the periods when Scott will be here. Those are my very favorite times. And to my great delight, he has come to the beach often over this past year.

When Scott is under our roof, along with Jim, our dog and cats, I feel completely peaceful.

Everyone is safe. My family is together. It is a beautiful world.

Cast of Characters

NOTE: *The following list does not include every single person mentioned in the body of* A Good Fight; *it is intended to help readers identify many key players. An asterisk (*) next to a name indicates that the person is now deceased.*

FAMILY MEMBERS

James ("Big Jim")* and Dorothy* Brady: Jim's parents, residents of Centralia, Illinois.

Edward Brady*, Margaret Burke,* and Helen Cain*: Big Jim's siblings.

James Scott Brady Jr.: Scott, Jim's and my son.

Melissa Jane "Missy" Brady: Jim's daughter from a brief first marriage.

Helen Dehner*: My mother's sister.

John and Maribelle Dehner: My cousin, a oncological radiologist, and his wife.

L. Stanley*, Frances,* and William Kemp: My parents and my brother Bill.

BRADY FRIENDS

Dick and Jeri Church: Old friends from Illinois; Jim met Dick at the University of Illinois, where they were fellow Sigma Chis.

David and Brandy Cole: Friends and neighbors from our years in Arlington, Virginia; David is Scott's godfather.

Bob* and Suzi Dahlgren: Close friends from Jim's years at the Department of Housing and Urban Development.

Jim and Mollie Dickenson: Mollie is the author of *Thumbs Up: The Life and Courageous Comeback of White House Press Secretary Jim Brady*. Jim, also a writer, worked with my Jim on the 1980 Reagan presidential campaign.

Jerry and Debbie File: Neighbors of my mother who befriended us all after Jim was shot and were especially good to Scott.

Courtney, Mickey, and Theresa Gardner: Courtney was my personal assistant at Handgun Control. Mickey and Theresa are her parents.

William and Charlene Greener: Bill was Jim's boss and mentor when they worked at the Department of Housing and Urban Development.

Sally Law: "Aunt Sally" became a great friend when her niece and Scott started seeing each other and remained close to us after they broke up more than two years later.

Dorothy Mann*: Dorothy and her family were neighbors of the Bradys in Centralia, Illinois.

Dick and Bobbie McGraw: Good friends from Jim's days at HUD.

Steve Neal: A Chicago newspaper columnist Jim befriended during the 1980 presidential campaign.

Dennis Thomas: A dear friend whom Jim got to know well during the 1970s, when they both worked for Senator Bill Roth of Delaware.

Jan and Otto Wolff: Longtime friends. Otto and I worked together at the Republican National Committee, and Jim and Jan worked together at the Department of Defense.

OUR YEARS IN POLITICS

Richard Allen: National security adviser for Ronald Reagan when Jim was shot; also a neighbor and friend.

James A. Baker III: Chief of staff for President Reagan at the time Jim was shot.

John* and Nellie Connally: Former governor of Texas and his wife; Jim worked for John Connally's unsuccessful 1980 bid for the Republican nomination for president.

Michael Deaver: President Reagan's deputy chief of staff.

Eddie Mahe: A longtime Republican Party strategist who lured me to the Republican National Committee and got Jim to work for John Connally.

Joseph Maraziti: Republican congressman from New Jersey—my boss from 1972 to 1974.

Sally McElroy* and Mark Weinberg: Two of Jim's aides in the White House press office. Jim met Sally in 1975 when they worked for the Defense Department; he met Mark when both worked for the 1980 Connally presidential campaign.

James D. "Mike" McKevitt*: A Republican congressman from Colorado for whom I worked from 1970 to 1972.

William Roth: Republican Senator from Delaware, Jim's boss in the late 1970s, and a good friend ever since.

Ed Terrill: My boss in the late 1960s at the Republican Congressional Campaign Committee.

THE BRADY CAMPAIGN AND ITS ALLIES

Mike Barnes: A former congressman from Maryland, Mike has been president of Handgun Control—now the Brady Campaign to Prevent Gun Violence—since March 2000.

Jane Clarenbach: An employee of the Center to Prevent Handgun Violence from 1984 through 1992; she played a critical role in winning support for the Brady bill from the law enforcement community.

Gail Hoffman: Legislative director of Handgun Control from 1988 to 1992 and currently a consultant to the Brady Campaign.

Victoria Kennedy: An attorney and president of Common Sense About Kids and Guns, Vicki is married to Senator Edward Kennedy; she is an extremely active member of the board of the Brady Center to Prevent Gun Violence.

Barbara Lautman: Communications director for Handgun Control when I joined; later, executive director of the Center to Prevent Handgun Violence.

Charles Orasin: President of Handgun Control from 1975 to 1992 and the originator of the Brady bill.

Janet Reno: Dade County prosecutor and later U.S. attorney general under the Clinton Administration; a tireless supporter of the Brady bill.

Phyllis Segal: Former chair of the Federal Labor Relations Authority, she succeeded me as chairman of the board of Handgun Control in February 2000; Phyllis teaches at Harvard Law School and runs a national mediation and facilitation law practice.

Nelson "Pete" Shields*: Chairman of Handgun Control when I joined as a volunteer.

Bob Walker: President of Handgun Control from 1992 until 2000.

Susan Whitmore: Communications director of Handgun Control from 1988 to 1995.

CONGRESSIONAL FRIENDS AND FOES

Joseph Biden: Democratic senator from Delaware; as chairman of the Senate Judiciary Committee, a key figure in trying to pass a 1992 crime measure that included the Brady bill.

Jack Brooks: Democratic congressman from Texas who, as chairman of the House Judiciary Committee, firmly opposed the Brady bill.

Dick Cheney: Republican Representative from Wyoming; an opponent of gun laws who went on to become vice president of the United States.

Howard Coble: Republican congressman from North Carolina who first voted for the Brady bill—then against it.

Dennis DeConcini: Democratic senator from Arizona who introduced a bill that outlawed civilian purchases of certain assault weapons.

Bob Dole: Republican senator from Kansas; although he was no friend of gun control, he worked hard to pass the Senate's version of the Brady bill.

Edward Feighan: Democratic congressman from Ohio; the Brady bill's first sponsor in the House of Representatives.

Dianne Feinstein: Democratic senator from California who forged a compromise assault-weapons bill that became law in 1994.

Thomas Foley: Democratic congressman from Washington who, as Speaker of the House, staunchly opposed the Brady bill.

Nancy Kassebaum: Republican senator from Kansas, one of Congress's most effective supporters of sensible gun laws.

Edward Kennedy: Democratic senator from Massachusetts and a longtime gun control activist.

William McCollum: Republican congressman from Florida who helped defeat the Brady bill when it came up for its first vote in 1988.

Howard Metzenbaum: Democratic senator from Ohio; the Brady bill's chief Senate sponsor.

George Mitchell: Maine Democrat and Senate Majority Leader who expanded the Brady bill and fought hard for its passage.

Charles Schumer: Democratic congressman (and later senator) from New York, eventually the Brady bill's chief sponsor in the House.

James Sensenbrenner: Republican Representative from Wisconsin who eventually became the Brady bill's primary Republican sponsor.

Paul Simon: Democratic senator from Illinois, one of the Brady bill's strongest supporters.

Alan Simpson: Republican senator from Wyoming, and one of my favorite opponents.

Harley Staggers: Democratic congressman from West Virginia who tried to defeat the Brady bill in 1991.

MEDICAL MATTERS

Emmy Bania, Dee Hardy, and Mary Dickerson: Jim's nurses and loyal companions for many years. Emmy is still with us, and we consider her a member of the family.

Sandra Butcher: The head social worker at the George Washington University Hospital when Jim was shot.

George Economos*: The doctor who eventually coordinated all of Jim's medical care.

David Ettinger: A specialist in cancer at the Johns Hopkins Oncology Center.

Arthur Kobrine: The neurosurgeon at GW Hospital who saved Jim Brady's life.

Mike Newman: The internist who was Jim's primary physician when we lived in Virginia.

Srihari Peri: The oncologist who supervised my chemotherapy at the Tunnell Cancer Center, part of the Beebe Medical Center in Lewes, Delaware.

James Spellman: My oncological surgeon at the Beebe Medical Center.

Charles Stanislav: The young Delaware doctor who ordered my first lung scan—and delivered the bad news.

Andrejs Strauss: My radiation oncologist at Beebe's Tunnell Cancer Center.

Index